W9-CPC-691

Strategic Thinking

An Executive Perspective

jfrederi
0928I9812

Strategic Thinking

An Executive Perspective

Cornelis A. de Kluyver

Henry Y. Hwang Dean and Professor of Management

Peter F. Drucker Graduate School of Management
Claremont Graduate University
Claremont, CA 91711

Prentice Hall, Upper Saddle River, New Jersey 07458

Senior Editor: Stephanie Johnson
Editorial Managing Editor: Jennifer Glennon
Editorial Assistant: Hersch Doby
Editor-in-Chief: Natalie Anderson
Marketing Manager: Michael Campbell
Production Manager: Gail Steier de Acevedo
Production Coordinator: Maureen Wilson
Permissions Coordinator: Monica Stipanov
Manufacturing Buyer: Natacha St. Hill Moore
Senior Manufacturing Manager: Vincent Scelta
Cover Design: Karen Salzbach
Cover Photo: Michael Simpson/FPG International LLC
Full Service Composition: Carlisle Communications, Ltd.

Copyright © 2000 by Prentice-Hall, Inc.
Upper Saddle River, New Jersey 07458

All rights reserved. No part of this book may be reproduced, in any form or by any
means, without written permission from the publisher.

Library of Congress Cataloging-in-Publication Data
De Kluyver, Cornelis A.
    Strategic thinking : an executive perspective / by Cornelis A. de
Kluyver.
        p. cm.
    Includes bibliographical references and index.
    ISBN 0-13-020995-3
    1. Strategic planning.   I. Title.
HD30.28.D396   2000
658.4′012—dc21   99-25828
                                                            CIP

Prentice-Hall International (UK) Limited, London
Prentice-Hall of Australia Pty. Limited, Sydney
Prentice-Hall Canada, Inc., Toronto
Prentice-Hall Hispanoamericana, S.A., Mexico
Prentice-Hall of India Private Limited, New Delhi
Prentice-Hall of Japan, Inc., Tokyo
Prentice-Hall (Singapore) Pte Ltd.
Editora Prentice-Hall do Brasil, Ltda., Rio de Janeiro

Printed in the United States of America

10 9 8 7 6 5 4

Contents

Preface

The competitive environment is changing at a furious pace. Businesses that were immune to global competition only a few years ago now find themselves locked in fierce competitive battles with rivals from around the world. Technology is changing the way we live and work and, in the process, is rewriting the rules of competitive strategy for many businesses. At the corporate level, new strategic options such as the use of alliances and joint ventures have become essential to building competitive advantage. And key concepts in global strategic thinking—from which global battles to enter to how to manage the value chain in a global setting—are being revisited in a climate of rising worldwide economic uncertainty. Keeping up with these changes, and with new ways of strategic thinking aimed at exploiting these new developments, is critical to success.

Given the importance of this topic, it is surprising that there are few if any short, up-to-date, readable overviews of the field of strategy aimed at its most important audience: executives who shape tomorrow's strategies. Most writings on the subject are highly academic in nature or focus on a particular aspect of strategy—business unit strategy, strategy in high-technology industries, and so forth. There is also a plethora of books that deal with more tactical, operational issues such as reengineering, total quality, and outsourcing. But executives who wish to refresh or update their knowledge about the major issues in strategy development must turn to corporate or university executive development programs or enroll in one of a growing number of executive MBA programs in which they are given notes, reprints of well-known articles, case materials, and other supplementary readings organized in voluminous loose-leaf binders. This book is an attempt to fill the gap.

WHO SHOULD READ THIS BOOK?

This book is written for practicing executives who are getting ready to assume broader responsibilities. *It is intended as background reading in executive MBA and corporate executive programs to a series of case discussions in which specific strategic issues are examined in greater detail, or as a stand-alone overview if time pressures make taking a formal course on strategy development impractical.* And, if the limited experience with preliminary versions of this treatment of the subject is any guide, the book should appeal to a select number of practice-oriented MBA programs.

ORGANIZATION AND APPROACH

The approach and organization of this book reflect years of experience in executive development. Its tone is conversational, its coverage topical, and its approach practical. The first chapter defines strategy as the act of *positioning* a company for *sustained com-*

petitive advantage by focusing on *unique* ways to *create value* for customers. It requires *choosing* what *industries* to participate in, what *markets* to pursue, and what *products* or *services* to offer, and how to *allocate resources* to make such a positioning a reality. Formulating a sound strategy requires both *analysis* and *synthesis,* and therefore is as much a *rational* as it is a *creative* act. Successful strategies are rooted in a deep understanding of what customers value, how markets behave, and how competition develops. They also reflect a clear *strategic intent* and *competitive innovation.* Generic strategies rarely propel a company to a leadership position. Knowing where you want to go and finding carefully considered, creative ways of getting there, combined with a measure of patient persistence, are the hallmarks of successful strategy.

Chapter 2 looks at the importance of changes in a firm's *external strategic environment*—driven by *economic, technological, political, and sociocultural* change—and the impact of the evolutionary forces that shape a company's *industry environment* on strategy formulation. In particular, we focus on two key issues that every strategist must confront: how to assess and deal with *change* and *uncertainty.*

Chapter 3 focuses on the company itself. Analysis of external change forces is critical to determining what strategic changes a company *should* consider. An assessment of internal strategic resources and capabilities and of pressures for and against change is important to determining what strategies a company successfully *can* (and should) pursue. A firm's *strategic resources* include its physical assets (*physical resources*), its relative financial position (*financial resources*), the quality of its people (*human resources*), and specific knowledge, competencies, processes, skills, or cultural aspects of the organization (*organizational resources*). A second aspect of assessing a company's internal strategic environment deals with identifying *pressures for strategic change* that come from within the organization or from its immediate stakeholders. Persistent disappointing performance, new owners or management, limitations to growth with current strategies, scarcity of critical resources, or internal cultural changes are examples of conditions that give rise to such pressures.

Chapter 4 deals with creating a sustainable and profitable competitive position for a business unit within a specific industry, segment, or served market. The principal focus of business unit or competitive strategy is on *how* to compete, in a given competitive setting as opposed to corporate strategy, the subject of chapter 5, which is concerned with *what* businesses a company should compete in and *how* a parent company can add value to its business units. The chapter begins by examining the *logic* behind strategic thinking at the business unit level. In this section we address the basic question, What determines profitability at the business unit level? We look at the relative importance of the industry in which a company competes and its competitive position within the industry, and identify the drivers that determine sustained competitive advantage. This logic naturally suggests a number of *generic strategy choices,* broad strategy prescriptions, which define the principal dimensions of competition at the business unit level. Which generic strategy is more attractive and what form it should take varies considerably according to the specific opportunities and challenges analyzed. Accordingly, the next section deals with the question of how to size up a strategic challenge at the business unit level. It introduces a variety of techniques such as *profit pool analysis, growth vector analysis, gap analysis, competitor analysis,* and *product life cycle analysis* useful for generating and assessing strategic alternatives. Since strategy is developed in a specific industry context, the next section considers six different industry environments. Three represent different stages in an industry's evolution—*embryonic, growth,* and *mature* industry settings. The other three—*fragmented* industries, *global,* and *deregulating* industry environments—are defined by their structure, scope, or external forces operating on them. We conclude the chapter with a number of special topics—the role of *innovation* in value creation, issues of *timing, entry-exit* decisions, *vertical integration,* and the *relationship between business unit and corporate strategy.*

Chapter 5 has several parts. We first look at the concept of *economics of scale and scope*—a fundamental underpinning of corporate strategy—and try to answer the question, Is bigger always better? Next, we turn to the context in which corporate strategy is developed and executed. In particular, we note the importance of the dispersion in the ownership of large corporations in the last 30 years and of emergence *of the market for corporate control.* With this background, we trace the *evolution of strategic thinking* at the corporate level. Four perspectives are identified—the *portfolio, value-based, generic strategy,* and *resource-based* points of view—and their relative merits assessed. This discussion leads us to the consideration of *strategy choices* at the corporate level. In this section we look at *concentrated growth strategies, diversification issues, merger and acquisition activities, cooperative strategies* including joint ventures and alliances, and *sell-offs, spin-offs, and liquidations.* Next, we look at the issue of *corporate parenting* and how a parenting style affects portfolio composition and management. We conclude the chapter with a discussion of *how to evaluate* strategy choices at the corporate level.

In chapter 6 we take a closer look at the opportunities and risks associated with staking out a global competitive position and identify the principal dimensions of a global strategy. To set the stage we first take a look at the driving forces behind the emerging global economy and characterize "globalization" in greater detail as an economic, political, social, and technological phenomenon. Industry globalization is the next topic of discussion. In this section we focus on such questions as: What is a global industry? What are the driving forces behind the globalization of industries? and What explains the dominance of particular countries or regions in global industries? The third major topic of this chapter is global strategic thinking. In this section we identify the principal dimensions of global strategy and introduce a framework for global strategic thinking that links global strategy options to the nature of the global industry environment. A major tenet of this discussion is that global strategy, more than strategy at the corporate or business unit levels, increasingly is played out in two arenas: a market and a nonmarket arena. Market dimensions of global strategic thinking concern questions such as: Which markets should we participate in? Why? In what form? To what extent should we standardize products and services? Where should we locate key value-added activities? Should we have a uniform market positioning worldwide? and How do we coordinate competitive moves across the globe? They are aimed at creating value through economic performance in a global context. Nonmarket dimensions of global strategy deal with shaping the global competitive environment. As many executives will attest, the rules of global competition are critical to performance. As a consequence, to enhance their global competitiveness, an increasing number of companies have concluded that they need to participate in the political process of shaping those rules. An integrated global strategy therefore consists of market and nonmarket components that act synergistically to create a sustained competitive advantage on a global scale. The effectiveness of different global postures depends importantly on the structure of the global industry. Accordingly, we evaluate the relative effectiveness of different global strategy options in the context of a number of generic global industry settings. We conclude this discussion by considering the various strategic risk factors associated with a global strategic posture.

Chapter 7 briefly looks beyond strategy formulation. It argues that because of the greater intensity of the competitive environment the need for effective *leadership*, at all levels of the organization, has never been greater. At the same time, the growing complexity of the strategic environment makes leadership not only more critical to success but also more difficult. This in part explains why companies are experimenting with new forms of *organization*; traditional models simply are not as effective anymore. This *reinventing the corporation* also reflects a broader paradigm shift about what management is all about. Getting comfortable with change is not an option any more; today it is a requirement for success. After all, no matter how well crafted a strategy is, success begins with implementation. And as many executives have learned, "Successful implementation is secured through commitment, not compliance."

ABOUT THE BOOK

As every author knows, writing a book about a vast subject such as strategy involves making compromises and trade-offs. This book is no exception. In choosing what to include, where, and at what level of depth, I was guided by the book's primary objective as a companion volume to case analysis in an executive MBA setting. To me, that positioning meant several things. First, the book had to be *relatively short,* and highly *readable.* Second, a *broad perspective* was needed—sometimes at the expense of details about particular techniques or analysis frameworks. Third, the focus should be on strategic *thinking*—not on recipe-driven strategy formulation. Fourth, the book should give the reader a sense of *context* through the use of real examples and, where appropriate, of relevant historical references. Finally, a fundamental premise underlying this book is that strategy development is a *dynamic* process. All companies have a strategy of some kind in place. What is more, few executives have the luxury of "starting over." This book recognizes therefore that most strategies *evolve over time,* and must take into account how things are done today.

Strategy formulation is as much a creative as an analytical process. To emphasize this point, each chapter begins with a quotation by a famous painter, composer, or dancer. Their words inspire new ideas about and new approaches to strategic thinking. Paul Cézanne's views on art, for example, known to us almost exclusively through letters to personal friends such as fellow artist Emile Zola, speak to the way in which he translated what he saw into what he painted. Executives today are confronted with a competitive environment that provides such a barrage of continuous stimuli that one wonders how they can effectively absorb it all. For Gauguin, the expression of feeling was essential, but Matisse recites the need to see the total picture. Judith Jamison connects her total being to the creative process of dance and shows what commitment to an idea is all about. And Picasso said, "In my opinion to search means nothing in painting. To find, is the thing. Nobody is interested in following a man who, with his eyes fixed on the ground, spends his life looking for the pocketbook that fortune should put in his path."[1] Perhaps these thoughts will spark creative strategic thinking.

---

[1]Pablo Picasso, Statement, 1923, as quoted in Herschell B. Chipp, *Theories of Modern Art: A Source Book by Artists and Critics* (Berkeley, CA: University of California Press, 1968), 263.

ACKNOWLEDGMENTS

Writing a book is a mammoth undertaking. Fortunately, I had a lot of encouragement along the way from members of my family, colleagues, and friends. I take this opportunity to thank them all for their constructive criticisms, their time, and their words of encouragement. A few individuals deserve special mention. Robert D. Buzzell patiently read early drafts of this work and his comments materially influenced the way I structured the book and approached certain topics. I am grateful for his advice and counsel. I am also indebted to Edgar A. Pessemier, who has been a mentor throughout my professional career. Without his constant encouragement this book may not have been written. Jack Pendray provided helpful feedback and cheered me on along the way. I am also grateful to the reviewers of this text: Mary Smidt, University of Phoenix; Lee McConaghy, Keller Graduate School of Management; Andrew Klein, Keller Graduate School of Management; Donald Wilson, Rochester Institute of Technology; Jordan Kaplan, Long Island University; Mary Eckenrod, Rockwell Automation; William K. Harper, Arthur D. Little School of Management; and Les Spero, Strategic Management Group, Inc. The idea of relating strategy to art is probably not original. The value of this suggestion, however, was brought home to me when I had the opportunity to discuss it at some length with Francine Neville. She read early drafts of the book, made valuable suggestions for change, helped select suitable quotations from the arts, and patiently listened as I related my frustrations about writing during a number of lunches. I am grateful to all of them and hope the end result meets their high expectations. It goes without saying that I alone am responsible for any remaining errors or misstatements. Finally, my heartfelt thanks go to my family: my wife Louise, and sons Peter and Jonathan. There were many weekends when, instead of attending a ball game, Dad was at the office trying to write some more. I hope they forgive me for the times I was not there, and thank them for their unwavering support.

CdK, April 1999

List of Figures

Strategic Thinking

An Executive Perspective

C H A P T E R

1

What Is Strategy?

*The painter chooses his color with the profound concentration suitable to him, just as the musician chooses the tone and intensity of his instruments. The color does not govern the design, but harmonizes with it.**
—HENRI MATISSE

INTRODUCTION

As we approach the twenty-first century, the competitive landscape is undergoing radical change. Globalization as a political, economic, social, and technological force appears unstoppable. While boundaries between countries and regions may be meaningful in political terms, they have all but disappeared on the global competitive map. The ever-faster flow of information across the world has made people aware of the tastes, preferences, and lifestyles of citizens in other countries. Through this information flow we are all becoming—at varying speeds and at least in economic terms—global citizens. Around the world, people increasingly take advantage of what a global economy has to offer—they write with a Waterman or Mont Blanc pen, wear Levi's jeans and Nike sneakers, drink Coca-Cola, eat McDonald's hamburgers, and carry Louis Vuitton luggage. This is equally true for the buying habits of businesses. The market boundaries for IBM and Compaq computers or GE aircraft engines are no longer defined in political or geographic terms. Rather, it is the intrinsic value of the products and services that defines their appeal. Like it or not, we are living in a global economy.

This deepening integration of the global economy implies a greater degree of interdependence—between the economies of individual countries and between industries—and has created a world in which a disturbance in one part of the world economy can have a major impact elsewhere, and in which developments in one sector increasingly affect the health of others. However, economic integration between countries is still far from universal. Indeed, the data suggest that the globalization of the world economy is a highly skewed phenomenon; U.S., German, British, and French companies still account for the largest foreign direct investment outflows. Inflows are similarly concentrated. But this too is changing. In the decades to come, as global competition heats up, the Asian and Latin American economies are widely expected to outpace those of the West.

---

*From "Temoignages" (observations assembled by Maria Lux and approved by Henri Matisse) XX Siecle (Paris) (January 1952): 66–80, as quoted in Herschell B. Chipp, *Theories of Modern Art: A Source Book by Artists and Critics* (Berkeley, Calif.: University of California Press, 1968), 143.

As recent world events indicate, however, neither the pattern nor the process of further globalization of the world economy is likely to be smooth. Only ten years ago—in the late eighties—the Japanese economy was exalted as the paragon of global competitive success while the United States was struggling with sluggish growth and European countries muddled along under an increasingly onerous regulatory burden. Japanese firms in many high-tech industries were rapidly becoming leaders in product quality, innovation, and market share around the globe whereas American and European companies were thought to have lost their competitive edge.

This illustrates why journalism only provides us with a first draft in the writing of history. Today, things look very different. The U.S. economy, while increasingly vulnerable to the ups and downs of the global economy, is once again the world leader. "The New Economy," as *Business Week* and others have described the recent burst in technological, business, and financial creativity, holds great promise for growth, low inflation, and low unemployment well into the next century.[1] European companies have begun to adopt a more entrepreneurial orientation to running their businesses, and await the tangible benefits that an economic and monetary union will bring. Asian economies, meanwhile, face a more formidable struggle to regain their former resiliency. In the end, however, the enormous pent-up demand for modern goods and services in that part of the world should provide them with a ready-made platform for future growth and prosperity.

This turbulent evolution of the competitive landscape has taken its toll. Traditional companies such as General Motors, Digital Equipment Corporation, Caterpillar Tractor, and AT&T have seen their fortunes fluctuate as executives grappled with the seemingly intractable problems of an ever-changing competitive landscape. At the same time, a host of new companies such as Microsoft, Dell, and Gateway now dominate the headlines. What is more, this competitive turbulence is not restricted to the United States. European firms such as DAF, Philips, Mercedes Benz, and ICI and Japanese giants such as Komatsu, Matsushita, and NEC faced the same challenge of responding to the new competitive realities. To keep up with the changes around them, companies today must continuously reinvent themselves. Even politicians and policymakers are beginning to realize that the laws and regulations they pass today may have little relevance tomorrow.

How should we think about *strategy* in this dynamic, continuously changing environment? Are the principles on which strategic thinking was founded years ago still valid today? These are some of the important issues we explore in this book. We begin with a discussion of "What is Strategy?" We define strategy in terms of delivering *value to stakeholders*, distinguish between *strategy* and *operational effectiveness*, and differentiate between strategy formulation at the *corporate, business unit*, and *functional* level. We also look at the *process* by which strategy is formulated and look at events that can trigger a strategy review. As part of this discussion, we ask whether strategy is necessarily a planned activity, clarify such concepts as *mission, vision, goals*, and *objectives*, and introduce the notions of *strategic intent* and *stretch*. To set the stage for the following chapters, the third section traces the evolution of strategic thinking at the corporate and business unit levels in broad strokes. This is followed by a discussion of new strategic questions that have arisen as a consequence of such forces as globalization and the technology revolution, and concludes that a number of strategic orthodoxies—market share is king, for example—may not always be applicable anymore. The fifth section introduces the challenge of evaluating different strategy proposals. Specifically, we ask whether strategic options can and should be evaluated purely on economic grounds or whether broader qualitative criteria play a role. In the sixth section, "What's Ahead," we detail the plan for the remainder of the book.

Throughout the book we implicitly address the four c's of strategy—*content, context, conduct,* and *change.* Content refers to what strategy formulation is all about—its scope, focus, and major dimensions. Context is important because strategy is not formulated in a vacuum; strategy development should be responsive to the needs and concerns of an organization's multiple stakeholders, the strategic environment in which it operates, and a realistic appraisal of what can be accomplished. Conduct refers to process. Not all organizations deal with strategy formulation the same way. In entrepreneurial organizations the process is often less formal than in large corporations; nonprofit organizations differ from for-profit enterprises; and strategy formulation often reflects leadership style. Finally, today, more than ever before, strategy must deal with continuous sometimes abrupt change in the broader economic, technological, political, and sociocultural environment as well as in the increasingly global competitive environment. Anticipating and capitalizing on change has therefore become a key determinant of success.

WHAT IS STRATEGY?

The Essence of Strategic Thinking

How did Bill Gates guide Microsoft to its dominant position in the software industry? Is its position sustainable? Or will it go the way other well-known companies have in the past and succumb in the next wave of brutal global competition? Will Lou Gerstner's remake of IBM have staying power or will its recent competitive resurgence prove temporary? Is the vision of the Internet as a major avenue for business realistic? Or is this a much-hyped idea that prudent executives should be wary of? These kinds of questions lie at the heart of strategic thinking.

It is hard to imagine a business conversation today that does not include the word *strategy.* We talk about Microsoft's strategy in software, Coca-Cola's strategy in China, McDonald's human resource strategies, IBM's marketing strategies, Intel's technology strategy, and so on. Its frequent use would suggest that the term *strategy* is unambiguous and its meaning well understood. Unfortunately, it is not. Much of what is labeled "strategy" in fact has little to do with it. And while numerous attempts have been made at providing a simple, descriptive definition of strategy, its inherent complexity and subtlety preclude a one-sentence description. Yet there is substantial agreement about its principal dimensions. Strategy is about *positioning* an organization for *sustainable competitive advantage.* It involves making *choices* about *which industries to participate in, what products and services to offer,* and *how to allocate corporate resources* to achieve such a sustainable advantage. And its primary goal is to *create value for shareholders and other stakeholders* by providing *customer value.*

Strategy is important because there is a proven link between a company's strategic choices and its long-term performance. Successful corporations tailor their strategy, structure, and processes to the demands of the environment and leverage their core competencies and skills for competitive advantage. Crafting an effective strategy is hard work; it requires both *analysis* and *synthesis,* and therefore is as much an *analytic* as a *creative* act. Sound strategy is rooted in a deep understanding of what current and potential customers value, how markets develop, how competition unfolds, and how such elements are likely to change. It should also reflect a clear *strategic intent* and *competitive innovation.* "Generic" or cookie-cutter strategies rarely propel a company to a leadership position.

Strategy Versus Tactics

In the last two decades an avalanche of new business concepts has come our way. Innovation, total quality, flexibility, and speed, among other factors, came to be regarded as essential to a company's competitive strength and agility. As a consequence, corporations embraced total quality management, time-based competition, benchmarking, outsourcing, partnering, reengineering, and a host of other concepts in an all-out effort to enhance competitiveness.

Many of these initiatives have produced dramatic results. General Motors, Ford, and Chrysler each have spent billions of dollars reengineering their design and production processes. As a result, unit costs have fallen dramatically; quality has gone up; relationships with component manufacturers and other suppliers are stronger; and the time needed to take a new car from concept to production has been cut in half. Such moves to enhance operational effectiveness are crucial in today's cutthroat competitive environment. But they are no substitute for a sound strategy. In fact, they may obscure the difference between strategy and the application of operational tools and managerial philosophies, or, as Michael Porter puts it, of the difference between *strategy* and *operational effectiveness.*[2] Both are essential to competitiveness. But whereas the application of managerial tools is aimed at doing things *better* than competitors and therefore is *tactical* in nature, *strategy* focuses on doing things *differently.* This distinction is crucial.

Long-term sustainable superior performance—the ultimate goal of strategy—can only be realized if a company can *preserve* meaningful differences with rivals. Total quality management, time-based competition, benchmarking, and other initiatives aimed at improved operational performance generally are fairly easily imitated. And while imitation may be the sincerest form of flattery, differences in performance attributable to such actions are at best temporary.

Strategy Forces Trade-offs

Strategic thinking, instead, focuses on taking *different* approaches to delivering customer value; on choosing *different* sets of activities that cannot easily be imitated and thereby provide a basis for sustainable competitive advantage. When Dell Computer pioneered the custom-built approach in the personal computer market, it designed every aspect of its manufacturing, sourcing, and inventory system around the direct-selling concept and created a formidable cost advantage. Rivals, stuck with traditional distribution-based approaches, had a hard time responding and were forced to rethink what value they delivered.

Thus, whereas tactics such as total quality management, time-based competition, and reengineering can be helpful in improving how different activities are being performed, they do not force companies to choose between entirely different, internally consistent *sets* of activities. Compaq and other competitors may choose to sell direct but unless they are willing to dismantle their traditional distribution structures they will never reap the benefits Dell realizes from its strategy. Choosing a *unique competitive positioning*—the essence of strategy—forces trade-offs in terms of what to do, and equally important, of what *not* to do. In other words, a well-thought-out strategy has built-in *barriers to imitation,* which is an essential ingredient to building a sustained competitive advantage.

Strategy as Value Creation

The ultimate goal of strategy is to create *value*—for shareholders and other stakeholders—by satisfying the needs and wants of customers. If a company can deliver value to its customers better than its rivals can over a sustained period of time, that company likely has a superior strategy. This is not a simple task. Customers' wants, needs, and preferences change, often rapidly, as they become more familiar with products and services, as new rivals enter the market, and as competition raises the bar that defines value. As a result, what is valuable today may not be valuable tomorrow. *Value, unless constantly maintained, nourished, and improved, erodes with time.*

Consider the challenges faced by one of the world's best-known brands, McDonald's, and how they illustrate this important strategic maxim.[3] While universally acknowledged as one of the great commercial success stories of this century, McDonald's decline in performance in the last few years has raised questions about the company's ability to adapt to America's changing tastes and preferences.

Without a doubt McDonald's is one of the great corporate success stories of our time and we should not underestimate its staying power. Since its founding in 1937, the company has grown to a world-class organization that has become an integral part of the American experience. With 1997 profits of $1.6 billion, on sales of $11.4 billion, a 42 percent share of the U.S. market, and a dominant position and even more potential abroad, its future appears secure. But questions about the future of the Golden Arches are being asked with greater frequency. Despite a steep increase in the number of restaurants, its U.S. share of the market has been slipping. Profits have not kept pace with inflation in recent years, and attempts to rejuvenate the menu have been largely unsuccessful. Also, surveys suggest that McDonald's reputation for quality and cleanliness is suffering.

Management realizes something needs to be done. It is hard to dismiss a persistently lagging stock price, several quarters of subpar profits, and investor uncertainty. Meanwhile, competitors such as Burger King and Wendy's are taking advantage of the current situation by innovating in every part of their business. McDonald's brand franchise is still formidable. But the time has come for management to apply some fresh strategic thinking; it has done it before and no doubt will do it again.

Figure 1-1 depicts this "competitive advantage cycle." It shows that "at any time, companies are endowed with a mixed bag of resources. Some of the assets and capabilities are no better than those of the competition, others are inferior, while a few are superior to the competition. These superior assets and capabilities are the source for positional advantages."[4] Whatever competitive advantage a firm creates, it must anticipate that ongoing change in the strategic environment and competitive moves by rival firms continuously work to erode it. Competitive strategy in this environment has a dual purpose: slowing down the erosion process by protecting the current advantage against the actions of competitors, and investing in new capabilities that form the basis for the next position of competitive advantage. Thus, the creation and maintenance of advantage is a continuous cycle.

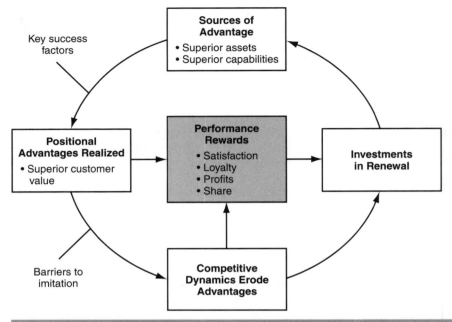

FIGURE 1-1 The Competitive Advantage Cycle

Source: George S. Day and David J. Reibstein, *WHARTON on Dynamic Competitive Strategy,* 1997. John Wiley & Sons, New York, NY. Reprinted by permission of John Wiley & Sons, Inc.

Strategy as a Portfolio of Options

When we speak of strategy as crafting a blueprint for an organization's future this does not mean deciding on a detailed long-term plan and following it to the letter. As noted earlier, change is one of the principal hallmarks of today's competitive environment. Strategy therefore embodies both ideas—a long-term vision of where we want to go and a degree of flexibility about how to get there. Learning therefore is an essential element of strategy formulation. As soon as we begin to implement a chosen direction, we start to learn about how well attuned the chosen direction is to the competitive environment, about how rivals are likely to respond, and about how well prepared the organization is to carry out its mission. Thus, rather than interpreting a strategy as a detailed long-term plan, it is more accurate and preferable to look at a strategy in terms of a portfolio of future options. Inherent in this characterization is the notion that at the time a strategy is crafted some elements of that strategy are more predictable than others. When Intel invests in a new technology, for example, it may know that this technology holds promise in several markets. Its precise returns in different applications, however, may not be known with any degree of certainty until much later.[5]

The Importance of Stakeholders

In recent years strategy formulation has begun to reflect the concerns and influence of the full range of an organization's *stakeholders* in a more serious manner. Historically, the amount of attention paid to stakeholders other than directly affected parties such as employees or major investors in crafting strategy, at least in the United States, has been limited. As executives learned that effective development of internal and external resources is increasingly important to an organization's success, however, *stakeholder analysis*—the process of identifying and prioritizing key stakeholders, assessing their needs and concerns, and incorporating their ideas and insights into the strategy formulation process—has become an important element of strategy development.

Most companies today rely, to a much greater extent than in the past, on a network of suppliers, partners, and even competitors in the value creation process. At the same time, the motivation of internal stakeholders—directors, top executives, middle managers, and employees—has come to be recognized as a critical determinant of success. As a consequence, paying attention to the needs and concerns of principal stakeholders is crucial. A misstep in managing suppliers, a critical error in employee relations, or a lack of communication with principal shareholders can set back a firm's progress for years or even precipitate its downfall in today's networked business environment. The importance of different stakeholders to strategy development is based on the *stake* they have in the organization and the kind of *influence* they can exert. Freeman distinguishes between groups or individuals with an *ownership stake* (shareholders, directors, among others), an *economic stake* (creditors, employees, customers, suppliers, etc.), and a *social stake* (regulatory agencies, charities, the local community, activist groups, etc.).[6] In a similar vein, we can distinguish between groups or individuals with *formal power, economic power, or political power.* Formal power is usually associated with legal obligations or rights; economic power is derived from an ability to withhold products, services, or capital; whereas political power is rooted in an ability to persuade other stakeholders to influence the behavior of an organization.

Levels of Strategy

Strategy formulation occurs at the *corporate, business unit,* and *functional* levels.[7] In a single product or service business, management's principal challenge is to decide what product or service to offer, how to manufacture or create it, and how to take it to the market place. Such choices are part of formulating a *business unit* strategy. In a multibusiness diversified corporation, a second set of issues relates to what kinds of businesses a firm should compete in, and how the overall portfolio of businesses should be managed. Such issues make up *corporate* strategy. *Functional* strategies typically involve more limited domains such as marketing, research and development, technology, and so on. All are part of *strategic management*—the totality of managerial processes used to chart and direct the future for a corporation.

FORMULATING STRATEGY

Process

The growing complexity of the competitive landscape, the rising importance of global issues in strategy formulation, and the enormous diversity in corporate identities, strategic postures, and challenges suggest that "recipe"-driven approaches to strategy formulation are doomed to failure. Nevertheless, at the broadest level, strategic thinking involves three principal steps: (1) a "*Where are we now?*" analysis, (2) a "*Where do we go?*" assessment, and (3) a "*How do we get there?*" appraisal (Figure 1-2).

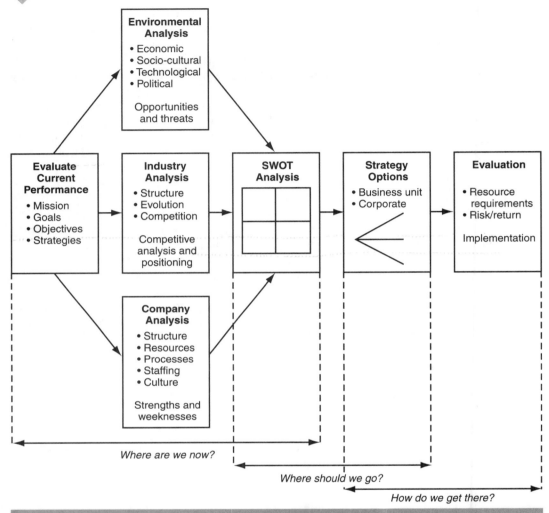

FIGURE 1-2 The Strategy Formulation Process

1. *"Where are we now?"* This part of the process is focused on taking stock of where the business, or the company as a whole, is today. It usually begins with a detailed evaluation of current performance. As part of this evaluation, it is useful to revisit such issues as "What is our mission?" "Who are our principal stakeholders?" and "What are our key objectives?" This analysis typically includes an assessment of pertinent trends in the broader sociopolitical, economic, legal, and technological environment in which the company operates; of opportunities and threats in the industry environment; and of internal strengths and weaknesses.

2. *"Where do we go?"* This second step is concerned with generating strategic alternatives based on the assessment of pertinent environmental and competitive trends, forces of change, and on the analysis of the sustainability of the current competitive po-

sitioning performed in the first step. At the business unit level, it contrasts options such as concentrating on growth in a few market segments with a wider market focus or even lessening the company's dependence on current product markets through diversification. At the corporate level, this step is concerned with making changes in the portfolio of businesses the company operates in and with making adjustments in parenting philosophies and processes. At both levels, the output is a statement of *strategic intent*— a broad (vision) statement that identifies the guiding business concept or driving force that will propel the company forward toward the achievement of that intent.

3. *"How do we get there?"* The third step deals with detailed questions of how to achieve the desired objectives. One of the most important issues addressed at this stage is how to bridge the *capability gap* that separates current organizational skills from the capabilities needed to achieve the stated strategic intent. It focuses on *core competence* building, and identifying the *key success factors* associated with successfully implementing the chosen strategy. The end product is a detailed set of strategies that forms the basis for communicating the chosen direction throughout the organization and for formulating intermediate and subordinate goals and plans.

Strategy and Planning

A strategy review can be triggered by a host of factors—new leadership, disappointing performance, changes in ownership, the emergence of new competitors or technologies—or be part of a scheduled, typically annual, review process.

Thirty years ago, "strategy formulation" and "strategic planning" were almost synonymous. Elaborate planning processes, supported by dedicated staff groups, could be found in almost every Fortune 500 company. The process, as much as the strategic concepts employed, provided focus to strategic thinking. Then a backlash developed. Almost overnight strategic planning fell out of favor. Disappointing corporate results, erosion in competitiveness, a lack of innovation, and a failure to take risks were all blamed on "strategic planning." An overreliance on simplistic planning models and the dubious numbers they generated was also cited as a major cause of failure and executives looked to free themselves from the barrage of forms, graphs, matrices, and volumes of planning documents. Interestingly, today the pendulum is beginning to swing back again toward more formal planning. To see why this is occurring we have to step back a few years in corporate history.

As corporate America faced the new challenges of the seventies and eighties posed by more intense global competition, it embraced leaner, more agile organizational structures that relied to a much greater extent on decentralized decision making. Formal bureaucratic processes were replaced by simpler, more effective ones; elaborate planning systems gave way to leaner, more decentralized forms of strategy development; and "staff" groups that had been the backbone of many corporate planning processes were eliminated. Strategy formulation became a line management function once again, and processes that were primarily "top-down" in nature were replaced by more "bottom-up"-oriented approaches reflecting the new culture of empowerment. In the process, thick strategic planning documents were exchanged for more easily grasped and communicated five-page strategic plans.

While the sentiments behind these changes—making strategy development a line responsibility once again, restoring the balance between top-down and bottom-up influences and simplifying planning processes—were laudable, their implementation often left a lot to be desired. As a result, for many companies these changes exacted a heavy price. In the frenzy of "catching up" with their competitors, executives became preoccupied with operational issues such as reengineering, benchmarking, downsizing, total quality initiatives, teamwork, and empowerment. Speed was considered all-important. Execution and implementation became the focal point of managerial effort. Strategy was easy, some thought; implementation was the real challenge.

As we now know, there are no shortcuts to reaching a position of long-term sustainable superior performance. We have also learned to distinguish between *strategic thinking* and *strategic planning*. Strategic thinking is the process used by leaders of organizations to create a vision for their organization, and to craft a clear, concise blueprint for realizing that vision. Strategic planning is a process used to develop supporting analyses, and to communicate and implement the chosen strategy. Only a CEO or senior management can "drive" the strategic thinking process. Strategic thinking starts at the top of the organization and therefore is very much a "trickle-down" process. Strategic planning, on the other hand, can and should have a major "bottom-up" component to make sure all relevant information about a strategic issue is captured.

As we approach the end of this century, we are witnessing a renaissance in strategic planning practices, albeit in much more modest proportions. General Electric, for example, once thought of as the paragon of old-style strategic planning, is now pioneering new "planning" concepts primarily aimed at making sure that strategic lessons learned in one part of the corporation are readily available to others. The focus of many of these new concepts and techniques is on communication, and on the transfer of usable knowledge from one part of the company to another, reflecting strategic planning's new supporting role in formulating business unit and corporate strategies.

Today, we also recognize that a strategy cannot be totally "planned." Planning assumes a degree of rationality, a dominance of systematic analysis, and a degree of certainty about the future that is often unwarranted. Lest we forget this, Mintzberg suggests we talk about "crafting" rather than "planning" strategy.[8] He reasons that strategies are as much plans for the future as they are patterns from the past and that strategies are not always the deliberate output of a onetime planning process but also emerge incrementally over time. What is more, strategies are not always crafted in gradually changing competitive environments—they sometimes represent responses to major discontinuities in the competitive environment that cannot be planned for.

Mission, Vision, Goals, Objectives

Many companies have a *mission* statement that documents the purpose for their existence and often contains a code of corporate conduct to guide management in implementing the mission. A *vision* statement represents senior management's strategic intent—a description of what competitive position the company wants to attain over a given period of time, and what core competencies it will need to acquire to get there. As such, it summarizes a company's broad strategic focus for the future. *Goals* are open-ended statements about desirable outcomes. "Being profitable" or "Having a concern for all corporate stakeholders" are examples. *Objectives*, on the other hand, are more specific and, as a consequence, should be measurable. "Becoming number one in our industry by the year 1999," for example, is a tangible, measurable statement about desired strategic outcomes.

Strategic Intent and Stretch

Most companies that have risen to positions of global leadership started from modest beginnings with ambitions that were far greater than their resource base and competencies would allow. To get to a position of market leadership, a focus on the drivers of competition is clearly not enough; strong leadership determined to realize a clear vision for the future, a *strategic intent,* is required. With such a mindset, disparities between resources and goals become challenges rather than constraints, and "winning" becomes a corporate "obsession" capable of sustaining a sense of urgency for a long period of time.[9]

Consider the much-analyzed competitive battle between Caterpillar and Komatsu over the last 25 years. In the early seventies, Komatsu was about one-third as large as Caterpillar in terms of sales. It produced primarily for the domestic Japanese market and had only one major product line—small bulldozers. In less than 20 years, the company became a global challenger in earthmoving equipment, industrial robots, and semiconductors. How did it accomplish this feat? *Strategic intent* surely provides a substantial part of the answer. "Encircle Caterpillar" became an "obsession" that guided the company's strategy for more than a decade. It inspired a whole series of competitive moves and programs aimed at building specific competencies and ultimately, securing a competitive advantage. It mastered new technologies, increased quality, reduced costs, developed new products, and cultivated export markets. By 1985, Komatsu had sales of more than $2.8 billion.

To be sure, Komatsu's rise was abetted by an unprecedented rise in the dollar against other major currencies, and by the Third World debt crisis, which caused orders for more expensive heavy earthmoving equipment to dry up almost overnight. Between 1980 and 1987, the dollar rose more than 80 percent against the yen and other major currencies, making it difficult for Caterpillar to compete domestically against cheaper Komatsu imports and around the world with its superior but relatively pricey aftersale service and support infrastructure. But while these environmental changes played an important role in shaping Komatsu's opportunities, its clear strategic intent enabled it to capitalize on them. In 1985 the U.S. government, persuaded that the dollar was substantially overvalued, intervened with help from other countries to drive its value down, helping Caterpillar to become competitive in world markets once again.[10]

Thus, *strategic intent* does more than paint a vision for the future; it signals the desire to win. It focuses the organization on key competitive targets, and provides clear goals about which competencies to develop, what kinds of resources to harness, and what segments to concentrate on. It also serves as a reminder that true strategic thinking has a long-term focus. When Komatsu decided it needed to increase the quality of its products, it did not worry excessively about costs. Only after its quality goals had been reached did cost reduction become a major objective.

A related idea is the concept of *stretch.* Most companies will not have the resources or capabilities to reach their most ambitious goals. As such, strategic intent forces the organization to think about how to obtain the necessary resources and develop key capabilities. Instead of worrying about the degree of "fit" between current resources and opportunities, the focus shifts to "how to close the capability gap." In this view, current resources and capabilities are starting points for strategy development, not constraints on strategy formulation.

Stretch reflects the recognition that successful strategies are built as much around *"what can be"* as around *"what is."* Ultimately, every company must create a fit between its resources and its opportunities. The question is over what time frame. Too short a time frame encourages a focus on *fit* rather than *stretch,* on resource *allocation* rather than getting *more value* from existing resources. The use of too long a time horizon, on the other hand, creates an unacceptable degree of uncertainty and threatens to turn stretch objectives into unrealistic goals.

THE EVOLUTION OF STRATEGIC THINKING

Early Contributions—
The Industrial Economics Perspective

Strategic thinking has evolved considerably over the last 40 years or so. From the early 1960s to the late 1980s, *environmental* influences—particularly those shaping industry structure—were thought to be the primary determinants of success. According to this view, a company's competitive environment imposed pressures and constraints, which made certain strategies more attractive than others. A second tenet was that most companies within an industry or segment were thought to control the strategically relevant resources they needed and, to the extent those resources were similar, their strategic responses would show similarities. Resource mobility was a third assumption of the industrial economics model. If a company did not have the requisite resources to execute a particular strategy, it could simply buy them. It is not surprising, therefore, that much of the strategic thinking of that era centered on choices about the competitive environment. Selecting the most attractive industries or industry segments to participate in became a dominant theme in strategy, both at the business unit and corporate levels.

Michael Porter's well-known "five forces" model, discussed in detail in chapter 2, is representative of this industrial economics-based perspective. It holds that at the broadest level, firm success is explained by two principal factors: the *attractiveness of the industry* a firm competes in and its *relative position* within that industry. Industry attractiveness, in turn, is explained in terms of five forces: the *threat of new entrants,* the *bargaining power of customers,* the *bargaining power of suppliers,* the *threat of substitute products* or *services* and the *jockeying among current rivals.*[11]

According to this model, within a particular industry, the relative profitability of rival firms depends on the *nature of their competitive* position, that is, on their ability to create a *sustainable competitive advantage* vis-à-vis their competitors. Porter identifies two generic forms of sustainable competitive positioning: a competitive advantage based on *lower delivered cost* and one based on the ability to *differentiate* products or services from those of competitors and command a price premium relative to the cost of doing so.[12]

The view of a corporation as a *portfolio of businesses* and the related *portfolio management concept* illustrate the industrial economics approach to strategic thinking at the corporate level. By the mid-1970s most large corporations had diversified primarily through acquisition. Corporate executives struggled with formulating a coherent strategy for their diverse array of semiautonomous divisions. The well-known *growth/share matrix* introduced in the seventies by the Boston Consulting Group, and discussed in detail in chapter 5, helped them confront these issues.[13] This simple framework provides a classification of different operating units, defined as *strategic business units* (SBUs), according to their market position and growth prospects. Businesses with a leading share of the market in relatively mature markets are "*cash cows.*" As a rule, they generate more cash than they can profitably reinvest. "*Question marks,*" poorly positioned business units in high growth markets, or "*stars,*" well-positioned businesses in attractive markets poised for further growth, on the other hand, generally need more capital than they can generate internally and therefore represent opportunities for further investments. In this framework, "*dogs*"—businesses with a relatively poor market position in low-growth markets—are considered less attractive and candidates for harvesting or divestment. Anxious to reverse a poor performance, many corporations adopted the BCG approach as the principal tool for rationalizing their portfolio. Its relative simplicity combined with a focus on cash flow and return on investment explain its rapid acceptance. The BCG concept, more than any other technique, shaped the corporate strategy of many companies during that time.[14]

The Resource-Based View of Strategic Thinking

By the late 1980s, a subtle but important shift marked the dominant logic underlying strategic thinking. In part, this shift reflected the increased pace of change in the competitive environment. As globalization, the technology revolution, and other major environmental forces picked up speed and began to radically change the competitive landscape, key assumptions underlying the industrial economics model came under scrutiny. Should the competitive environment be treated as a constraint on strategy formulation, for example, or was strategy really about shaping competitive conditions? Was the assumption that businesses controlled most of the relevant strategic resources needed to compete in a particular industry still applicable? And were strategic resources really as mobile as the traditional model assumed and was the advantage associated with owning particular resources and competencies therefore necessarily short-lived?

This point of view was further developed in an influential article entitled "The Core Competence of the Corporation."[15] It urged a shift in the focus of strategic thinking from positioning a company within environment-dictated constraints to strategy development based on a company's unique resources and capabilities. It advocated the building of core capabilities that transcend the boundaries of traditional business units, the creation of corporate portfolios around *core businesses,* and the adoption of goals and processes aimed at enhancing *core competencies.* It recognized, of course, that not all of a firm's resources and capabilities lend themselves to or can be leveraged to build a sustainable competitive advantage. The focus, therefore, was on developing and nurturing those resources and capabilities that are *valuable* to a company's chosen direction, *hard or costly to imitate,* and that *cannot easily be substituted.*

This perspective was later extended to what is known today as the resource-based view of the firm. Its central thesis is that a corporation is a collection of tangible and intangible assets that collectively define its "distinctive competence," and that strategy is about the creation of value through the configuration and coordination of a set of multimarket activities. Instead of emphasizing potential synergies between component businesses to create a competitive advantage, it stresses the importance of a fit between existing and to-be-developed corporate resources and product markets. Three elements—*resources; businesses;* and *structure, systems;* and *processes*—represent the foundations of the resource-based model of strategic thinking. It holds that when aligned in pursuit of a *vision* and motivated by the right *goals* and *objectives,* a *corporate advantage* can be created that justifies the corporation's existence as a multibusiness entity.[16]

More recently, a related perspective focusing on the fit between the capabilities of the corporate parent and the needs of the various businesses in the portfolio has been added.[17] This "*parenting framework*" focuses on the competencies of the parent organization and on the value created from the relationship between the parent company and its component businesses.

While there are important differences between these perspectives they are not mutually exclusive. Contemporary thinking about strategy contains elements of both schools of thought. It holds that *value creation* is the fundamental purpose of strategy; that companies should focus on how to create value through the *configuration* and *coordination* of their multimarket activities; and that the value of a multibusiness corporation should be greater than the sum of its component parts.

STRATEGY FORMULATION IN THE TWENTY-FIRST CENTURY: NEW ISSUES

The Changing Strategy Context

Whether the "New Economy" comes to pass or not, one thing is clear: The pace of change is more likely to accelerate than decelerate. The drivers of this change in the strategic environment include the relentless pace at which competition is becoming *global*. From oil to aircraft, from semiconductors to accounting services, and from soft drinks to furniture, small and large companies alike are feeling the impact of globalization. It has intensified competition, increased the diversity of rivals, and enriched product and service offerings. At the same time, the more intense rivalry has raised the stakes in almost all industries—potential rewards are larger but so are the risks.

The *technology revolution* is a second major force that is changing the competitive landscape in important ways. The structural change in the computer industry provides a good example. Twenty years ago the industry was fairly concentrated and major players such as IBM and DEC seemed unassailable with their vertically integrated lock on suppliers and customers. Today, the industry is fragmented and vertical integration has been all but abandoned. Compaq, Dell, Gateway, and IBM now focus mainly on hardware; Microsoft's strategy is built around operating systems; while others including Intuit and Broderbund concentrate on writing application software. In the meantime, Intel has come to dominate the semiconductor market.

Deregulation is a third environmental force that is reshaping the competitive landscape in many industries. In the United States, first the airline and telecommunications industries and now financial services have experienced major changes as barriers to entry are brought down, competition heats up, and upstarts challenge the existing order.

In this climate of sweeping change and competitive turbulence it is not surprising that "strategic orthodoxies" are questioned with greater frequency. Many "old-line" corporations—Wang, Honeywell, Digital Equipment, Sears, and Kmart to name a few—either have seen their fortunes wane or completely disappear in recent years. Oblivious to the changes around them or overconfident in their ability to ride out the storm, they have fallen victim to new, more agile competitors not burdened by tradition, obsolete structures, or entrenched ways of doing things. Many others were or are in the process of being taken over in a merger and acquisition frenzy driven by the belief that competitive salvation can be found in scale and scope. Only a few including IBM and

General Electric have managed to reinvent themselves and once again have begun to reassert their competitiveness around the world.

Challenging Conventional Wisdom

The changing dynamics of competition have forced us to reconsider a number of basic premises underlying traditional strategy frameworks. Conventional wisdom, for example, holds that market share is the most appropriate measure of market influence, that relative share is a proxy for competitive strength, and therefore that market share is a principal driver of profitability. The structural changes we have witnessed in a number of industries, however, particularly in the high-tech sector, coupled with the rise in cooperative strategies between firms in the form of joint ventures, alliances, and other forms of so-called *cooptition,* have triggered a reexamination of such basic premises.

Is market share the best measure of market influence in today's competitive climate? And what does market share mean? Increasingly, companies compete with branded as well as nonbranded product entries. Should we focus on brand share or on total market share? Do we mean domestic market share or global market share? With outsourcing becoming a more important element of a company's strategy, how do we deal with the mismatch it creates between market share and manufacturing share? Is market share a proxy for the ability to develop and launch new products and therefore a measure of core competence?

New questions are also being asked about the focus of strategic analysis.[18] As firms increasingly compete as "families"—the Western equivalent of the Japanese *Keiretsu*—should we focus more on the performance of such families rather than solely that of companies? Do companies primarily compete at the business unit level or the corporate level? Should we focus on regional performance rather than that of individual business units? How does the fact that boundaries between industries are becoming increasingly permeable enter our analysis? Will Citicorp compete with Microsoft or AT&T as the electronic revolution reaches the next stage? Apple with Sony? Should we analyze rivalry at the business unit level? The corporate level? Does real competition start before a market has been developed? When core competencies are being built? When rivals engage in a battle for standards?

As these questions suggest, analyzing competitive rivalry is becoming increasingly complex. In a world in which competitors do not always compete, where rival firms simultaneously may be suppliers, competitors, and customers of one another, where short-term "failure" may be necessary to build long-term success, simplistic strategy "prescriptions" will not suffice. Hamel and Prahalad have gone further. They assert that the widespread reliance on traditional concepts such as *"strategic fit"*—between resources and opportunities—*"generic strategies"*—low cost versus differentiation—and the use of a *"strategy hierarchy"*—goals, strategies, and tactics—has in fact contributed to competitive decline.[19]

Hamel and Prahalad note, for example, that few Western companies have been successful in anticipating competition from new global rivals and suggest that the explanation lies in the *way* most companies approach issues such as competitor analysis. They observe that all too frequently competitor analysis focuses on the *current* resource base—technical, financial, human—of *present* competitors, and that more important questions such as "Which companies *could* pose a threat in the future?" rarely are seriously entertained.

EVALUATING STRATEGY OPTIONS

Criteria

The ultimate test of any strategy is whether it produces a sustainable competitive advantage with above-average returns. Thus, it is not surprising that to many executives strategy evaluation is principally a matter of how well a business or company performs. Are we making money? Is the business growing? Although intuitive, this approach by itself, however, is not sufficient. Measures of current performance are not necessarily indicative of future performance. Instead, strategy evaluation should focus on a firm's future competitiveness and ask whether objectives set for the future are appropriate; whether strategies chosen to attain such objectives are consistent, bold enough, and achievable; and whether they are likely to produce a sustainable competitive advantage with above-average returns.

Quantifying such judgments is difficult. While financial returns are important, the key question is whether strategic intent and specific proposals aimed at realizing intent always can or should be reduced to a cash flow forecast. Of course, the financial impact on the corporation of specific strategy options such as acquisitions at the corporate level or specific new product or market entries at the business unit level can and should be quantified. But a good argument can be made that not all strategic thinking lends itself to a purely quantitative assessment. Historically, corporate and business unit strategies were limited to market-based competitive initiatives and economic analysis was the dominant if not sole component of strategic analysis. Today, political and public policy analyses are rapidly gaining in currency as nonmarket strategies such as initiatives targeted at governments and international regulatory agencies aimed at creating a level, competitive playing field abroad, are becoming an essential part of an integrated strategic posture. Putting a value on such nonmarket elements of strategy is extremely difficult. What is more, even when strategy options can be quantified, the accuracy of such forecasts varies greatly. Finally, simply adding forecasts associated with different business units in a multibusiness organization often does not adequately reflect the value of a company's strategy as a whole.

Notwithstanding these concerns, executives face enormous pressure—from within the organization as well as from external sources such as the financial community—to forecast business unit and corporate performance and, implicitly, to quantify anticipated strategic outcomes. Traditionally, measures such as *return on investment* (ROI) were most commonly used to evaluate a strategy's efficacy. Today *shareholder value* is one of the most widely accepted yardsticks for evaluating strategy alternatives.

Shareholder Value

The *shareholder value approach* (SVA) to strategy evaluation holds that the value of the corporation is determined by the discounted future cash flows it is likely to generate. Value is created when companies invest capital at returns that exceed the cost of that capital. New strategic initiatives therefore must be treated as any other investment the company makes and evaluated on the basis of shareholder value. A whole new managerial framework—*value-based management* (VBM)—has been created around it.[20]

Companies such as American Hospital Supply, Borg-Warner, Westinghouse, Marriott, and others have publicly endorsed the approach.[21] They claim that the use of shareholder value for evaluating strategy proposals is more appropriate than traditional, accounting-oriented or qualitative criteria because it focuses directly on important questions such as "Will the proposed strategy create value for shareholders?" "Which business units are creating value?" "Which are not?" and "How would alternative strategies affect shareholder value?" While conceptually appealing—any strategy proposal can in theory be translated into a cash flow forecast after all—its practical application has proved challenging, however. Many operating executives, not always fully conversant with its intricate, technical details, object to its complexity and rigid assumptions, and cite the lack of support they get from traditional accounting mechanisms in implementing the approach. Others, frustrated by a preoccupation with numbers, fear it inhibits strategic thinking. And, in the wrong hands, complex quantitative techniques such as shareholder value analysis can become a political instrument.[22]

Today, the use of shareholder value or related measures such as *economic value added* (EVA), defined as after-tax operating profit minus the cost of capital, is still highly contentious as the principal yardstick for evaluating alternative strategy proposals. Besides implementation problems, there is a perceived lack of transparency in the relationship between "shareholder value" on the one hand and "positioning for sustained competitive advantage" on the other. While shareholder value and strategy formulation are ultimately about the same thing—generating long-term sustained value—they use different conceptions of value and view the purpose of strategy from a fundamentally different point of view.

Strategists focus on creating a sustainable competitive advantage through *value delivered to customers.* SVA measures *value to shareholders.* Whereas in the long run the two should be highly correlated, individual strategy proposals may force (short-term) trade-offs between the two. It is not surprising, therefore, that shareholder value has not been universally embraced as the preferred method for measuring a strategy's potential. It also explains why less restrictive but possibly less rigorous evaluation schemes, such as the "balanced scorecard" approach advanced by Kaplan, have gained prominence in the last few years.[23]

WHAT'S AHEAD

The remainder of this book is organized in six chapters. An effective strategy anticipates and capitalizes on relevant changes in a company's strategic environment. In chapter 2 we look at the importance of changes in a firm's *external strategic environment*—driven by *economic, technological, political, and sociocultural* change—and the impact of the evolutionary forces that shape a company's *industry environment* on strategy formulation. In particular, we focus on two key issues that every strategist must confront: how to assess and deal with *change* and *uncertainty.* Significant current trends analyzed include the globalization of the competitive environment, the information and biotechnology revolutions, the changes in demographics around the world, and the changing domestic and international regulatory environment. We then turn to the analysis of the industries and address questions such as "What is an industry?" and "How do industries evolve?" As part of this discussion we introduce a number of well-known analytic frameworks and techniques including Michael Porter's five forces framework for analyzing industry attractiveness.

Analysis of external change forces is critical to determining what strategic changes a company *should* consider. An assessment of internal strategic resources and capabilities, and of pressures for and against change, is the subject of chapter 3. This is important in determining what strategies a company successfully *can* (and should) pursue. A firm's *strategic resources* include its physical assets (*physical resources*), its relative financial position (*financial resources*), the quality of its people (*human resources*), and specific knowledge, competencies, processes, skills, or cultural aspects of the organization (*organizational resources*). A second aspect of assessing a company's internal strategic environment deals with identifying *pressures for strategic change* that come from within the organization or from its immediate stakeholders. Persistent disappointing performance, new owners or management, limitations to growth with current strategies, scarcity of critical resources, or internal cultural changes are examples of conditions that give rise to such pressures. To make such judgments, we survey techniques such as *financial analysis, stakeholder analysis,* and *SWOT (strengths, weaknesses, opportunities, and threats) analysis.*

Chapter 4 looks at strategy formulation at the *business unit* level. We consider the relative importance of the industry in which a company competes, its competitive position within the industry, and identification of the drivers that determine sustained competitive advantage. This logic naturally suggests a number of *generic strategy choices*—broad strategy prescriptions that define different ways of competing at the business unit level. The relative attractiveness of such generic strategy choices crucially depends on the specific opportunities and challenges analyzed. Accordingly, the next section deals with the question of how to size up a strategic challenge at the business unit level. It introduces a variety of techniques such as *growth vector analysis, value chain analysis, profit pool analysis, gap analysis, competitor analysis* and *product life cycle analysis* that are useful for generating and assessing strategic alternatives. Because strategy is developed in a specific industry context, the next section considers six different industry environments. Three represent different stages in an industry's evolution—*embryonic, growth,* and *mature* industry settings; the other three—*fragmented* industries, *global* and *deregulating* industry environments—are defined by their structure, scope, or by external forces operating on them. We conclude the chapter with a number of special topics—how value creation relates to *innovation,* the importance of *timing* in strategy, *entry-exit* decisions, *vertical integration,* and the *relationship between business unit and corporate strategy.*

In chapter 5 we turn our attention to strategic thinking at the corporate level. The opening section takes a look at the concepts of *economics of scale and scope*—of fundamental importance to corporate strategy—and tries to answer the question: Is bigger always better? Next, we turn to the context in which corporate strategy is developed and executed. In particular, we note the importance of the dispersion in the ownership of large corporations in the last 30 years and emergence of *the market for corporate control.* With this background, we trace the *evolution of strategic thinking* at the corporate level. Four perspectives are identified—the *portfolio, value-based, generic strategy,* and *resource-based* points of view—and their relative merits assessed. This includes a discussion of the principal *analysis techniques* used to dissect corporate portfolios and major *strategy choices* at the corporate level. Next, we look at the issue of *corporate parenting* and how a parenting style affects portfolio composition and management. We conclude the chapter with a discussion of *how to evaluate* strategy choices at the corporate level.

In chapter 6 we take a closer look at the opportunities and risks associated with staking out a *global* competitive position and identify the principal dimensions of a global strategy. To set the stage we first take a look at the driving forces behind the emerging global economy and characterize "globalization" in greater detail as an economic, political, social, and technological phenomenon. *Industry globalization* is the next topic of discussion. In this section we focus on such questions as "What is a global industry?", "What are the driving forces behind the globalization of industries?", and "What explains the dominance of particular countries or regions in global industries?". The third major topic of this chapter is global strategic thinking. In this section we identify the principal dimensions of global strategy and introduce a framework for global strategic thinking that links global strategy options to the nature of the global industry environment. A major tenet of this discussion is that global strategy, more than strategy at the corporate or business unit levels, increasingly is played out in two arenas—a *market* and a *nonmarket* arena. Market dimensions of global strategic thinking concern questions such as "Which markets should we participate in?" "Why?" "In what form?" "To what extent should we standardize products and services?" "Where should we locate key value-added activities?" "Should we have a uniform market positioning worldwide?" and "How do we coordinate competitive moves across the globe?" These questions are aimed at creating value through economic performance in a global context. Nonmarket dimensions of global strategy deal with shaping the global competitive environment. As many executives will attest, the rules of global competition are critical to performance. As a consequence, to enhance their global competitiveness, an increasing number of companies have concluded that they need to participate in the political process of shaping those rules. An *integrated global strategy* therefore consists of market and nonmarket components that act synergistically to create a sustained competitive advantage on a global scale. The effectiveness of different global postures depends importantly on the structure of the global industry. Accordingly, we evaluate the relative effectiveness of different global strategy options in the context of a number of *generic global industry settings.* In the last section of this chapter, we consider the various strategic *risk* factors associated with a global posture.

The epilogue to this book (chapter 7) entitled "Strategy and the (r)Evolution in Management" looks beyond issues of strategy formulation. Specifically, it notes that in today's fast-changing competitive climate effective *leadership* has become a critical determinant of success. Companies are also seeking ways to become more adaptable by experimenting with new forms of *organization.* This reinvention of the corporation reflects a broader paradigm shift about what management is all about. Instead of thinking about the strategic environment as essentially in equilibrium, subject to occasional shocks and disturbances that strategies must address, the new paradigm emphasizes constant, often chaotic change. Getting comfortable with change is not an option anymore; it is a requirement for success. After all, no matter how well crafted a strategy is, success begins with implementation. And as many executives have learned, successful implementation is secured through commitment, not compliance.

A FINAL WORD BEFORE WE GET STARTED

As this chapter has attempted to show, strategy formulation involves both *analysis* and *synthesis.* Each is important. Understanding a company's current position, analyzing what forces drive competition in the industries it competes in, how customers perceive value, and what capabilities can be leveraged to effect a long-term sustainable posture are key to developing a sound strategy. Much of this insight is gained through *analysis*. The ultimate act of creating a strategy based on these insights, however, is creative in nature and relies largely on *synthesis*.

Hamel noted that in any industry there are three kinds of competitors: *rule makers, rule takers, and rule breakers,* and observed that rule breakers—often revolutionary in their approach to strategy—have flourished in the new competitive environment. This book is written for rule makers and rule breakers, *not* rule takers.

Notes

1. "The 21st Century Economy," *Business Week,* August 24–31, 1998.

2. Michael E. Porter, "What is Strategy," *Harvard Business Review,* November–December, 1996, pp. 61–78.

3. "McDonald's: Can it regain its golden touch?" *Business Week,* March 9, 1998.

4. George S. Day, "Maintaining the Competitive Edge: Creating and Sustaining Advantages in Dynamic Competitive Environments," chap. 2, p. 52, in George S. Day and David J. Reibstein (eds.), *Wharton on Dynamic Competitive Strategy* (New York: John Wiley & Sons, 1997).

5. These ideas are based on Timothy A. Luehrman, "Strategy as a Portfolio of Real Options," *Harvard Business Review,* September–October, 1998, pp. 89–99.

6. R. E. Freeman, *Strategic Management: A Stakeholder Approach* (Boston: Pittman, 1984).

7. See, e.g., John A. Pearce, II and Richard B. Robinson, Jr., *Strategic Management: Formulation, Implementation and Control,* 6th ed., (Chicago: Irwin, 1996).

8. Henry Mintzberg, "Crafting Strategy," *Harvard Business Review,* July–August, pp. 66–75. See also Henry Mintzberg and James Brian Quinn, *The Strategy Process: Concepts, Text, and Cases,* 3d ed. (Upper Saddle River, New Jersey: Prentice Hall, 1996.)

9. Gary Hamel and C. K. Prahalad, "Strategic Intent," *Harvard Business Review,* May–June, 1989, pp. 63–76.

10. For a detailed description of the competitive battle between Caterpillar and Komatsu, consult the Harvard Business School case studies: Caterpillar Tractor Co. (9-385-276), Komatsu Ltd. (9-385-277), and Caterpillar-Komatsu in 1986 (9-387-095).

11. See, e.g., Michael E. Porter, *Competitive Strategy: Techniques for Analyzing Industries and Competitors* (New York: Free Press, 1980).

12. Michael E. Porter, in Richard P. Rumelt, Dan E. Schendel, and David J. Teece, *Fundamental Issues in Strategy* (Boston: Harvard Business School Press, 1994): 423.

13. Note on the Boston Consulting Group Concept of Competitive Analysis and Corporate Strategy, Harvard Business School, 1975 (175-175).

14. David J. Collis and Cynthia A. Montgomery, *Corporate Strategy: Resources and Scope of the Firm* (Chicago: Irwin, 1997): 17.

15. C. K. Prahalad and G. Hamel, "The Core Competence of the Corporation," *Harvard Business Review,* May–June, 1990, pp. 79–91.

16. Collis and Montgomery, 1997, op. cit., p. 7.

17. Andrew Campbell, Michael Goold, and Marcus Alexander, "Corporate Strategy: The Quest for Parenting Advantage," *Harvard Business Review*, March–April, 1995, pp. 120–132.

18. These thoughts can be found in C. K. Prahalad, "Weak Signals Versus Strong Paradigms," *Journal of Marketing Research* vol. 32 (August 1995): iii–viii.

19. See Gary Hamel and C. K. Prahalad, "Strategic Intent," *Harvard Business Review,* May–June, 1989, pp. 63–76; C. K. Prahalad and Gary Hamel, "The Core Competence of the Corporation," *Harvard Business Review,* May–June, 1990, pp. 80–91; Gary Hamel and C. K. Prahalad, "Strategy as Stretch and Leverage," *Harvard Business Review,* March–April, 1993, pp. 76–84; Gary Hamel, "Strategy as Revolution," *Harvard Business Review,* July–August, 1996, pp. 73–82.

20. See, e.g., Tom Copeland, Tim Koller, and Jack Murrin, *Valuation: Measuring and Managing the Value of Companies* (New York: McKinsey & Company, Wiley & Sons, 1995).

21. See Michael L. Blyth, Elizabeth A. Friskey, and Alfred Rappaport, "Implementing the Share-

holder Value Approach," *Journal of Business Strategy*, Winter 1986, pp. 48–58; and Alfred Rappaport, "Selecting Strategies that Create Shareholder Value," *Harvard Business Review,* May–June, 1981, pp. 139–149.

22. See George S. Day and Liam Fahey, "Putting Strategy into Shareholder Value Analysis," *Harvard Business Review,* March–April, 1990, pp. 156–162.

23. R. S. Kaplan and D. P. Norton, "Using the Balanced Scorecard as a Strategic Management System," *Harvard Business Review,* January–February, 1996, pp. 75–85; and R. S. Kaplan and D. P. Norton, "The Balanced Scorecard—Measures That Drive Performance," *Harvard Business Review,* January–February, pp. 71–79.

C H A P T E R

Change and Uncertainty in the External Strategic Environment

*I'm trying to get at the fundamental shape of an idea. To articulate that shape, you have to pare off an awful lot of chaos or surrounding information.**

—SARAH CHARLESWORTH

INTRODUCTION

An effective strategy anticipates and capitalizes on relevant changes in a company's strategic environment. In this chapter we look at the importance of changes in a firm's *external strategic environment*—driven by *economic, technological, political, and sociocultural* change—and the impact of the evolutionary forces that shape a company's *industry environment* on strategy formulation. In particular, we focus on two key issues that every strategist must confront: how to assess and deal with *change* and *uncertainty*. In the next chapter we will look at the impact of a firm's internal company environment.

Why Environmental Change Matters

Changes in the external environment, often beyond the control of any single company, can have a profound impact on success. In the previous chapter we saw how Komatsu benefited from a steep rise in the dollar in its competitive battle with Caterpillar in the early eighties. Other environmental forces such as demographic or social changes—the aging of the population, the entry of large numbers of women into the labor force, or the renewed interest in quality-of-life issues—may create new opportunities or threaten existing businesses. The technology revolution is changing the way we live, work, and unwind and spawning entire new industries; and globalization has increased the interdependence among the world's major economies and intensified competition in many industries.

Changes in a company's *industry environment* typically have a more direct and pronounced effect on a company's strategic options. Consider the enormous changes taking place in the telecommunications industry. Twenty years ago, the industry consisted of a number of well-defined regulated services. Deregulation changed all that. Instead of talking about telecommunications, today it may be more useful to speak of "information transmission" services. Traditional telecommunications options are making inroads into mail and the overnight delivery of information, the Internet is progressively supplanting voice communications, cable TV is poised to enter the two-way communications race while broadcast TV and satellite-based communications are about to go

---

*From Judy Glantzman, "Sarah Charlesworth," *Journal of Contemporary Art* (Spring 1988): 59, as taken from Susan Fisher Sterling, *In-Photography: The Art of Sarah Charlesworth* (Santa Fe: SITE, 1997), 80.

digital. Even electric utilities are getting into the act by exploring possibilities to carry information over copper wires.

Some of these changes, such as demographic shifts, are predictable. Others, the oil crisis of the seventies, for example or, more recently, the collapse of a number of Far Eastern economies, take us by surprise. Scanning the environment for forces that potentially have a major impact on a company's fortunes is therefore an important element of strategic analysis. Most companies routinely follow economic trends such as GDP (Gross Domestic Product) growth, interest rates, inflation, employment, and so on. Monitoring new technological developments has also become an integral part of many companies' strategic development process. Trends in the legal/political arena or in sociocultural aspects of our environment are typically followed on a less formal basis but are assuming greater importance in many industries as the pace of change picks up.

CHANGE IN THE EXTERNAL ENVIRONMENT

Identifying relevant trends and change forces in the external strategic environment that can materially impact a company's competitive position is the first step in the process of analyzing external opportunities and threats. Publications such as the *Wall Street Journal, Business Week, The Economist, Fortune, Forbes,* and the *Harvard Business Review* regularly carry features dealing with new trends and issues. The writing of books on "life in the twenty-first century" has become a growth industry. Television, radio, and the Internet regularly feature documentaries, talk shows, and other programs that shape our perceptions of how environmental change affects business. Widely quoted futurists such as Alvin Toffler and John Naisbitt have tried to integrate much of what we know about the changes that are occurring in technology, our culture, and the economy and to paint a picture of life in the next century.[1] The challenge is to decide whom to listen to, what to read, and how to assess the relative importance of different trends to a company's strategic future.

The following sections will identify—in no particular order of importance—some of the most important issues, trends, and forces in the external strategic environment.

Globalization

As the economies of the industrialized nations mature, growth prospects for many industries in traditional markets are diminishing. At the same time, other parts of the globe—the Far East, Central and Eastern Europe, Latin America—are experiencing faster economic development causing the "center of gravity" of the world's business climate to swing from the developed economies to the developing nations. This shift in global economic activity is driven by many factors: living standards in developing countries are rising; free enterprise is spreading, slowly but surely, across the globe; technology is exploding; barriers to trade are coming down; communication is becoming instantaneous worldwide; and global financial systems deliver capital efficiently to where it is used most productively.

The globalization of the competitive landscape has forced many companies to fundamentally rethink their strategies. Whereas once only a few businesses such as oil could be labeled truly global, today all kinds of industries—from pharmaceuticals to aircraft to computers, and many more—are becoming global in scale and scope. Others, a number of service industries, for example, may never become totally global but will increasingly have characteristics commonly associated with global industries. In this changing environment, "thinking globally" is no longer a luxury but a prerequisite for success. Customers around the world are increasingly demanding the same high levels of product quality and service we take for granted. As a consequence, issues such as how to successfully penetrate foreign markets, how to exploit diverse capabilities and take advantage of regional cost advantages, how to coordinate competitive activity on a global basis, and how to develop, source, manufacture, and distribute products and services for world markets have become the key to building and sustaining global competitive advantage.

Today, car companies use global networks to design new models, source parts from suppliers in Japan, Korea, Germany, and a host of other countries, assemble them in key locations around the world, and arrange financing in local markets. This book is written on a computer made in Asia, using software developed in Washington State, and probably will be printed on a German printing press using ink from Korea and paper from Canada.

Globalization has not only increased competitive intensity but has also raised business risk. Greater exposure to international markets means venturing into other, often unfamiliar cultures, dealing with different regulatory agencies and structures, and progressing to a higher level of political and currency risk. Few companies, however, can afford to ignore the issue of globalization. For most the question is not "Should we adopt a more global posture?" but "To what extent and how?"

The Information Age

The speed by which technology is changing our lives is nothing short of astonishing. Ten years ago the Internet was still a dream. Today, customers routinely tap into Federal Express's package-tracking database to check on the status of their shipment. Meanwhile, other companies including AT&T and Levi Strauss are putting together Intranets for their information bases so that employees can reallocate investments in their 401(K) plans, work together with corporate offices around the globe, and connect to their homes.[2]

Computing power continues to increase exponentially. What once took a machine the size of an average living room several days can now be done in seconds on a desktop. Entire new industries have sprung up in a matter of years, while others have been totally restructured, merged into others, or disappeared. Deregulation and the advent of digital technology have created a battle between phone companies, publishing houses, studios, broadcasters, cable television operators, and information technology companies for market share in what is expected to be a trillion-dollar telecommunications industry. A new wave of megamergers is already underway. In the future we can expect the emergence of a new group of "supercarriers"—companies that either on their own or through alliances will offer a full menu of electronic communications.[3]

Through improvements in products and services, technology is also changing the quality of our lives. For many people the days of the maddening commute through endless streams of traffic and congestion are already over. Flexible work hours, the emergence of the fully equipped home office, and new forms of communication are making new lifestyles possible, which allow for a blend of work with family life.

The Biotechnology Revolution

Although much of the focus in recent years has been on the enormous changes brought about by the information technology revolution, another, equally important sequence of scientific developments is just around the corner: the biotechnology revolution. Public understanding of the impact this revolution is likely to have is still low. For many people news of the successful cloning of a sheep in Scotland in early 1997 represents the first and only exposure to the challenges and opportunities this revolution may open up. But while the birth of "Dolly" may be an important scientific feat, it represents but a tiny part of the coming biotechnology revolution. The rapid advances in humankind's ability to understand and manipulate the basic elements of life are likely to fundamentally alter scientific inquiry and allow solutions to problems that could not be solved before.

Business Week forecast that farmers will grow plants that make plastic—enough to lessen our dependence on oil, that whole families of new drugs will allow the eradication of many types of disease, and that major advancements in pollution cleanup will become possible. In the meantime, companies such as Motorola have begun to investigate the potential of genetic engineering in computing—the first step toward a DNA computer.[4]

The biotechnology revolution is thought to have the greatest potential in three areas: medicine, environmental matters, and agriculture. It is also possible that in the long run advances in the biosciences will shake up the world of electronics and make silicon obsolete. Along with these breakthroughs, the biotechnology revolution will bring a host of new challenges. Already questions are being asked about the moral and legal implications of our increasing ability to manipulate life. How far should doctors go in testing for genetic conditions? Who owns the test results? Should companies be able to use such information in forging their strategic direction? The answers to these questions are by no means obvious. What is clear, however, is that the biotechnology revolution is here and we can no longer avoid thinking about its impact on our future.

Changing Demographics

Of all the social changes in the Western world—increased participation of women in the workforce, postponement of marriage, more divorces, smaller families, the emergence of ethnic consumer groups, and the proliferation of more varied lifestyles—none will have as great an influence as the gradual aging of the population.

The average age of the U.S. population is expected to increase from 27.9 in 1970 to 34.9 by the end of the century. This aging of the population is not limited to the United States; European countries and Japan are experiencing a similar trend. This massive increase in the number of senior citizens—the result of lower birthrates, advances in healthcare, and a host of other societal factors—creates enormous opportunities for companies attuned to this trend. For others, it can be threatening. Demand for specialized products and services targeted at senior citizens—assisted living, healthcare, new forms of transportation, and a whole array of specialized financial services—will grow substantially in the years to come. At the same time, those banking on a continuation of today's "youth culture" may be in for a rude awakening.

The impact of this massive demographic shift is not limited to the private sector. We already read how federal and state budgets may be unable to cope with the projected increased expenditures on Social Security and a host of other entitlements. Will taxes have to be raised? Are there other ways of providing security with dignity for our seniors? These and related questions will increasingly occupy the minds of politicians and strategists alike.

A New Business Cycle?

As technology continues to become more important to the health of the economy, questions such as "Has the familiar business cycle been repealed?" or "Are we in a new economic era?" are heard with greater frequency. With continued global economic expansion, steady job growth, record levels of corporate profits, and inflation under control, it would be easy to conclude that "that old bugaboo of capitalism—the business cycle—has been tamed."[5]

There can be no question that high technology has replaced traditional cyclical industries as the principal engine of economic growth. More than one-third of the growth in the U.S. gross national product now comes from such sectors as information technology and telecommunications. The rapid advances in the state of the art in these areas have produced a high level of growth with low inflation because falling equipment prices have counterbalanced rising wages. But does this mean that the business cycle has been repealed? Most likely, no. If anything, high-tech industries are more volatile than their traditional counterparts. Product life cycles of high-tech products and the technologies behind them tend to be shorter and characterized by patterns of fast growth and decline. What is more, because much of the economy's growth is now dependent upon high technology, there is a substantial multiplier effect—a decline in the high-tech sector is likely to have a major effect on the state of health of other parts of the economy. Thus, the more dominant role of high technology in the economy may well foreshadow greater volatility in the future.

The Euro

Jeffrey Garten, dean of the Yale School of Management and *Business Week* guest columnist, made a bold prediction: "Europe's impending creation of a monetary union with a single currency, the euro, will be the most important change in the global economy well into the next century. It will have a more lasting impact than virtually any other economic event that can be imagined—such as the reemergence of Japan as a powerhouse or the extension of NAFTA throughout South America. And it could pose a serious challenge to America's economic supremacy."[6]

Whether or not this prediction will come to pass, there can be no doubt that the introduction of the euro marks a major milestone for European integration. When fully operational, the European Economic and Monetary Union (EMU) area will be the world's second-largest economy, consisting of 288 million people and a gross domestic product of nearly 20 percent of the global total. Businesses and individuals will be able to buy and sell products and services across European borders more easily; trade and competition will increase; a Pan-European capital market is likely to develop, and the EMU may encourage more flexible labor markets and further harmonization of taxation and regulatory policies.

Regulatory Issues

If the competitive landscape has become more uncertain so have the rules that govern competitive behavior. *Business Week* noted that the Justice Department and the Federal Trade Commission appear to be "crafting the rules and the rationale for them as they go along."[7] In past simpler times, an approval for a merger proposal principally depended on the resulting degree of market concentration. Clearly, more recent antitrust decisions defy this simple logic. As examples, consider the approval of the merger between Boeing Co. and McDonnell Douglas Corp., creating a powerhouse in the domestic commercial aircraft market, and the reservations about the WorldCom Inc.—MCI Communications Corp. combination because of a concern that the combined company would control 50 percent of the Internet "backbone." And then there are questions about whether or not or how to prevent Microsoft from dominating the Information Superhighway. Executives can be forgiven if they are confused. Have the criteria changed? What are the rules of the game?

It may be too early to tell. Clearly the concern has shifted from simple measures of concentration in mainly mature industries to one of promoting competition, protecting consumers, and preserving innovation in a quickly evolving, global, high-tech marketplace where consolidation is gaining momentum and new monopolies may be taking hold. How to do this, however, is still very much open to question.

Take the Microsoft case. The old adage, "Tall trees catch more wind" certainly seems apt. The Justice Department, acting on complaints from Microsoft's rivals and corporate customers, is putting pressure on the company to loosen its grip on the market for operating software. It maintains Microsoft has a monopoly and suspects that the company has reached its current position using anticompetitive tactics. It appears to be considering a range of options including forcing Microsoft to decouple its browser from its operating system. On the other side, Bill Gates says that complaints about Microsoft are misdirected; that browsing is a natural extension to an operating system; and that rivals are merely envious of Microsoft's innovative accomplishments. Who is right?

Resolving these issues will take years and protracted court battles. The stakes are high. Microsoft is poised to move into every business where operating software is critical—from mainframe computing to household appliances. Future decisions by the Justice Department will determine which markets the company can enter, how, and at what pace. The outcomes will not only determine Microsoft's future but redefine the playing field for current and potential rivals for years to come.[8]

Until progress in solving these problems is made, confusion over the competitive rules of the game will persist. In the meantime, we can expect more court battles and high-level lobbying. The Baby Bells are holding on to their monopolies in local phone service by tying up the Federal Communications Commission (FCC) in court while the cable-TV industry is fighting to keep out competition from satellite providers using an alliance with broadcasters. And because these issues increasingly are contested in the political arena, all will attempt to pressure Congress to create or preserve competitive advantage.

Nostalgia Time?

A number of social studies indicate that stress levels are rising and many people feel increasingly overwhelmed by the demands of the Information Age. This explains why a growing number of companies find there is money to be made by marketing a vision of a simpler, more peaceful and less stressful time. Volkswagen, for one, is capitalizing on this "nostalgia boom" with its new Beetle. With its U.S. market share down to less than

1 percent, VW is hoping its new 1998 Beetle, clearly reminiscent of the past but equipped with all the modern features car buyers demand, such as air bags and power outlets for cell phones, can revive its fortunes. Its appeal to a simpler past is evident in its advertising, "If you sold your soul in the '80s," proclaims one ad, "here's your chance to buy it back."[9]

Volkswagen is not alone in going back to the future. As *Business Week* notes, "These days, nostalgia marketing is everywhere, from almost forgotten brands such as Burma Shave to jingles that borrow from classic rock. Pepsi uses the Rolling Stones' *Brown Sugar,* while James Brown's *I Feel Good* helps sell Senokot Laxatives. Hollywood is awash with remakes of movies and TV shows plucked from an earlier era. Even retired slogans and mascots are being resurrected. Maxwell House has dusted off "Good to the last drop," and Charlie the Tuna is swimming his way through Starkist tuna ads once again."[10]

CHANGES IN THE INDUSTRY ENVIRONMENT

Changes in the industry environment often have a more direct impact on a company's strategic position. The entrance of a new competitor, for example, or a major breakthrough in product or process technology that materially changes the existing cost structure or a product or service's functionality or quality can radically alter the competitive balance in an industry. Analysis of the industry environment should therefore be focused on identifying forces of change that potentially have a major impact on the structure and the drivers of competition in an industry.

What Is an Industry?

When we speak of industries we tend to think in terms of a group of companies or organizations that compete directly with each other in the marketplace. While intuitive, the simplicity of this definition masks a complex issue. In many instances, there is more than one way in which an industry may be reasonably defined. Do makers of facsimile machines compete with each other, with manufacturers of personal computers, telephone companies, the U.S. Postal Service, or overnight delivery companies? Is competition primarily between products or companies? Should we therefore analyze rivalry at the business unit level or at the corporate level? Should we distinguish between regional competition and global rivalry? As these questions suggest, deciding on industry boundaries is difficult. What is more, errors of judgment can be extremely costly. The use of too narrow a definition—"railroads competing with other railroads"—can lead to strategic myopia and cause us to overlook important opportunities or threats. The use of too broad a definition on the other hand—"we're in a high-tech industry"—may render analysis meaningless.[11]

Abell and Hammond suggest defining industries along four dimensions: (1) *products,* (2) types of *customers,* (3) *geography,* and (4) *stages* in the *production-distribution pipeline.*[12] The first dimension—products—can be further broken down into two components: *functions* and *technologies.* Function refers to what the product or service does. Some cooking appliances merely cook; others cook and roast; still others fry, boil, or do it all. It is important to note that functionality can be actual or perceived. Some over-the-counter remedies, for example, are positioned as "cold relievers," while others are promoted as "allergy medicines." This is as much a matter of positioning and perception

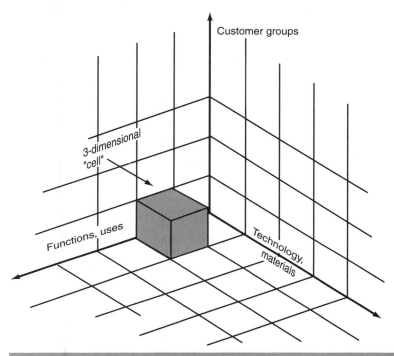

FIGURE 2-1 Dimensions of Industry Definition

Source: From Robert D. Buzzell, *Note on Market Definition and Segmentation,* 579–083 Boston: Harvard Business School, 1978. Copyright © 1978 by the President and Fellows of Harvard College. Reprinted by permission.

as of actual functionality. Technology is a second distinguishing factor; some cooking appliances use gas while others are electric, for example.

Defining an industry's boundaries requires the simultaneous consideration of all of these dimensions. In addition, it is important to distinguish between the *industry* a company competes in and the *market(s) it serves*. For example, a company may compete in the appliance *industry* but choose refrigerators as its *served market*. Figure 2-1 reflects these considerations. It depicts an industry as a collection of (adjacent) three-dimensional cells; each comprising a particular combination of functions/uses, technologies/materials, and types of customers. The task of defining an industry therefore consists of identifying a group of market cells thought most relevant to the strategic analysis at hand.

In the process of generating strategic alternatives, it is often useful to use multiple definitions. Assessing a company's growth potential, for example, may require the use of a different industry/market definition than, say, assessing its relative cost position. The issue is one of scope.

Industry Structure and Porter's Five Forces Model

The publication of the book *Competitive Strategy* fundamentally changed the way we approach industry and competitive analysis.[13] Based on an extensive study of a large number of industries, Michael Porter concluded that an industry's profit potential is

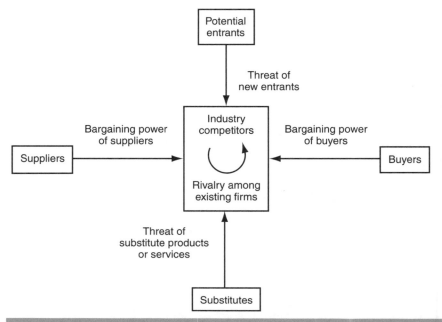

FIGURE 2-2 Porter's Five Forces Model

Source: Reprinted with the permission of The Free Press, a Division of Simon & Schuster, Inc. from *Competitive Strategy: Techniques for Analyzing Industries and Competitors* by Michael E. Porter. Copyright © 1980 by The Free Press.

largely determined by the intensity of the *competitive rivalry* within that industry. Rivalry, in turn, is explained in terms of five forces: the *threat of new entrants,* the *bargaining power of customers,* the *bargaining power of suppliers,* the *threat of substitute products* or *services* and the *jockeying among current rivals.* Let us briefly consider Porter's so-called *five forces model* (Figure 2-2).

The Threat of Entry   When it is relatively easy to enter an industry, we expect the industry to be highly competitive. Potential new entrants threaten to increase the industry's capacity and drive down prices and margins, to intensify the fight for market share, and to upset the balance between demand and supply. Whether or not this threat is real depends on two factors: (1) what barriers to entry exist, and (2) how entrenched competitors are likely to react.

Porter identifies six major barriers to entry: (1) economies of scale, (2) product differentiation (brand equity), (3) capital requirements, (4) cost disadvantages independent of size, (5) access to distribution channels, and (6) government regulations. Consider, for example, the difficulty of entering the soft drink industry and competing with advertising giants such as Coca-Cola and Pepsi Cola. Or the plight of microbrewers trying to gain distribution for their brands of beer against major companies such as Anheuser Busch. In high-tech industries, capital requirements and accumulated experience comprise major barriers. This said, industry conditions can change and strategic windows of opportunity can open up. A prime example is deregulation. When airlines were deregulated in the early eighties, a host of new carriers was able to enter the industry because existing barriers were removed.

Powerful Suppliers and Buyers   Buyers and suppliers can sometimes exercise considerable influence over the participants in an industry by exerting a major influence on prices, quality, or the quantity demanded or sold. Consider, for example, how soft drink concentrate producers, by raising prices in the late eighties, contributed to the erosion of the profit margins of bottlers because they could not pass the increases on to the final customer.

Generally, suppliers are more powerful when (1) there are a few dominant companies and they are more concentrated than the industry they serve, (2) the component supplied is differentiated, making the switching of suppliers difficult, (3) there are few substitutes, (4) suppliers can integrate forward, and (5) the industry comprises but a small portion of the suppliers' revenue base.

Buyers have substantial power when (1) there are few of them and/or they buy in large volume, (2) the product is relatively undifferentiated, making it easy to switch to other suppliers, (3) the buyers' purchases represent a sizable portion of the sellers' total revenues, and (4) buyers can integrate backwards, among other factors. Wal-Mart, for example, due to its size and industry position has considerable leverage in negotiating with suppliers.

Substitute Products or Services   Substitute products or services continually threaten most industries and in effect place a lid on prices and profitability. HBO and Pay-per-View are substitutes for the movie rental business and effectively limit what the industry can charge for its services. Moreover, if cost structures can be changed, for example, by employing new technology, substitutes can take substantial market share from existing businesses. The increased availability of pay-per-view entertainment over cable networks, for example, has begun to erode the competitive position of movie rental companies. From a strategic perspective, therefore, substitute products or services that deserve the closest scrutiny are those that (1) show improvements in price performance relative to the industry average, and (2) are produced by industries with deep pockets.

Andrew Grove, founder of Intel, has suggested adding a sixth force to Porter's model: the influence of *complementary products*. Complementors are businesses from whom customers buy complementary products. Computers need software and software needs hardware; cars use gasoline and gasoline needs cars. When the interests of the industry are aligned with those of complementors, the status quo is preserved. New technologies or approaches can upset the existing order, however, and cause their paths to diverge.[14] One example is a change in technological standards that renders previously compatible products and services incompatible.

Rivalry among Participants   How competitive an industry is also depends greatly on the number, relative size, and competitive prowess of its participants, the industry's growth rate, and related characteristics. Porter suggests intense rivalry can be expected when (1) competitors are numerous and relatively equal in size and power, (2) industry growth is slow and the competitive battle is more about market share than creating new customers, (3) fixed costs are high or the product or service is perishable, (4) capacity increases can only be secured in large increments, and (5) exit barriers are high making it expensive to discontinue operations.

Strategic Groups

A *strategic group* is a set of firms that face similar threats and opportunities in an industry but which differ from the threats and opportunities faced by other sets of companies in the same industry.[15] Rivalry is generally more intense within strategic groups than between them because members of the same strategic group focus on the same market segments with similar strategies and resources. In the fast-food industry, for example, hamburger chains tend to compete more directly with other hamburger chains than with chicken or pizza restaurants. Similarly, in pharmaceuticals, strategic groups can be defined in terms of what disease categories companies tend to focus on. Analysis of strategic groups helps explain how competition evolves within and between competitors with a similar strategic focus over time. Strategic groups can be mapped using broad characteristics, such as price and product line breadth, or other pairs of variables, for example, the degree of vertical integration that differentiates competitors within an industry.

Industry Evolution

Industry structures change over time. Entry barriers may fall away as in the case of home publishing, or may go up significantly, as has happened in a number of industries where brand identity became an important competitive weapon. Other industries are becoming more concentrated as real or perceived benefits of scale and scope cause the industry to consolidate. Models of *industry evolution* can help us understand how and why industries change over time. Perhaps the word "evolution" is somewhat deceptive; it suggests a process of slow, gradual change. Sometimes structural change occurs with remarkable rapidity as in the case of deregulation or when a major technological breakthrough enhances the prospects of some companies at the expense of others.

The personal computer industry provides a good example of the importance of understanding the forces that shape industry evolution. As recently as the late seventies, personal computers were beyond the reach of most Americans. The technology was, by today's standards, primitive; equipment prices were high and software was cumbersome and mainly aimed at business applications and office productivity. What a difference 20 years makes! In 1997, PC household penetration stood at almost 40 percent. And, as technology advances further and prices drop well below the $1,000 level, a new segment of buyers, many of whom do not currently own a PC, is pushing this number higher. Forrester Research estimates that PC penetration is likely to reach 60 percent of U.S. homes by 2002. If this forecast proves correct the PC will become a nearly ubiquitous tool for most households—like the telephone or the automobile. Universal access, in turn, foreshadows further growth in Internet traffic, and will drive up advertising rates, thereby allowing electronic commerce to fulfill its long-awaited promise and quickly change the way business is done in all kinds of industries, as companies such as Amazon.com already demonstrate.[16]

The *product life cycle model*—based on the theory of diffusion of innovations and its logical counterpart, the pattern of acceptance of new ideas—is perhaps the best-known model of industry evolution. It contends that an industry passes through a number of stages—introduction, growth, maturity, and decline—in the course of time. The different stages are defined by changes in the rate of growth of industry sales, generally thought to follow an S-shaped curve reflecting the cumulative result of first and repeat adoptions of a product or service over time (Figure 2-3).[17]

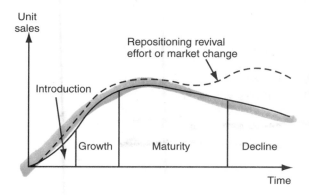

FIGURE 2-3 The Product Life Cycle Concept

Source: William M. Moore and Edgar A. Pessemier, *Product Planning and Management: Designing and Delivering Values.* Copyright © 1993 McGraw-Hill Company, Inc., New York, NY. Reproduced with permission.

Although useful as a general construct for understanding how the principle of diffusion can shape industry sales in the course of time, the product life cycle concept has little predictive value. Empirical studies have repeatedly shown that industry growth does not always follow an S-shaped pattern and industries can recycle a number of times before declining. In some instances stages are skipped, while at other times they repeat themselves. More importantly, the product life cycle concept does not allow for the possibility that companies, through strategic actions such as increasing the pace of innovation or repositioning their offerings, can *affect* the shape of the growth curve. Taking an industry growth curve as a given, therefore, can become a self-fulfilling prophecy.[18] We will discuss this model and its implications for strategy in greater detail in chapter 4.

Dimensions of Industry Evolution

For analytic purposes, it is often useful to analyze changes in industry structure in terms of a number of key dimensions such as the movement from a primarily *vertical* to a more *horizontal* structure or vice versa, changes in the degree of industry *concentration,* increases or decreases in the degree of *product differentiation,* and changes in the relative *maturity* of the industry.

These dimensions are illustrated by the convergence of three industries that originated some 50 years apart—telecommunications, computers, and television—which have spawned a new "multimedia industry" in which traditional industry boundaries have all but disappeared. Instead of consisting of three distinct "vertical" businesses in which being vertically integrated was the key to success, the new industry appears to have evolved toward a structure of five primarily "horizontal" segments: content (products and services), packaging (bundling of content and additional functionality), the network (physical infrastructure), transmission (distribution), and display terminals (devices to capture and display information).

In the new structure, strategic advantage for many companies is primarily determined by their relative position within one of the five value-chain components. Of course, vertical integration may once again become an important strategy when economics of scale and scope become more critical to competitive success and the principal driver behind another round of industry consolidation. It is equally predictable that not all participants or affected companies are likely to survive this kind of a shake-up.

Quality broadline competitors, such as Disney, can be confident about their future. Some content providers will team up with distribution companies anxious to secure content for their mode of delivery. Transmission companies will focus, individually or jointly, on upgrading their networks. Computer companies will face new challenges as the game shifts from a hardware to a content/access battle. And terminal producers will have the opportunity to dazzle consumers with a whole new array of display devices and ancillary products.[19] This illustration shows that industry evolution can move in cycles.

The preceding example also shows that when economies of scale are important, that is when market share and total costs are inversely related, industry structures are often more *concentrated.* Observing that in many such industries the size distribution of business firms is highly skewed, the Boston Consulting Group coined the "Rule of Three and Four" stating that many stable markets will have only three significant competitors and their market shares will roughly be proportioned as four-to-two-to-one.[20] Subsequently, studies have shown that as markets evolve, they sometimes become less concentrated, suggesting that the relationship between relative share and cost position is less pronounced in *mature* markets than it is for *immature* markets. The latter explains why larger companies often lose market share as the industry matures—their cost advantage diminishes over time.[21]

In contrast, in *fragmented* industries, characterized by a relatively *low* degree of *concentration,* no single player has a major market share. Such industries are found in many areas of the economy. Some are highly *differentiated* (application software) while others tend to *commodity* status (concrete products). In the absence of major forces for change, fragmented industries can remain fragmented for a long time.

New Patterns

Many new industries such as the cellular telephone or high definition television industries cannot evolve without some convergence in *technological standards.* Competition for standards or formats is frequently waged by a group of companies led by the developer of a standard competing with another group of companies favoring a different standard. This new competition for standard or format share is important because the winning standard will garner a substantial share of future profits. Consider, for example, the battle between the VHS and Betamax formats in the field of videorecording or that between Intel and Motorola over hardware standards in the PC industry.

For industries in which competition for standards has become an important determinant of strategic success, Prahalad has proposed a new model that describes industry evolution in three phases.[22] In the first phase, competition is mostly focused on ideas, product concepts, technology choices, and the building of a competency base. The primary goal at this stage is to learn more about the future potential of the industry and about the key factors that will determine future success or failure. In the second phase, competition is more about building a viable coalition of partners that will support a standard against competing formats. Companies cooperating at this stage may compete vigorously in phase three of the process—the battle for market share for end products and profits.

As competition becomes more global, industries consolidate and technology becomes more pervasive, the lines between customers, suppliers, competitors, and partners are increasingly becoming blurred. With greater frequency companies competing in one market collaborate in others. At times, they may be each other's customers or suppliers.

This complex juxtaposition of roles suggests that questions such as "What will this industry look like in five or ten years time?" are often extremely difficult to answer and that relying on simple, stylized models of industry evolution can be dangerous. And as industry boundaries become more permeable, structural changes in *adjacent* industries—industries serving the same customer base with different products or services, or industries using similar technologies and production processes—or *related* industries—industries supplying components, technologies, or complementary services—increasingly influence an industry's outlook for the future. Finally, it is worth remembering that change sometimes is simply a function of time. For example, buyers generally become more discriminating as they become more familiar with a product and its substitutes and, as a consequence, are likely to be more explicit in their demands.

DEALING WITH UNCERTAINTY*

Uncertainty Is a Given

Documenting the kinds of change and counterforces that are likely to impact a company's future competitive position is the first step toward formulating a strategic posture. For this analysis to be actionable, we must also assess the degree of *uncertainty* associated with the *speed* with which such forces occur and the possible *outcomes* they foreshadow. Some change processes occur gradually and are knowable if not predictable. We may not be able to determine exactly when and how they affect a specific industry or issue but their broad impact is relatively well understood. The globalization of the competitive climate and most demographic and social trends fall into this category. The prospect of new industry regulations creates a more immediate kind of uncertainty—the new regulatory structure will either be adopted or it will not. The collapse of boundaries between industries constitutes yet another scenario—the change forces themselves may be identifiable but their outcomes are not totally predictable. And there are change forces such as the sudden collapse of foreign governments, outbreaks of war, or major technological discoveries that are inherently random in nature and cannot easily be foreseen.

An important, related question is how can we relate strategic *choice* to different levels of uncertainty? Should we think about high stake bets in an attempt to shape the future as Kodak did when it decided to invest $500 million a year aimed at redefining digital photography? Or is it better to be somewhat risk-averse and make a series of smaller investments designed to reserve the right to play?

The Concept of a Change Arena

The *strength* of a change or counterforce—whether it originates within or outside a company—is determined by its current and future impact on the firm's competitive position. A strong change force can substantially erode a company's market position if it does not anticipate, prepare, and respond appropriately at the right time. On the other hand, "aware" companies have an opportunity to strengthen their competitive position by leveraging the momentum generated by the change force. Consider the shift from mainframe to distributed computing. A number of companies including IBM substantially

*Hugh Courtney, Jane Kirkland and Patrick Viguerie, "Strategy Under Uncertainty." *Harvard Business Review* (November–December, 1997) pp. 66–79.

underestimated the strength or timing of this change force and saw their competitive position substantially eroded. Meanwhile, a number of start-up firms carefully staked out a position in the distributed computing arena or simply were in the right position at the right time. Whether by chance or design, their positioning created the opportunity to "ride the wave" of this change force to prosperity.

A *change arena* is a pictorial representation of the relative strength of strategic forces of change and forces of resistance in terms of four domains (Figure 2-4).[23]

Domain 1: Weak Change Forces, Strong Resistance

Many stable or highly regulated industries are sheltered from the winds of change and are controlled by a few dominant firms with the lion's share of the market. Subsequently, strategic positions in these industries are generally well understood by all players and tend to be fairly stable. As long as resistance forces dominate the forces for change, strategic behavior will be highly predictable—its essence is continuity. Provided the strength of the change forces does not increase, this situation can last indefinitely.

Domain 2: Strong Change Forces, Weak Resistance

In this scenario the forces of change far exceed the threshold of resistance and change occurs continuously. This represents a strategic environment in which no individual player or even a small group can block the forces of change. A number of high-tech industries, populated by a larger number of small, innovative players, share this trait of continuous adaptation.

Domain 3: Weak Change Forces, Weak Resistance

Industries with weak but finely balanced forces of change and resistance tend to experience sporadic, relatively minor turning points when the balance is upset by events such as the occasional entry of a new competitor, relative minor changes in technology, or small shifts in economic conditions. On the whole, the industry and the companies that comprise the industry adapt relatively easily to the new conditions, and the fundamentals that determine industry behavior remain intact. A number of retailing sectors fit this profile.

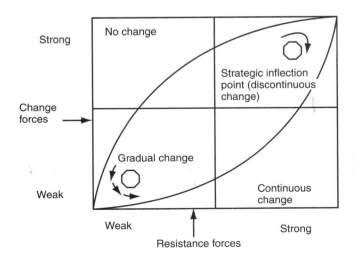

FIGURE 2-4 The Concept of a Change Arena

Copyright © 1994, by The Regents of the University of California. Reprinted from the *California Management Review,* vol. 36, no. 2. By permission of The Regents.

Domain 4: Strong Change Forces, Strong Resistance

When strong change forces duel with strong forces of resistance, change can be sharply discontinuous. Think of the impact the invention of the semiconductor had or of events such as deregulation in the airline and telecommunications industries. Such shocks to the system are characterized by a massive shift from the status quo to a new order. Such upheavals are often called *strategic inflection points.*

Strategic inflection points are relatively rare in most industries but when they occur their impact is significant. They are not confined to high-tech environments. The advent of privatization, for example, defines a strategic inflection point in many industries in the former Communist world. Anticipating strategic inflection points and capitalizing on the opportunities they represent is one of the greatest challenges in strategy development.

Scenario Planning

Originally developed at Royal Dutch/Shell in London, *scenario planning* is probably the most widely used technique for constructing alternative plausible futures of a business's external environment.[24] Its purpose is to analyze the impact of various uncontrollable change forces on the strategic playing field and to test the resiliency of specific strategy alternatives. It is mostly used by businesses that are highly sensitive to external forces—energy companies, for example. Industries that are traditionally less sensitive to external change forces such as the packaged consumer goods industry, however, are increasingly feeling the winds of change. As a result, scenario planning has become a standard environmental analysis tool.

The first step in scenario planning is to carefully define the boundaries of the planning effort. Which elements of strategy are we focused on? What possible future developments need to be probed? Are we dealing with technological change, demographic trends, or resource issues? What time horizon are we considering? Three years, five, ten? The second step consists of identifying the most important determinants of the strategic environment. The key question here is, what forces or developments are likely to have the greatest ability to shape the future? The third step involves the construction of a comprehensive set of future scenarios based on different combinations of possible outcomes. Some combinations will be of greater interest than others, either because they have greater impact on the strategic issue at hand, or because they are more or less likely to occur. As a result, a few scenarios usually emerge that become the focus of a more detailed analysis. In the fourth and final step scenario-specific forecasts are generated that allow us to assess the implications of the alternative futures for strategic postures and choices.

An Example

Planning Review published a case study describing how in 1987 researchers at Statoil, Norway's state-owned oil and gas company, used scenario planning to assist in the development of a technology strategy.[25] First, the team developed four alternative planning scenarios for the 1987–2010 period around three high-impact/high-uncertainty dimensions: (1) The structure of the energy market—whether it would be a seller's or buyer's market, (2) the state of the Norwegian economy—moving toward energy dependence or toward diversified restructuring, and (3) the way technology could evolve—in a fragmented or integrated fashion.

The four scenarios analyzed were

- *Scenario A.* Norway's future is primarily an oil and gas economy; the oil and gas industry is a seller's market; the economy is energy dependent; technology is still fragmented
- *Scenario B.* Oil and gas benefits spur a restructuring of the economy; the oil and gas industry is a seller's market; the economy has diversified; an integrated oil industry technology is emerging
- *Scenario C.* The country struggles; a buyer's market for oil and gas develops; energy dependence persists; technology remains fragmented
- *Scenario D.* Norway is driven from oil dependence by global restructuring; a buyer's market for oil and gas develops; energy dependence continues; technology remains fragmented

At the same time, they prepared a detailed assessment of Statoil's current technology portfolio in terms of (1) how much each technology contributed to operating goals, (2) satisfying market needs, and (3) advancing the state of the art. With these insights, they analyzed what each scenario might mean for key technology issues such as R&D (Research and Development) funding, government relations, and so on. By focusing on the commonalities and differences between these implications, a complete set of technology strategy options could be identified including one that appeared relatively resilient and would therefore serve the company well under a variety of alternative futures.

Dealing with Uncertainty

Courtney, Kirkland, and Viguerie noted that a binary approach to dealing with uncertainty in which the future is either thought to be known or unknown can be dangerous and that forcing precise predictions in inherently uncertain situations can lead to seriously deficient strategic thinking.[26] Instead, they suggest we focus on the degree of *residual* uncertainty present in the strategic environment—the uncertainty that remains after all knowable change forces have been analyzed—and distinguish between four levels of residual uncertainty (Figure 2-5).

Level 1: A Clear Enough Future
Some strategic environments are so sufficiently transparent and stable that a single forecast of the future can be made with a reasonable degree of confidence. A number of mature, low-tech industries fall into this category. It also applies to more narrowly defined strategic challenges such as countering a specific competitor in a specific market or region.

Level 2: Alternate Futures
At times the future can be envisioned in terms of a small number of *discrete* scenarios. In such cases we may not be able to forecast with any precision which outcome will occur but the set of possible outcomes is fully understood. Businesses that are affected by major legislative or regulatory changes fall into this category.

Level 3: A Range of Futures
Level three defines a higher level of uncertainty in which we can identify the key variables that are likely to shape the future but we cannot reduce this knowledge to a

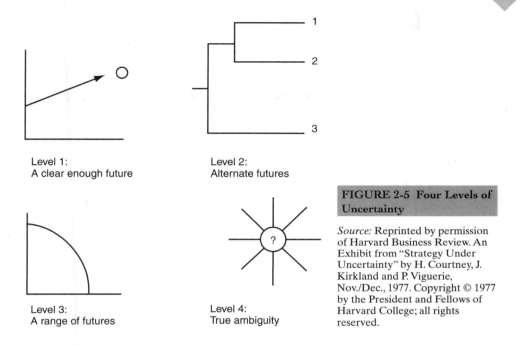

Level 1:
A clear enough future

Level 2:
Alternate futures

Level 3:
A range of futures

Level 4:
True ambiguity

FIGURE 2-5 Four Levels of Uncertainty

Source: Reprinted by permission of Harvard Business Review. An Exhibit from "Strategy Under Uncertainty" by H. Courtney, J. Kirkland and P. Viguerie, Nov./Dec., 1977. Copyright © 1977 by the President and Fellows of Harvard College; all rights reserved.

few discrete, plausible outcomes. Instead, a range of almost *continuous* outcomes is possible. Courtney et al. cite the example of a European consumer goods company trying to decide whether to introduce its products to the Indian market. The best available market research might identify only a broad range of potential market shares.

Level 4: True Ambiguity

At this level even the driving forces that are likely to shape the future are hard to identify. As a consequence, no discrete scenarios or even range of outcomes can be predicted. While level four situations are rare, they do exist. Take, for example, the challenges faced by companies that considered entering post-Communist Russia in 1992. Every aspect of the strategic environment was fraught with uncertainty. There was uncertainty about the legal aspects of doing business, about the availability of raw materials and components, about the likely demand for various products and services, and about the political stability of the new order. In such situations, traditional analysis techniques and forecasting tools are of little assistance.

Situations characterized by *level one* uncertainty lend themselves to conventional analysis. Simple trend extrapolation may be sufficient to identify what is happening in the broader sociopolitical, economic, and technological environment whereas Porter's five forces framework and standard techniques of competitor analysis can be used to clarify the picture at the industry level. At *level two,* standard techniques can be used for analyzing each discrete set of outcomes but a different analysis may be needed for different scenarios. This can make it difficult to compare them. In addition, we must then assess the likelihood that each scenario will occur with the use of decision analysis techniques. *Level three* situations are prime candidates for techniques such as scenario planning, described previously. *Level four* environments are most difficult to analyze. At best a partial, mostly qualitative analysis can be performed. In these situations it may be useful to analyze comparable past environments and extract strategic lessons learned.

Implications for Strategy

Courtney et al. use the terms *strategic posture*—a company's strategic intent—and *strategic moves* to construct a generic framework for formulating strategy in uncertain environments. In characterizing how firms deal with uncertainty, they distinguish between *shapers, adapters,* and *companies reserving the right to play.*

Shapers drive the industry toward a structure that is to their benefit. They are out to change the rules of the competitive game and try to control the direction of the market. An example is Kodak's attempt to fundamentally change the way people create, store, and view pictures with its new digital photography.

Adapters are companies that exhibit a more reactive posture. They take the current industry structure as a given and often bet on gradual evolutionary change. In strategic environments characterized by relatively low levels of uncertainty, adapters position themselves for competitive advantage within the current structure. At higher levels of uncertainty, they may behave more cautiously and fine-tune their abilities to react quickly to new developments.

The third posture, also reactive in nature, *reserves the right to play.* Companies pursuing this posture often make incremental investments to preserve their options until the strategic environment becomes easier to read or less uncertain. Making partial investments in competing technologies, taking a small equity position in different start-up companies, or experimenting with different distribution options are examples of reserving the right to play.

Strategic moves are action patterns aimed at realizing strategic intent. *Big bets* are large commitments mostly used by companies with shaping postures such as Kodak. They often carry a high degree of risk—potential payoffs are large but so are potential losses. *Options* target high payoffs in best-case scenarios while minimizing losses in worst-case situations. Licensing an alternative technology in case it proves superior to current technology is a good example. Finally, a *no-regrets* move has a positive or neutral outcome under all scenarios and is often associated with a reserve the right to play posture.

In *level one* strategic environments—a clear enough future—most companies are *adapters.* The industry structure is fairly stable, its evolution relatively predictable, and conventional analysis techniques can assist with positioning the company for sustained competitive advantage. Because of the high degree of predictability, such strategies by definition consist of a sequence of no-regrets moves. This state of relative tranquillity is maintained until a *shaper* upsets the apple cart, usually with a big bet move. Consider, for example, the actions of Wayne Huizinga's Republic Industries in the movie rental and waste management industries, and now with automobile dealerships.

Although *shapers* in level one environments raise the level of uncertainty by challenging the existing order, at levels two, three, and four their objective is to reduce uncertainty through determined action. At *level two*—alternate futures—a shaping strategy is designed to tilt the probabilities toward a specific outcome. Making a big commitment to building new capacity as a way of deterring a potential rival from entering the industry is illustrative of a shaping strategy. A heavy lobbying effort for or against a piece of legislation is an example of a nonmarket shaping posture. At level two, *adapting* or *reserving the right to play* are easier than at higher levels of uncertainty because the forces of change are known and only a few discrete scenarios are thought to occur.

At level two, *shaping* was about forcing a particular outcome; at *level three* no discrete outcomes can be identified. As a result, at this level of uncertainty shaping strategies focus on limiting the range of possible outcomes to a smaller set of more desirable futures. Consider the earlier example of a European manufacturer wishing to enter the Indian market. A shaping strategy might involve local partnerships or tie-ins with already established products. *Adapter* and *reserving the right to play* strategic postures are more common at this level. Both are aimed at keeping the company's options open. Adapters are generally more aggressive and will craft strategy in real time as opportunities emerge while companies adopting a reserve the right to play posture often wait until a more definitive strategy can be adopted. At this level, options and no-regrets moves are more common than big bets.

Level four environments are the most uncertain. Extreme uncertainty, however, may represent enormous opportunities to *shapers* who can exploit it. When true ambiguity prevails, the situation invites new rules and a sense of order. As a consequence, shaping strategies may not require big bets and in fact can be less risky at this level than at levels two or three. Alternatively, adaptive strategies or a reserve the right to play posture may represent opportunities lost. Battles for technological standards, discussed earlier, come to mind.

SUMMARY

In this chapter we looked at a company's external and industry environments and their importance to strategy formulation. We saw how changes in the strategic environment can have a major impact on a company's current and future competitive position. Identifying relevant change forces and capitalizing on them therefore is a major challenge in formulating strategy. We also noted that merely identifying such forces is not enough. A more sophisticated analysis considers their relative strength and the degree of uncertainty associated with their occurrence and timing. Such analysis has direct consequences for adopting a particular strategic posture—a statement of strategic intent that reflects the degree of uncertainty in a company's strategic environment. Strategic posture, in turn, defines the kinds of strategic moves a company can and should consider in crafting strategy at the business unit or corporate level.

Notes

1. See, e.g., John Naisbitt, *Megatrends: Ten New Directions Transforming Our Lives* (New York: Warner Books, 1982); and Alvin Toffler, *Future Shock* (New York: Random House, 1970).
2. "Here Comes the Intranet," *Business Week,* Feb. 26, 1996.
3. "Telecom's New Age," *Business Week,* April 8, 1996.
4. "The Bio-Tech Century," *Business Week,* March 10, 1997.
5. "The New Business Cycle," *Business Week,* March 31, 1997.
6. "The Euro Will Turn Europe into a Superpower" (Economic Viewpoint), *Business Week,* May 4, 1998.
7. "What Do the Trustbusters Want?" *Business Week,* March 23, 1998.
8. "Microsoft's Future," *Business Week,* Jan. 19, 1997.

9. "The Nostalgia Boom," *Business Week*, March 23, 1998.

10. Ibid.

11. For a thorough discussion of this issue, consult Robert D. Buzzell, Note on Market Definition and Segmentation, Harvard Business School, 1978 (9-579-083).

12. Derek Abell and John Hammond, *Strategic Market Planning: Problems and Analytical Approaches* (Englewood Cliffs, New Jersey: Prentice Hall, 1979).

13. Michael Porter, *Competitive Strategy* (New York: Free Press, 1980).

14. Andrew S. Grove, *Only the Paranoid Survive*, Doubleday, New York, 1996.

15. Caves, Richard E. and Michael Porter, "From Entry Barriers to Mobility Barriers: Conjectural Decisions and Contrived Deterrence to New Competition," *Quarterly Journal of Economics*, vol. 91, 1977, pp. 241–262.

16. "PCs for Everyone," *Business Week*, March 23, 1998.

17. See, e.g., Philip Kotler, *Marketing Management*, 9th ed., Prentice Hall, Englewood Cliffs, New Jersey, 1997.

18. Levitt, Theodore, "Exploit The Product Life Cycle," *Harvard Business Review*, November–December, 1965, pp. 81–94.

19. P. William Bane, Stephen P. Bradley, and David J. Collis, "Winners and Losers: Industry Structure in the Converging World of Telecommunications, Computing and Entertainment," http://www.hbs.edu/mis/multimedia/link/p_winners_losers.html, 1995.

20. Boston Consulting Group, "The Rule of Three and Four," *Perspectives*, no. 187, Boston, 1976.

21. Robert D. Buzzell, "Are There 'Natural' Market Structures?" *Journal of Marketing*, vol. 45, Winter 1981, pp. 42–51.

22. C. K. Prahalad, "Weak Signals Versus Strong Paradigms," *Journal of Marketing Research*, vol. 32, 1995, pp. iii–ix.

23. This categorization is based on Paul Strebel, "Choosing the Right Change Path," *California Management Review*, vol. 36, no.2, Winter 1994, pp. 29–51.

24. For more information on scenario planning, see e.g., the May–June 1992 issue (vol. 20, no. 3) of *Planning Review;* for other techniques, see e.g., L. Fahey, W. R. King, and V. K. Narayanan, "Environmental Scanning and Forecasting in Strategic Planning—the State of the Art," *Long Range Planning*, February 1981; K. Nair and R. Sarin, "Generating Future Scenarios—Their Use in Strategic Planning," *Long Range Planning*, June 1979; and S. W. Edmonds, "The Role of Future Studies in Business Planning," *Journal of Business Strategy*, Fall 1982.

25. "Case Study: Statoil—Using Scenarios to Develop Technology Strategy," *Planning Review*, vol. 20, no.3, May–June, 1992, p. 23.

26. This section is substantially based on Hugh Courtney, Jane Kirkland, and Patrick Viguerie, "Strategy Under Uncertainty," *Harvard Business Review*, November–December, 1997, pp. 66–79.

CHAPTER

Leveraging Internal Resources and Change Drivers for Strategic Advantage

Only after strenuous labor have I at last succeeded in making the form of my compositions correspond, more or less, with their contents. Formerly I was careless and did not give sufficient attention to the critical overhauling of my sketches. Consequently my "seams" showed, there was no organic union between my individual episodes ... but the form of my works will never be exemplary, because, although I can modify, I cannot radically alter the essential qualities of my musical temperament.*

—PETER ILYICH TCHAIKOVSKY

INTRODUCTION

Analysis of external change forces is critical to determining what strategic changes a company *should* consider. An assessment of internal strategic resources and capabilities and of pressures for and against change is important to determining what strategies a company successfully *can* (and should) pursue. A firm's *strategic resources* include its physical assets (*physical resources*), its relative financial position (*financial resources*), the quality of its people (*human resources*), and specific knowledge, competencies, processes, skills, or cultural aspects of the organization (*organizational resources*). A second aspect of assessing a company's internal strategic environment deals with identifying *pressures for strategic change* that come from within the organization or from its immediate stakeholders. Persistent disappointing performance, new owners or management, limitations to growth with current strategies, scarcity of critical resources, or internal cultural changes are examples of conditions that give rise to such pressures.

Analyzing a company's internal strategic environment therefore has two principal components: (1) cataloguing and valuing current resources and core competencies that can be used to create a competitive advantage, and (2) identifying internal pressures for change and forces of resistance that may reduce the firm's capacity for strategic change.

This chapter is organized in four sections. In the first section we characterize a company's strategic resource base in terms of *physical, financial, human resource,* and *organizational* assets, define the concepts of a *value chain* and *core competencies,* and survey a number of techniques that can be used in analyzing company resources. The second section deals with analyzing *internal change drivers* and *counterforces to change* that can have a major influence on what strategy options a company can or should consider. Two well-known models, *the company life cycle concept* and *McKinsey's 7-S framework,* useful in analyzing a company's internal dynamics, are described. In the

---

*From a letter to Nadezhda von Meck, Kamenka (June 25, 1878), as quoted in Josiah Fisk (ed.), *Composers on Music: Eight Centuries of Writings* (Boston: Northeastern University Press, 1956), 159.

third section we introduce *SWOT (strengths, weaknesses, opportunities, and threats) analysis* as a convenient framework for summarizing the principal findings of an analysis of the strategic environment. In the final section we take the first step toward strategy formulation. Specifically, we ask what the findings revealed in a SWOT analysis imply for the articulation of a strategic *vision*—a statement of *strategic intent*.

RESOURCES AND CORE COMPETENCIES

Resources

Strategic resources consist of *physical, financial, human resource,* and *organizational* assets. *Physical* assets such as state-of-the-art manufacturing facilities or plant or service locations near important customers or markets can materially impact a company's competitiveness. *Financial* strength—excellent cash flow, a strong balance sheet, and a strong track record of financial performance—is important. The quality of a company's *human resources*—strong leadership at the top, experienced managers, and well-trained, motivated employees—may well be the most important strategic resource a company will ever have. Finally, strategic *organizational* resources—specific competencies, processes, skills, or knowledge under the control of a corporation—include such qualities as a firm's manufacturing experience, brand equity, innovativeness, relative cost position, or ability to adapt and learn as circumstances change.

To evaluate the relative worth of a company's strategic resources, four specific questions should be asked: (1) How *valuable* is a resource; does it help build and sustain competitive advantage? Honda applies its expertise in engine design and manufacture to a broad array of industries; General Electric uses its financial services skills to great effect in all of its other businesses. To be truly valuable, not only resources must benefit the company but also value to external stakeholders such as customers and suppliers is important. (2) Is this a *unique* resource or do other competitors have similar resources? If competitors have substantially similar resources or capabilities or can obtain them with relative ease, their strategic value is diminished. That does not mean they are not valuable; it simply means that their value as a potential *differentiating* factor is limited. (3) Is the strategic resource easy to *imitate?* This is related to uniqueness. Ultimately, most strategic resources, with the exception of patents and trademarks, can be duplicated. The question is at what cost. The more expensive it is for rivals to duplicate a strategic resource, the more valuable it is to a company. (4) Is the company *positioned* to exploit the resource? Possessing a strategic resource is one thing; being able to exploit it is quite another. A strategic resource that has little value to one company may be an important strategic asset for another; the issue is whether it can be leveraged for competitive advantage.[1]

The Value Chain

Porter introduced the concept of a *value chain* to help identify and evaluate potential sources of competitive advantage.[2] It depicts a company's value creating process in terms of a number of distinct organizational processes. *Primary* activities include those related to logistics, operations, marketing, sales, and service. Specific administrative functions, the management of human resources, and the development of technologies are examples of *support* activities. (Figure 3-1). In analyzing a firm's value creation

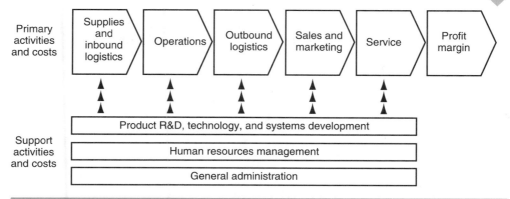

FIGURE 3-1   The Concept of a Value Chain

Source: Adapted with the permission of The Free Press, a Division of Simon & Schuster, Inc. from *Competitive Advantage: Creating and Sustaining Superior Performance* by Michael E. Porter. Copyright © 1985 by Michael E. Porter.

process, explicit consideration should be given to *potential synergies* between the different sources as suggested by linkages between different value creating activities in the value chain. Specific marketing activities, for example, may affect other activities in the value chain such as manufacturing or quality control.

Analyzing a Company's Financial Resource Base

A complete review of strategic resources includes an evaluation of a company's financial performance and position. At the corporate level, this involves a thorough analysis of the company's income statement, balance sheet, and cash flows. At the divisional or business unit level such an evaluation is usually limited to an analysis of the income and cash flow statements. For a full discussion of techniques of financial analysis, readers are encouraged to consult books or articles dedicated to that subject. In this section, we simply identify some of the better-known approaches.

   Financial ratio analysis can provide a quick overview of a company or business unit's recent or past profitability, liquidity, leverage, and activity. *Profitability* ratios measure how well a company is allocating its resources, *liquidity* ratios focus on cash flow generation and a company's ability to meet its financial obligations, *leverage* statistics may suggest potential improvements in the financing of operations, and *activity* ratios measure productivity and efficiency. Such ratios (Figure 3-2) can be used to assess (1) the business's position in the industry, (2) the degree to which certain strategic objectives are being attained, (3) the business's vulnerability to revenue and cost swings, and (4) the level of financial risk associated with the current (or proposed) strategy.

   The so-called *DuPont* formula for analyzing a company's or business unit's return on assets directly links operating variables to financial performance. Return on assets, for example, is computed by multiplying earnings, expressed as a percentage of sales, by asset turnover. Asset turnover, in turn, is the ratio of sales to total assets employed (Figure 3-3). A careful analysis of such relationships allows pointed questions about a strategy's effectiveness and the quality of its execution.

Ratio		Definition
1. Profitability		
a. Gross profit margin:	$\dfrac{\text{sales} - \text{cost of goods sold}}{\text{sales}}$	Total margin available to cover operating expenses and yield a profit
b. Net profit margin:	$\dfrac{\text{profits after taxes}}{\text{sales}}$	Return on sales
c. Return on assets:	$\dfrac{\begin{array}{c}\text{earnings}\\\text{before interest}\\\text{and taxes (EBIT)}\end{array}}{\text{total assets}}$	Return on the total investment from both stockholders and creditors
d. Return on equity:	$\dfrac{\text{profits after taxes}}{\text{total equity}}$	Rate of return on stockholders' investment in the firm
2. Liquidity		
a. Current ratio:	$\dfrac{\text{current assets}}{\text{current liabilities}}$	The extent to which the claims of short-term creditors are covered by short-term assets
b. Quick ratio:	$\dfrac{\text{current assets} - \text{inventory}}{\text{current liabilities}}$	Acid-test ratio; the firm's ability to pay off short-term obligations without having to sell its inventory
c. Inventory to net working capital:	$\dfrac{\text{inventory}}{\text{current} - \text{current liabilities}}$	The extent to which the firm's working capital is tied up in inventory
3. Leverage		
a. Debt-to-assets ratio:	$\dfrac{\text{total debt}}{\text{total assets}}$	The extent to which borrowed funds are used to finance the firm's operations
b. Debt-to-equity ratio:	$\dfrac{\text{total debt}}{\text{total equity}}$	Ratio of funds from creditors to funds from stockholders
c. Long-term debt-to-equity ratio:	$\dfrac{\text{long} - \text{term debt}}{\text{total equity}}$	The balance between debt and equity
3. Activity		
a. Inventory turnover:	$\dfrac{\text{sales}}{\text{inventory}}$	The amount of inventory used by the company to generate its sales
b. Fixed-asset turnover:	$\dfrac{\text{sales}}{\text{fixed assets}}$	Sales productivity and plant utilization
c. Average collection	$\dfrac{\text{accounts receivable}}{\text{average daily sales}}$	The average length of time required to receive payment

FIGURE 3-2 Ratio Analysis

Source: A. J. Rowe, R. O. Mason, K. E. Dickel, and N. A. Snyder, *Strategic Management: A Methodological Approach,* 3rd edition, 1989, Addison-Wesley Longman, Glenview, IL. Reprinted by permission.

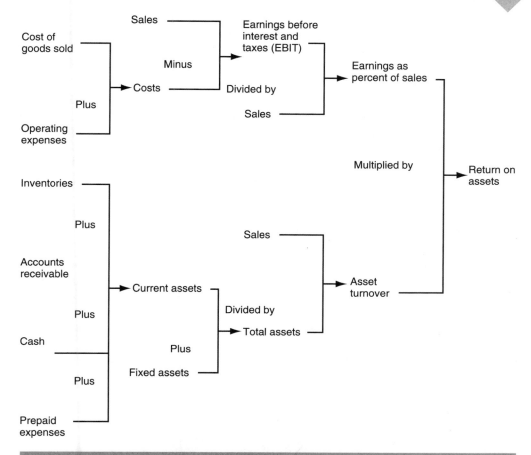

FIGURE 3-3 The DuPont Formula for Computing Return on Assets

Source: A. J. Rowe, R. O. Mason, K. E. Dickel, and N. A. Snyder, *Strategic Management: A Methodological Approach,* 3rd edition, 1989, Addison-Wesley Longman, Glenview, IL. Reprinted by permission.

Whereas once most companies relied on simple measures such as *return on investment (ROI)* to assess current performance, today many, including Coca-Cola, General Electric, Whirlpool, and AT&T, have adopted broader *shareholder value-based* measures such as *economic value added (EVA)* and *market value added (MVA)*. Their popularity stems from evidence that accounting-based measures are not particularly strong indicators of a business unit's economic value. Shareholder value analysis, instead, focuses on cash flow generation, the principal determinant of shareholder wealth. Shareholder value analysis therefore is helpful in answering such questions as (1) Does the current strategic plan create shareholder value, and how much? (2) How does the business unit's performance compare to others in the corporation? and (3) Would an alternative strategy increase shareholder value more than the current one in use?

Cost analysis deals with the identification of *strategic cost drivers*—those cost factors in the value chain that determine long-term competitiveness in the industry. Examples of strategic cost drivers include product design, factor costs, scale and scope of operations, and capacity utilization. Such analysis should focus on costs and cost drivers that are of strategic importance, in other words, can be influenced by strategic choice. Whereas operational cost control is focused on *doing things right,* strategic cost analysis is concerned with *doing the right things.*

Cost benchmarking is useful for assessing cost competitiveness relative to competing firms or for comparing a company's performance against best-in-class companies.[3] The process involves five steps: (1) selecting which areas or operations to benchmark, (2) identifying key performance measures and practices, (3) identifying best-in-class companies or key competitors, (4) collecting cost and performance data, and (5) analyzing and interpreting the results. This technique is extremely practical and versatile. It allows a direct comparison of the relative efficiency by which different operations—that is, parts of the value chain—are being performed. *It is dangerous, however, to rely exclusively on benchmarking—an operational tool—for strategic guidance because of its focus on similarities rather than differences between rival firms' strategic designs.*

A complete evaluation of a company's financial resources should include a *financial risk analysis.* Most financial models in use today are essentially deterministic in nature. That is, managers can specify a single estimate for each key variable. Yet many of these estimates are made with a great deal of uncertainty. Together, such uncertainties can mask high levels of risk. It is important, therefore, that risk is explicitly considered. This involves determining which variables—market growth rate, market share, price trends, the cost of capital, the useful life of the underlying technology, to mention a few—have the greatest impact on revenues and costs as a basis for assessing the exposure to and likelihood of different risk scenarios.

People: A Company's Most Valuable Strategic Resource

Companies are run by and for people. While most strategic resources can be duplicated in time, the people that make up an organization or its immediate stakeholders are unique. Understanding their concerns, aspirations, and capabilities is therefore key to understanding a company's strategic position and options for the future.

Stakeholder analysis is aimed at identifying key stakeholders inside and outside the organization, the roles they play in fulfilling the organization's mission, and the values they bring to the process. A firm's internal stakeholders include its owners, board of directors, CEO, executives, managers, and employees. The CEO (chief executive officer) has primary responsibility for setting the strategic direction of the company; the others are more immediately concerned with approving strategic plans (owners and the board of directors) or with implementing the chosen strategic direction (management and employees). This division of roles suggests that the quality of a CEO's strategic leadership, of the board's contributions to and oversight of the strategy formulation process, and of the work managers and employees do in executing a strategy are all critical to a company's success. The annals of business history include many references to the importance of strategic leadership. CEOs such as Sam Walton (Wal-Mart), Lee Iaccoca (Chrysler), and Bill Gates (Microsoft) are all regarded as visionary and charismatic. A strong board of directors can also make a difference as recent evidence that strong corporate governance has a positive effect on valuation confirms.[4] Motorola's decision to build its next major production facility in Japan, despite intense competition for talent in the Japanese market and higher cost, was motivated in part by the high quality of Japan's labor force. As these examples suggest, assessing the quality and depth of a firm's talent pool at all levels of the organization is an essential part of strategic resource analysis.

External stakeholders—key customers, suppliers, alliance partners, and, particularly in regulated industries, governmental and other regulatory agencies—can also have a major influence on a firm's strategic options. The importance of productive relationships with external stakeholders and their influence on a firm's strategy is illustrated by the experience of Apple Computer in the seventies. For years, it resisted partnering with other companies in hardware and software development through licensing. By insisting on "going it alone," it reduced its own potential for growth. By the time the company recognized its strategic error it was too late; it had lost its position as an industry leader.

Organizational Strategic Resources and Core Competencies

Core competencies represent collective learning toward unique capabilities that allow a company to build a sustainable competitive advantage. Typically, they *transcend* organizational boundaries and *are more than skills.* Sony has learned to "miniaturize" better than any other company, 3M has developed a core competence in coatings, and Canon has core competencies in optics, imaging, and microprocessor controls. Sony's expertise in miniaturization gives it a head start over potential competitors in developing next generation products. Procter & Gamble's marketing prowess allows it to adapt more quickly than its rivals to changing opportunities. As companies increasingly compete globally as corporations rather than business units, the development of core competencies has become a key element in building a long-term strategic advantage. An assessment of strategic resources and capabilities therefore must include questions about what core competencies a company has or is developing, how they are nurtured, and how they can be leveraged into core products and services.

Hamel and Prahalad suggest three tests for identifying core competencies. First, core competencies should provide *access to a broad array of markets.* Honda's expertise in engines is an example. Second, a core competence should help *differentiate core products and services.* Sony's miniaturization of many electronics products clearly sets them apart from rival entries. Third, true core competencies should be *hard to imitate* because they represent multiple skills, technologies, and organizational elements.[5] Experience shows that only a few companies have the resources to develop more than a handful of core competencies. Picking the right ones, therefore, is the key. "Which resources or capabilities should we keep in-house and develop into core competencies and which ones should we outsource?" is a key question to ask. Pharmaceutical companies, for example, increasingly outsource clinical testing in an effort to focus their resource base on drug development. Generally, *the development of core competencies should focus on key skills and knowledge, not products; lead to long-term platforms capable of adapting to new market circumstances; focus on unique sources of leverage in the value chain; on areas where the firm thinks it can dominate; and on elements that are important to customers in the long run.*[6]

ANALYSIS OF INTERNAL CHANGE FORCES

Internal Change Drivers

In chapter 2 we focused on change forces that emanate from a company's *external* strategic environment. A second set of drivers for strategic change comes from within the organization or from its immediate stakeholders. Persistent disappointing performance, new owners or management, limitations to growth with current strategies, scarcity of critical resources, or internal cultural changes are examples of conditions that give rise to such pressures.

Although analysis of external change forces is essential to determining what strategic changes a company *should* consider, an assessment of internal change forces is important to determining what strategies a company successfully *can* and should pursue. This points to a key difference between external and internal forces for change. Whereas in the external environment *counterforces to change* often hold as much strategic potential as the change forces that spawn them, *internal resistance to change* is mostly unproductive and often inhibits strategy development. For example, the rising interest in ethnic, cultural, and religious issues, an external counterforce to homogenizing change forces such as globalization and technological change in our culture, has created numerous opportunities. Ethnic restaurants, products, and services rooted in specific cultures and membership in religious activity all are flourishing. Similarly, counterforces that originate in a company's industry environment—players dedicated to the status quo, for example—provide start-ups and challengers with extra time to establish opposition. *Internal resistance to change is different. It reduces a company's capacity to adapt and chart a new course.* And because it usually reduces a company's strategic freedom to act, it deserves a strategist's careful attention.

Resistance Forces

Organizational resistance to change can take four basic forms: (1) *structural, organizational rigidities;* (2) *closed mind-sets* reflecting obsolete business beliefs and strategies; (3) *entrenched cultures* reflecting values, behaviors, and skills that are not conducive to change; and (4) *counterproductive change momentum* driven by historical or other change drivers that is not in tune with current strategic requirements.[7]

These four forms of resistance represent very different strategic challenges. Internal structures and systems, including technology, can be changed relatively quickly in most companies. Converting closed minds to the need for change, or changing a corporate culture, is considerably harder. Counterproductive change is the most difficult to remedy because it typically involves altering all three—structures and systems may have to be rethought, mind-sets must be changed, and new behaviors and skills have to be learned.

The Company Life Cycle

Which type of organizational resistance should be anticipated and how strong it is likely to be greatly depends on a company's history, performance, and culture. Nevertheless, some patterns can be observed. Like human beings, companies go through a *life cycle*.[8] It begins when a founder or founding team organizes a start-up. At this point a vision or purpose must be established; the initial direction for the company set; and the necessary resources marshaled to transform this vision into reality. In these early stages, the identities of the founders and that of the company are difficult to separate. This is positive if there is capable leadership, but can be a major impediment if individual and organizational needs become entangled.

As companies grow, more formal systems are needed to handle a variety of functions. The transition from informality to a more formal organizational structure can stimulate or hinder strategic change. This passage to organizational adulthood, often described as the "entrepreneurial-managerial" transition, poses a dilemma familiar to many companies: how to maintain an entrepreneurial spirit while moving toward an organizational structure increasingly focused on control. Some companies—Lotus Development Corporation, for example—have made this transition with relative ease; others, including Apple Computer Corporation, continue to struggle with this dilemma.

With growth it becomes necessary for an *organization* rather than particular individuals to learn. The evolution of processes such as the delegation of authority, coordination of effort, and collaboration between organizational units increasingly can have a significant influence on a company's effectiveness in responding to new environmental and internal challenges. In younger companies the internal operating environment is frequently characterized by greater ambiguity than in established organizations. This can be an advantage or a disadvantage. Sometimes, ambiguity encourages entrepreneurship and innovation. At other times, a lack of control can cause a company to lose its strategic focus.

Evolving and established companies share one pervasive strategic challenge albeit with a different twist—growth. For many evolving companies growing too fast is a major concern. As they try to cope with explosive growth they find that success can cover up a host of underlying problems of organizational development: dilemmas of leadership can develop, loss of focus becomes an issue, communication becomes harder, skill development falls behind, and stress becomes evident. In established companies, the pressure to grow faster can skew strategic thinking. Ill-considered acquisitions or market expansions, forays into new, untested technologies, straying from core skills, and frequent exhortations for more entrepreneurial thinking are indicative of the stresses endured in more mature companies.

Assessing a Company's Capacity for Change— The 7-S Framework

The increased importance of a firm's capacity to effectively deal with change has made a strategic perspective on this issue essential. As any CEO knows, a host of internal factors can reduce a company's capacity for change. Sometimes structural rigidities, a lack of adequate resources, or an adherence to dysfunctional processes inhibit change. Most often, however, resistance to change can be traced to cultural factors.

Perhaps one of the best-known frameworks for analyzing how organizational factors such as structure, systems, and style interact with strategy is the so-called 7-S model, originally developed at McKinsey & Company.[9] Its central idea is that organizational effectiveness stems from the interaction of a number of factors, of which strategy is just one (Figure 3-4). Intentionally, its structure is not hierarchical; it depicts a situation in which it is not clear which factor is the driving force for change or the biggest obstacle to change. The different variables are interconnected. Change in one variable will force change in another or, put differently, progress in one area must be accompanied by

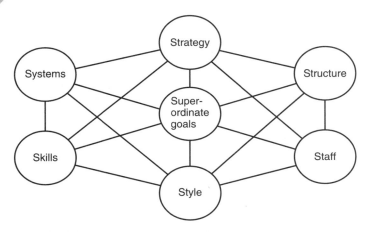

FIGURE 3-4 McKinsey's 7-S Framework

Source: Reprinted from *Business Horizons,* June 1980, Robert H. Waterman Jr., Thomas J. Peters, and Julien R. Phillips, "Structure Is Not Organization." Copyright © 1980, p. 40, with permission from Elsevier Science.

progress in another to effect meaningful change. As a consequence, it holds that solutions to organizational problems that invoke just one or a few of these variables are doomed to fail. An emphasis on "structural" solutions—"Let's reorganize"—without paying attention to strategy, systems, and all the other variables, therefore, can be counterproductive. McKinsey & Co. have shown that style, skills, and superordinate goals—the main values around which a business is built—are observable, even measurable, and can be at least as important as strategy and structure in bringing about fundamental change in an organization. The key to orchestrating change, therefore, is to assess the potential impact of each factor, align the different variables in the model in the desired direction, and then act decisively on all dimensions. In other words, strategy alone is not enough.

Waterman, Peters, and Phillips note that the problem of "How to organize?" has evolved from one of dividing up tasks to one focused on issues of coordination.[10] The issue of *structure* therefore is not whether to centralize or decentralize decision making. Rather, it involves identifying dimensions that are crucial to an organization's ability to adapt and evolve strategically, and adopting a structure that allows a company to refocus when needed. The right *systems* should enhance organizational effectiveness and facilitate strategic change. As many companies have learned, however, systems can also be a powerful drag on an organization's ability to adapt. Checking what impact, if any, current systems are likely to have on a company's ability to implement a particular strategy is therefore well advised. The importance of *style* is frequently overlooked. "Soft" issues, in general, tend to get under emphasized in analyzing a company's ability to effect change. Style, essentially manageable, has two principal components. First, we can think of style as the basic personality of the top management group—What attitude does the group project to the rest of the organization? How does it spend its time? What gets rewarded, rebuked? A second element is more symbolic. Companies tend to attract people, fund projects, and publicize accomplishments in areas where they are most successful. Strategies designed to alter this focus should recognize this fact. *Staffing* issues have gained enormously in currency in recent years. After several years of mindless downsizing and rightsizing, many companies have recognized how expensive it is to replace talent. As a result, much greater emphasis is being placed on attracting, rewarding, and retaining talent at all levels of the organization. Related to the staffing issue is *skill* development. Many companies have come to realize that developing tomorrow's skills, individually and collectively, is the key to strategic flexibility. Finally, *superordinate goals*—another soft issue meaning guiding philosophies, values, and aspirations—are now recognized as more than fundamental ideas around which the enterprise is built. They are the core values top executives want to promote throughout the organization. They define key aspects of corporate culture, essential in harnessing and coordinating organizational energies toward specific strategic goals.

STRENGTHS, WEAKNESSES, OPPORTUNITIES, AND THREATS

SWOT analysis—the sizing up of a company's *strengths, weaknesses,* external *opportunities,* and *threats*—is a helpful tool for generating a *summary* of a strategic situation. *Strengths and weaknesses* can include skills, expertise or technological know-how, particular organizational resources, competitive capabilities, or positional advantages or disadvantages defined by such variables as market share, name or brand recognition, or distribution capabilities. Increasingly, strengths and weaknesses depend on cooperative arrangements. SWOT analysis therefore should include an assessment of alliances and other partnering arrangements. *Opportunities and threats* typically stem from a company's external competitive environment. The exit of a competitor, for example, may spell opportunity. New regulation or the emergence of lower-cost technologies, on the other hand, may pose threats. In evaluating opportunities, it is important to distinguish between industry opportunities and company opportunities. Not every competitor is equally well positioned to pursue all new opportunities that emerge in an industry. Figure 3-5 documents examples of issues to consider in evaluating a company's strengths, weaknesses, opportunities, and threats.

Determining whether a company's competitive position is strong or weak relative to that of key competitors is a critical part of SWOT analysis. In trying to answer the question "How strongly does the firm hold its current competitive position?" it is useful to ask four related questions: (1) Will the company's competitive position become stronger or weaker if the present strategy is continued? (2) How does the company rank relative to its principal competitors on key dimensions of competitive strength and key success factors? (3) Does the firm enjoy a distinct, sustainable competitive advantage? and (4) How well and how long can the company defend its current position in light of the forces that drive the industry and competitive strategies?[11]

There is no simple formula for answering these questions. Managers must look for relevant indicators of competitive strength or weakness, make judgments about their relative importance and about the company's relative position, and then decide whether the company's competitive position is secure or at risk. Explicitly identifying key success factors is helpful. It allows assigning weights to each factor and rating of the company and its principal competitors on each dimension. Many indicators of competitive strength, however, are not that easily quantified. For example, in looking

Potential Internal Strengths	*Potential Internal Weaknesses*
• Core competencies in key areas • Adequate financial resources • Well-thought-of by buyers • An acknowledged market leader • Well-conceived functional area strategies • Access to economies of scale • Insulated (at least somewhat) from strong competitive pressures • Proprietary technology • Cost advantages • Better advertising campaigns • Product innovation skills • Proven management • Ahead on experience curve • Better manufacturing capability • Superior technological skills • Other?	• No clear strategic direction • Obsolete facilities • Subpar profitability because… • Lack of managerial depth and talent • Missing some key skills or competencies • Poor track record in implementing strategy • Plagued with internal operating problems • Falling behind in R&D • Too narrow a product line • Weak market image • Weak distribution network • Below/average marketing skills • Unable to finance needed changes in strategy • Higher overall unit costs relative to key competitors • Other?
Potential External Opportunities	*Potential External Threats*
• Ability to serve additional customer groups or expand into new markets or segments • Ways to expand product line to meet broader range of customer needs • Ability to transfer skills or technological know-how to new products or businesses • Integrating forward or backward • Falling trade barriers in attractive foreign markets • Complacency among rival firms • Ability to grow rapidly because of strong increases in market demand • Emerging new technologies	• Entry of lower-cost foreign competitors • Rising sales of substitute products • Slower market growth • Adverse shifts in foreign exchange rates and trade policies of foreign governments • Costly regulatory requirements • Vulnerability to recession and business cycle • Growing bargaining power of customers or suppliers • Changing buyer needs and tastes • Adverse demographic changes • Other?

FIGURE 3-5 SWOT Analysis

Source: From Arthur A. Thompson Jr. and A. J. Strickland III, *Strategic Management*, 9th edition, 1996. Reprinted by permission of McGraw-Hill Company, Inc., New York, NY.

for potential strengths, we may inquire about particular core competencies, the degree to which products or services are differentiated, changes in the loyalty of a company's customer base, the emergence of new strategic groups in the industry, or the relative creativity and talent of the different management teams. Potential indicators of weaknesses include a slippage in reputation with customers, suppliers, or partners, slowness in responding to emerging threats, or a lack of continuity in new product development.[12]

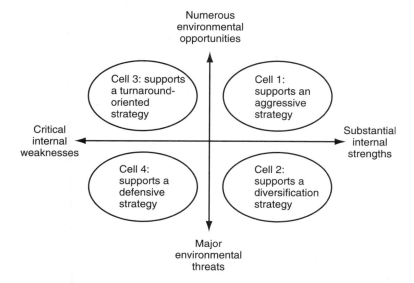

FIGURE 3-6 SWOT and Strategic Posture

Source: From Arthur A. Thompson, Jr., and A. J. Strickland, III, *Strategic Management: Formulation, Implemen- tation and Control,* 6th edition, 1997. Reprinted by permission of McGraw-Hill Company, Inc.,

TOWARD STRATEGIC INTENT

The process of identifying internal and external forces of change (and resistance), and of evaluating a company's strategic resource base and key stakeholder concerns, combined with feedback about current performance, acts to stimulate creative thinking about future strategic options. While it may be too soon to arrive at any conclusions, it is important to begin the process of creating a *vision* for the future of the organization, a broad statement of *strategic intent.*

In chapter 2 we saw that the degree of uncertainty in the external strategic environment has important implications for the *strategic posture* a company should consider. Highly uncertain environments sometimes call for an *adaptive* posture that "reserves the right to play." On the other hand, true ambiguity may also give *shapers* an opportunity to write new competitive rules and impose new structure on the competitive landscape. SWOT analysis is helpful in diagnosing uncertainty as a basis for choosing an appropriate strategic posture. Figure 3-6 shows how we can link the evaluation of external opportunities and threats with the assessment of internal strengths and weaknesses.[13] The combination of substantial environmental opportunities with considerable internal strengths calls for an aggressive, even bold, posture. On the other hand, the presence of major threats in the strategic environment, coupled with critical organizational weaknesses, suggests a far more defensive posture.

Mission and Vision

As noted in chapter 1, many companies have a *mission* statement, which documents the purpose for their existence, and often contains a code of corporate conduct to guide management in implementing the mission. A *vision* statement represents senior management's *strategic intent*—a description of what competitive position the company wants to attain over a given period of time, and what core competencies it will need to acquire to get there. As such, it summarizes a company's broad *strategic focus* for the future.

In crafting a vision, there are two important lessons worth heeding. First, *few organizations have achieved greatness by being all things to all people.* Focusing on relatively few activities and doing them extremely well is the hallmark of most successful companies. McDonald's became successful precisely because it stuck to hamburgers, H&R Block concentrates on tax preparation, and Michael Dell focuses on PCs. This suggests that effective strategizing is as much about deciding what *not* to do as it is about choosing what activities to focus on. The second lesson is that *most successful companies achieved their leadership position by adopting a vision far greater than their resource base and competencies would allow.* To get to a position of market leadership a focus on the drivers of competition is not enough; strong leadership aimed at "creating a new future" is required. With such a mind-set, disparities between resources and goals become challenges rather than constraints, and "winning" becomes a corporate "obsession" capable of sustaining a sense of urgency for a long period of time.[14]

Kotter argues that a good vision provides both *strategic guidance* and *motivational focus.* He suggests that an effective vision statement meets three criteria: (1) it must be *clear* but not so constraining that it inhibits initiative, (2) it should be *desirable* in the sense that it meets the legitimate interests and values of all stakeholders, and (3) it must be *feasible,* that is, it must be implementable.[15]

Thus, *strategic intent* does more than paint a vision for the future; it signals the desire to win and recognizes that successful strategies are built as much around *what can be* as around *what is.* It focuses the organization on key competitive targets, and provides clear goals about which competencies to develop, what kinds of resources to harness, and what segments to concentrate on. Instead of worrying about the degree of "fit" between current resources and opportunities, the focus shifts to "how to close the capability gap." In this view current resources and capabilities are starting points for strategy development, not constraints on strategy formulation.

Ultimately, every company must create a fit between its resources and its opportunities. The question is over what time frame. Too short a time frame encourages a focus on *fit* rather than *stretch,* and on resource *allocation* rather than getting more value from existing resources. The use of too long a time horizon, on the other hand, creates an unacceptable degree of uncertainty and threatens to turn stretch objectives into unrealistic goals.

Expectations

A good vision statement sets a direction for the future and identifies major challenges for the organization. It also frames and manages expectations. Strategic redirection takes time and effort, and results will not always immediately be visible. The time and effort needed to effect a new strategic thrust depends on the magnitude of the change as well as the degree to which the current strategy is entrenched. Figure 3-7 shows a typical change path for a company that has perfected the execution for a strategy that is no longer viable. Inevitably at first, execution of the new strategy will be less than perfect,

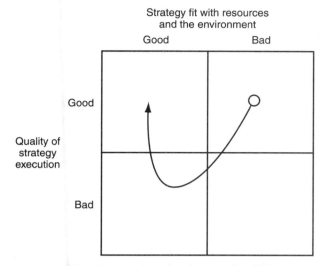

FIGURE 3-7 Performance Expectations under Strategic Change

reflecting initial confusion about the new direction—within and outside the company—and the relearning that needs to take place before the new strategy effectively takes hold. Putting a time frame on this adaptation process helps all stakeholders understand the nature of the challenge, sets expectations for management, employees, suppliers, partners, customers, and the financial markets, and prevents panic-driven corrections to a sound strategic choice.

SUMMARY

In this chapter we characterized a company's strategic resource base in terms of *physical, financial, human resource,* and *organizational* assets; defined the concepts of a *value chain* and *core competencies,* and surveyed a number of techniques that can be used in analyzing company resources. We emphasized the importance of analyzing *internal change drivers* and *counterforces to change* that can have a major influence on what strategy options a company can or should consider, and presented two well-known models, *the company life cycle concept* and *McKinsey's 7-S framework,* to guide the analysis of a company's internal dynamics. Next we discussed *SWOT (strengths, weaknesses, opportunities, and threats) analysis* as a convenient framework for summarizing the results of an analysis of relevant change forces in the external and internal strategic environment. We concluded the chapter by taking a first step toward formulating a strategy by asking what the findings revealed in a SWOT analysis imply for the articulation of a strategic *vision*—a statement of *strategic intent.*

Notes

1. J. B. Barney, *Gaining and Sustaining Competitive Advantage* (Reading, Mass.: Addison-Wesley, 1997), 145–164.

2. Michael E. Porter, *Competitive Advantage: Creating and Sustaining Superior Performance* (New York: Free Press, 1985), chap. 2.

3. See e.g., "Strategic Benchmarking: How to Pick the Right Target," special issue of *Planning Review* 21 (Jan.–Feb. 1993).

4. Robert F. Felton, Alec Hudnut, and Jennifer van Heeckeren, "Putting a Value on Board Governance," *McKinsey Quarterly,* no. 4 (1996): 170–175.

5. C. K. Prahalad and Gary Hamel, "The Core Competence of the Corporation," *Harvard Business Review* (May–June 1990): 79–93.

6. James Brian Quinn and Frederick G. Hilmer, "Strategic Outsourcing," *Sloan Management Review* 35 (Summer, 1994): 19–31.

7. Paul Strebel, "Choosing the Right Change Path," *California Management Review* 36 (winter 1994): 30.

8. This section is based in part on John J. Kao, *The Entrepreneurial Organization* (Englewood Cliffs, New Jersey: Prentice Hall, 1991), chap. 1.

9. Robert H. Waterman Jr., Thomas J. Peters, and Julien R. Phillips, "Structure Is Not Organization," *Business Horizons* (June 1980): 14–26.

10. Waterman, Peters, and Phillips, "Structure Is Not Organization," 14–26.

11. Arthur A. Thompson Jr., and A. J. Strickland III, *Strategic Management: Concepts and Cases,* 9th ed. (Chicago: Irwin, 1996), chap. 4.

12. Ibid.

13. This discussion is based on John A. Pearce II and Richard B. Robinson Jr., *Strategic Management: Formulation, Implementation and Control,* 6th ed. (Chicago: Irwin, 1997), chap. 6.

14. Gary Hamel and C. K. Prahalad, "Strategic Intent," *Harvard Business Review* (May–June 1989): 63–76.

15. John Kotter, *A Force for Change* (New York: Free Press, 1990).

CHAPTER 4

Business Unit Strategy

I carry my thoughts about with me for a long time, often for a very long time, before writing them down. I can rely on my memory for this and can be sure that, once I have grasped a theme, I shall not forget it even years later. I change many things, discard others, and try again and again until I am satisfied; then, in my head, I begin to elaborate the work in its breadth, its narrowness, its height, its depth and because I am aware of what I want to do, the underlying idea never deserts me. It rises, it grows . . . . You may ask where I obtain my ideas. I cannot answer this with any certainty: they come unbidden, spontaneously or unspontaneously. I may grasp them with my hands in the open air, while walking in the woods, in the stillness of the night, at the early morning. Stimulated by those moods that poets turn into words, I turn my ideas into tones, which resound, roar and rage until at last they stand before me in the form of notes.*

—LUDWIG VON BEETHOVEN

INTRODUCTION

Business unit strategy, sometimes referred to as competitive strategy, deals with creating a sustainable and profitable competitive position for a business unit within a specific industry, segment, or served market. Its principal focus is on *how* to compete in a given competitive setting as opposed to corporate strategy, the subject of chapter 5, which is concerned with *what* businesses a company should compete in and *how* a parent company can add value to its business units.

Deciding how to compete in a specific market is a complex issue. What is best for a given company, industry, product or service, and competitive environment depends on many factors including the *nature of the industry,* the company's *mission, goals* and *objectives,* its *current position* and *core competencies,* and major *competitors' strategic choices.* Fortunately, however, much has been learned in the last 30 years about what strategies work, why, and under what circumstances.

We begin our discussion by examining the *logic* behind strategic thinking at the business unit level. In the first section we address the basic question "What determines profitability at the business unit level?" We look at the relative importance of the industry in which a company competes, of its competitive position within the industry, and identify the drivers that determine sustained competitive advantage. This logic naturally suggests a number of *generic strategy choices*—broad strategy prescriptions that

---

*From a written conversation with Louis Schlosser (1822 or 1823), as quoted in Josiah Fisk (ed.), *Composers on Music: Eight Centuries of Writings* (Boston: Northeastern University Press, 1956), 56.

define the principal dimensions of competition at the business unit level. Which generic strategy is more attractive and what form it should take varies considerably according to the specific opportunities and challenges analyzed. Accordingly, the second section deals with the question of how to size up a strategic challenge at the business unit level. It introduces a variety of techniques such as *growth vector analysis, profit pool analysis, gap analysis, competitor analysis,* and *product life cycle analysis* that are useful for generating and assessing strategic alternatives. Because business unit strategy is typically developed in a specific industry context, the next section considers six different industry environments. Three represent different stages in an industry's evolution—*embryonic, growth,* and *mature* industry settings; the other three—*fragmented* industries, *global* and *deregulating* industry environments—are defined by their structure, scope, or by external forces operating on them. We conclude the chapter with a number of special topics—the role of *innovation* in value creation, issues of *timing, entry-exit* decisions, *vertical integration,* and the *relationship between business unit and corporate strategy.*

FOUNDATIONS

Strategic Logic at the Business Unit Level

What are the principal factors behind a business unit's sustained profitability? How important are product superiority, cost, marketing, and distribution effectiveness? And how important is the nature of the industry? Executives ask such questions every day all over the world in all kinds of businesses.

While there are no simple answers to such questions and the attractiveness of different strategic options varies greatly depending on the competitive situation analyzed, much has been learned about what drives competitive success at the business unit level. In a number of acclaimed books Michael Porter, expanding on earlier work by other academics and consultants, has articulated a "strategic logic" (Figure 4-1) that guides much of our strategic thinking at the business unit level today.[1]

This logic begins with the observation that at the broadest level, firm success is explained by two principal factors: the *attractiveness of the industry* a firm competes in and its *relative position* within that industry. In other words, business unit profitability depends on the industry as well as the position the company occupies within the industry. The success of some firms is almost entirely attributable to the industry in which they compete. The early history of the software industry provides a good example. The seemingly insatiable demand for new products did not just guarantee big profits for the industry leaders; many of their rivals were successful too. In the fiercely competitive beer industry, on the other hand, relative positioning is comparatively a far more important determinant of profitability. As Porter notes, "the distinction between industry structure and relative position is important because firms can choose strategies that improve one while harming the other."[2]

How Much Does Industry Matter?

In a comprehensive study of corporate performance in 4-digit SIC "Standard Industry Classification" industry categories, McGahan and Porter provided an answer to the question "How much does industry matter?" They found that variation in year effects, industry effects, segment-specific effects, and corporate parent effects accounted for 2

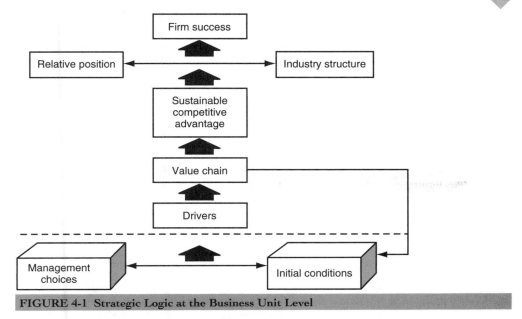

FIGURE 4-1 Strategic Logic at the Business Unit Level

Source: Reprinted by permission of Harvard Business School Press. An Exhibit from the book title by author Michael E. Porter, "Toward a Dynamic Theory of Strategy," in Richard P. Rumelt, Dan E. Schendel, and David J. Teece (Eds.), *Fundamental Issues in Strategy*. Boston, MA 1994, p. 432. Copyright © 1994 by the President and Fellows of Harvard College; all rights reserved.

percent, 32 percent, 4 percent, and 19 percent, respectively, of the aggregate variance in business segment profits. These results support the conclusion that industry characteristics are an important determinant of profit potential. In this study, industry directly accounted for 19 percent of the aggregate variation in business-specific profits and 36 percent of the explained total variation in profitability. The study also revealed marked differences between the relative importance of industry effects, segment-specific effects, and company-specific influences on profits across economic sectors. Industry effects were smaller in manufacturing, for example, than in lodging/entertainment, services, wholesale/retail trade, and transportation. Finally, the results indicate that industry effects tend to be more persistent over time, which is consistent with the observation that most industries evolve relatively slowly.[3, 4]

Relative Position

Within a particular industry, the relative profitability of rival firms depends on the *nature of their competitive position,* that is, on their ability to create a *sustainable competitive advantage* vis-à-vis their competitors. Porter identifies two generic forms of sustainable competitive positioning: a competitive advantage based on *lower delivered cost* and one based on the ability to *differentiate* products or services from those of competitors and command a price premium relative to the cost of doing so.[5] Which (generic) form of competitive advantage is most effective depends, among other factors, on a firm's choice of *competitive scope.* The scope of a competitive posture includes such elements as the number of product and buyer segments served, the number of different geographic locations in which the firm competes, the extent to which it is vertically integrated, and the degree to which it has to coordinate its positioning with that of related businesses in which the firm competes. As Porter notes, "competitive advantage is attained within some scope, and the choice of scope is a central one in strategy. Scope choices can also influence industry structure."[6]

Decisions about scope and how to create a competitive advantage are made on the basis of a detailed understanding of what customers value and what capabilities and opportunities a company has relative to its competitors. In this sense a firm's strategy defines its configuration and how the different elements interrelate. Competitive advantage results when a company has a better understanding of what customers desire and when it learns to meet those customer needs at a lower cost than rivals, or to create buyer value in unique ways that allow it to charge a premium.

How Important Is Market Share?

The relative importance of market share as a strategic goal at the business unit level has been the subject of considerable controversy. In their book *The Profit Zone: How Strategic Business Design Will Lead You to Tomorrow's Profits,* Adrian Slywotzky and David Morrison titled their opening chapter "Market Share Is Dead."[7] Arguing that profitability should be the primary goal of strategy, they believe executives have been led astray by a blind pursuit of market share. Citing examples such as the fact that A&P once had a high share of grocery sales, Intel had a high share of memory products, and WordPerfect once was the preferred word processor, they urge executives to ask themselves, "Am I managing for volume growth or value growth?"[8]

While their warning is timely and no manager should pursue growth for growth's sake, there is a pervasive body of evidence that indicates that market share is an important determinant of long-term profitability. Bradley Gale and Robert Buzzell, in reviewing the evidence on this subject, put it succinctly: "Large market share is both a reward for providing better value and a means of realizing lower costs. Under most circumstances, enterprises that have achieved a large share of the markets they serve are considerably more profitable than their smaller-share rivals. This connection between market share and profitability has been recognized by corporate executives and consultants, and it is clearly demonstrated in the results of our research over the last fifteen years."[9]

Findings from the PIMS Project

In the early seventies the Marketing Science Institute at the Harvard Business School undertook important research into the relative profitability of different market strategies. This so-called PIMS (profit impact of market strategy) project involved more than six hundred businesses over a period of more than 15 years.[10] Key questions included (1) What factors influence business profitability and how much influence does each one have? and (2) How does ROI (return on investment) vary with changes in strategy and market conditions?

The major findings of the PIMS study included (1) absolute and relative market share are strongly correlated with ROI, businesses with higher market shares were generally more profitable because of economies of scale, experience effects, market power, and the quality of management; (2) product quality is important to market leadership and allows companies with larger market shares to charge higher prices and therefore achieve higher margins; (3) ROI is positively correlated with market growth; (4) vertical integration can be beneficial later in the product life cycle, partway vertical integration should be avoided, forward integration is more profitable than backward integration; (5) the relationship between ROI and new product activity, the R&D to sales ratio, and marketing to sales ratio is most pronounced in the later stages of the product life cycle, as market share gets bigger, the potential benefits of such investments increases; (6) high investment intensity tends to depress ROI, as do high inventory levels; and (7) capacity utilization is critical for businesses with a high level of capital intensity, companies with small market shares are particularly vulnerable.

PORTER'S GENERIC STRATEGIES

Differentiation or Low-Cost?

Earlier, we distinguished between two *generic* competitive strategic postures: *low cost* and *differentiation*. They are called generic because in principle they apply to any business and any industry. It was also noted, however, that the relative attractiveness of different generic strategies is related to choices about competitive scope. If a company such as Wal-Mart chooses a relatively broad target market, a low-cost strategy is aimed at *cost leadership*. Such a strategy aggressively exploits opportunities for cost reduction through economies of scale and cumulative learning (experience effects) in purchasing and manufacturing and generally calls for minimal expenditures on R&D, marketing, and overhead. Cost leaders generally charge less for their products and services than rivals do, and aim for a significant share of the market by appealing primarily to budget-sensitive customers. Their low prices serve as an entry barrier to potential competitors and as long as they maintain their relative cost advantage, cost leaders can maintain a defensible position in the marketplace.

With a more narrow scope a low-cost strategy is based on *cost focus*. As with any focus strategy a small, well-defined market niche—a particular group of customers or geographic region—is selected to the exclusion of others and only activities directly relevant to serving that niche are undertaken at the lowest possible cost.

Differentiation postures can similarly be tied to decisions of scope. A *differentiation* strategy aimed at a broad mass market seeks to create uniqueness on an industry-wide basis. Walt Disney Productions and Nike are examples. Broadscale differentiation can be achieved through product design, brand image, technology, distribution, service, or a combination of these elements. Finally, like cost focus, a *differentiated focus* strategy is aimed at a well-defined segment of the market and targets customers willing to pay for value added (Figure 4-2).

Requirements for Success

The two generic routes—*low cost and differentiation*—are fundamentally different. Achieving *cost leadership* requires a ruthless devotion to minimizing costs through continuous improvement in manufacturing, process engineering, and other cost-reducing strategies. Scale and scope effects must be leveraged in all aspects of the value

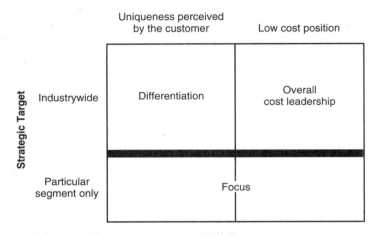

Strategic Advantage

FIGURE 4-2 Generic Strategy Choices

Source: Reprinted with the permission of The Free Press, a Division of Simon & Schuster, Inc. from *Competitive Strategy: Techniques for Analyzing Industries and Competitors* by Michael E. Porter. Copyright © 1980 by The Free Press.

creation process from the design of products and services to purchasing practices and distribution. And organizationally, achieving and sustaining cost leadership requires tight control and an organizational structure and incentive system supportive of a cost-focused discipline.

Differentiation requires an altogether different approach. Here, the focus is on value added. And while there may be only a limited number of ways to reduce cost, there are numerous ways to differentiate a company's products and services. Differentiation has multiple objectives. The primary objective is to redefine the rules by which customers arrive at their preferences and make their purchase decisions, by offering something unique that is valuable. In doing so, companies also seek to erect barriers to imitation. Differentiation strategies are often misunderstood. "Spray painting the product green" is *not* differentiation. Differentiation is a strategic choice to provide something of value to the customer other than a low price. One way to differentiate a product or service is to add functionality. There are, however, many other more effective ways to differentiate. R&D aimed at enhancing product quality and durability (Maytag) is a viable element of a differentiation strategy. Investing in brand equity (Coca-Cola) or pioneering new ways of distribution (Avon Cosmetics) are others.

There is considerable evidence that the most successful differentiation strategies use multiple sources of differentiation. Purchasing higher-quality raw materials, unique product design, more reliable manufacturing, superior marketing and distribution programs, and quicker service all contribute to set a company's offering apart from rival products. Consequently, the use of more than one source of differentiation makes it harder for competitors to effectively imitate. In addition to using multiple sources, integrating the different dimensions of value added—added functionality, economic, and psychological value—is important. Effective differentiation thus requires explicit decisions about how much value to add, where to add such value, and how to communicate such added value to the customer. Customers must be willing to pay a premium relative to the cost of achieving the differentiation. Successful differentiation therefore requires a thorough understanding of what customers value, what relative importance they attach to the satisfaction of different needs and wants, and what they are willing to pay extra for.

Risks

Each generic posture carries its own unique risks. Cost leaders must worry about technological change that can nullify past investments in scale economics or accumulated learning. In an increasingly global economy, cost leadership is particularly vulnerable to new entrants from other parts of the world that can take advantage of lower factor costs. And until recently, inflation threatened to reduce the price differential cost leaders could maintain vis-à-vis competitors using differentiation strategies. The biggest challenge to differentiators is imitation. Imitation narrows actual and perceived differentiation. If this occurs, buyers may change their minds about what constitutes differentiation and change their loyalties and preferences.

The biggest challenge under each generic posture is creating sustainability. For cost leaders, it means continually improving efficiency, looking for less-expensive sources of supply, and seeking ways to reduce manufacturing and distribution costs. For differentiators, the challenge is to erect barriers to entry around their dimensions of uniqueness, to use multiple sources of differentiation, and whenever possible, to create switching costs for customers. Organizationally, a differentiation strategy calls for strong coordination among R&D, product development and marketing, and incentives aimed at value creation and creativity.

A Success Story: Dell Computer

The story of Dell Computer's rise in the PC industry illustrates how a relentless pursuit of cost leadership and a close alignment between strategy and business design can pay off. Michael Dell, the company's founder and a consummate entrepreneur, defied critics who predicted that his mail-order model would not work.

Convinced he had a winning formula for selling personal computers, he turned a low-margin mail-order operation into a high-profit, high-service business that is the envy of the industry by challenging every aspect of PC selling and manufacturing. The company successfully applied its just-in-time manufacturing philosophy to the rest of its supply chain by requiring, for example, that the majority of critical components be warehoused within 15 minutes of a Dell factory. And by marrying this low-cost, speed-based business model to the new principles of electronic commerce Dell has created a competitive advantage that is hard to beat.

In relatively short order Dell has moved from a challenger to the number one seller of PCs over the Web; many corporations that were willing to buy over the phone now prefer electronic purchasing. "The Internet," says Dell, "is the ultimate direct model."[11] As a consequence, Dell has become one of the best high-tech growth stocks and its business model the envy of the industry. According to *Business Week,* Dell converts an average sale into cash in less than 24 hours, by emphasizing credit cards and electronic payment. By contrast, industry giant Compaq Computer Corp., which sells primarily through dealers, takes 35 days, and even mail-order rival Gateway 2000 takes more than 16 days.[12]

Competitors are working hard to catch up. IBM, Compaq, and Hewlett-Packard are trying to cut production time and improve service. IBM, for example, was forced into letting dealers assemble PCs for its corporate customers. And Compaq is designing its own Internet connection, allowing customers to manage everything from ordering a machine to scheduling software updates on-line. But imitation strategies have limitations, especially when the underlying business model is hard to change. Consider production, for example. While machines from Compaq and IBM can sit on dealer shelves for months, Dell does not order components until an order is booked. With rapidly falling prices that can translate into a significant profit advantage in components alone.

Value Disciplines

Treacy and Wiersema coined the term *value disciplines* to describe different ways successful companies can create value for customers. Specifically, they identify three different kinds of generic strategies that have successfully been used by companies such as Nike, Dell Computer, and Home Depot—*product leadership, operational excellence, and customer intimacy.*[13]

Companies pursuing *product leadership* typically produce a continuous stream of state-of-the-art products and services. Such companies are innovation-driven and constantly raise the bar for competitors by offering more value and better solutions. The authors cite Johnson & Johnson as an example of a company that creates value through product leadership.

Operational excellence—the second value discipline—describes a strategic approach aimed at better production and delivery mechanisms. Dell Computer focuses on operational excellence. Other companies pursuing this strategy include Wal-Mart, American Airlines, and Federal Express.

A strategy based on *customer intimacy* concentrates on building customer loyalty. Nordstrom and Home Depot are companies that continually tailor their products and services to changing customer needs. Pursuing customer intimacy can be expensive, but the long-term benefits of a loyal clientele can pay off handsomely.

Most successful companies, whether by accident or by design, try to excel in one of these three dimensions. Explicitly choosing a value discipline and focusing all available resources on creating a gap between the company and its immediate competitors can sharpen a company's strategic focus. Becoming a "master of two" (customer intimacy and operational excellence for example) as some companies, United States Automobile Association (USAA) for example, have succeeded in doing, is a particularly powerful way of creating sustainable competitive advantage.

STRATEGIC ANALYSIS AT THE BUSINESS UNIT LEVEL

Process

The process of formulating competitive strategy at the business unit level is shown in Figure 4-3.[14] It identifies four specific steps that fit with the *where are we now, where do we go,* and *how do we get there* framework introduced earlier. They are (1) analyzing the

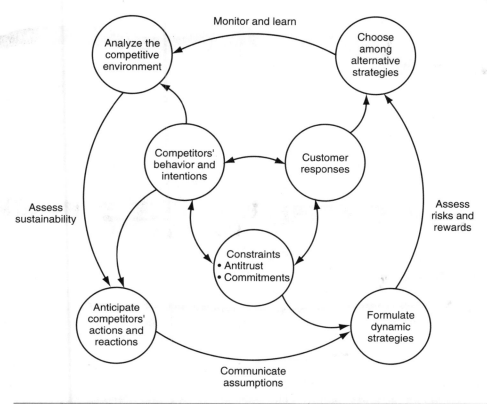

FIGURE 4-3 Formulating Business Unit Strategy

Source: From George S. Day, David J. Reibstein, *Wharton on Dynamic Competitive Strategy,* 1987. Copyright © 1997 John Wiley & Sons, New York, NY. Reprinted by permission of John Wiley & Sons, Inc.

competitive environment, (2) anticipating key competitors' actions, (3) formulating strategic options, and (4) choosing among the different alternatives.

Step one—analyzing the competitive environment—deals with two questions: "With whom do we compete, now and in the future?" and "What relative strengths do we have as a basis for creating a sustainable competitive advantage?" Answering these questions requires an analysis of the external strategic environment, of the (industry) competitive environment, and of internal strengths and weaknesses. Step two—anticipating key competitors' actions—focuses on understanding how competitors are likely to react to different strategic moves. Industry leaders tend to behave differently from challengers or followers. A detailed competitor analysis is helpful in gaining an understanding of how competitors are likely to respond and why. Step three—formulating strategic options—requires a balancing of opportunities and constraints and a consideration of a diverse array of strategic options ranging from defensive to preemptive moves. Step four—choosing among alternatives—consists of narrowing the various options down to a final choice. To assist in this process, we next look at a number of widely used techniques and analysis frameworks.

Profit Pool Analysis

An industry's *profit pool* is the total amount of profit earned at all points along the industry's value chain. Analyzing who makes the most profit where in the value chain and why is important to understanding industry economics. Profitability typically varies by customer group, product category, geographic area, or distribution channel. Additionally, the pattern of profit distribution is often quite different from that of revenue concentration. In the automobile industry, for example, car manufacturing and distribution generate the highest revenues but auto leasing, insurance, and auto loans are the most profitable activities. "Mapping" the industry's profit pool therefore provides important insight into profit potential. It also helps understand how the industry is evolving by raising such questions as "Why have profit pools formed where they have?" and "How is the profit distribution likely to change?" Mapping a profit pool involves four steps: (1) defining the pool's boundaries, (2) estimating its overall size, (3) allocating profits to the different value chain activities, and (4) verifying the results.[15]

Analyzing Product/Market Scope

Growth vector analysis (Figure 4-4) is based on the recognition that there are two primary ways a company can increase its strategic scope within an industry, by offering more products/technologies, or by tapping more (or new) segments. The group of product-market combinations a firm currently serves defines its current product/market scope. This constitutes a baseline for future growth. Further growth *within* the current market scope is called *market penetration;* growth by moving into related or new customer segments is referred to as *market development;* while *product/technology development* defines growth into related or new products. A change in both customer segments served and products/technologies offered is called *diversification,* which we discuss in greater detail in chapter 5, "Corporate Strategy."

When analyzing alternative directions for future growth or growth vectors, it is useful to perform a similar analysis for key competitors. The combined analysis allows us to determine whether the original assumptions about growth, the business's competi-

FIGURE 4-4 Product/Market Scope Analysis

Market Options		Present products	Improved products	New products
	Existing market	Market penetration	Product extension	Product development
	Expanded market	Market extension	Market/product extension	Product development/ market extension
	New market	Market development	Product extension/ market development	Diversification

Product Alternatives

Source: Marketing Management: Analysis, Planning and Control, 6th ed., © 1989. Reprinted by permission of Prentice-Hall, Inc., Upper Saddle River, NJ.

tive position, or the potential for improvement are still tenable, as well as to gain insight into competitors' intentions and the way the specific product markets are evolving.[16]

There is substantial evidence that companies that stay close to their current core competencies—whether core technologies or detailed knowledge about particular customer segments—and concentrate their growth into related markets and products are more successful than companies that diversify widely.[17] This suggests that it may be strategically more attractive to consider growth into related products and segments before looking farther afield.

Gap Analysis

Plotting alternative growth vectors for a company and its primary competitors often reveals *gaps* in the way a market is served, that is, where industry sales are below their potential and the causes for such shortfalls. *Gap analysis*—the process of comparing an industry's market potential to the combined current market penetration by all competitors—can lead to the identification of additional avenues for growth (Figure 4-5). Gaps between a market's potential and current sales levels can be the result of (1) product line gaps—the unavailability of product versions for specific applications or usage occasions, (2) distribution gaps—overlooked customer segments that have difficulty accessing the product, (3) usage gaps—underdeveloped applications for the product, and (4) competitive gaps—opportunities to displace competitors with weak product entries or questionable performance.

Segmentation

Most executives are familiar with *market segmentation*—the process of dividing a market into relatively homogeneous, minimally overlapping segments that benefit from distinct marketing approaches. Whether done on the basis of demographics, buying patterns, or

---

FIGURE 4-5 Gap Analysis

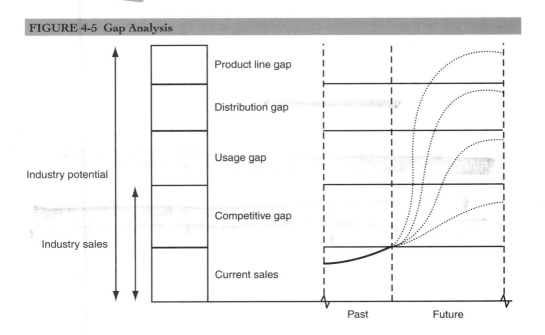

other data about products and customers, market segmentation helps tailor the specification and delivery of value to specific customer groups.

Strategic segmentation has a slightly broader focus; it focuses on finding out which segments of an industry offer the best prospects for long-term, sustainable results. It also considers the long-term defensibility of different segments by analyzing barriers to entry—capital investment intensity, proprietary technologies and patents, geographical location, and tariffs and other trade barriers.

Competitor Analysis

The greater complexity that characterizes industry evolution today has important consequences for how we analyze competition. For many businesses assumptions such as (1) our market is distinct and its boundaries are well-defined, (2) competition is mainly about capturing market share, (3) customers and competitors are known, and (4) competition primarily occurs at the business unit or product line level, are no longer tenable. The new competitive realities call for adopting a broader perspective and for asking new questions. Do consumer electronics companies compete primarily at the business unit level, at the corporate level, or both? Do automobile companies compete as stand-alone entities or as extended families that include their supplier base? When we define competition, should we therefore focus on the portfolios of which the businesses are a part? What are the competitive advantages of a portfolio of businesses against stand-alone companies? Should Citicorp in financial services look at Microsoft or AT&T as potential competitors? Which is more important to sustainable competitive advantage, access to money or information technology? Who will write the industry rules of tomorrow?

As these questions suggest, competitive analysis can no longer be conducted in isolation of an analysis of the drivers of industry evolution or be neatly compartmentalized at the business unit or corporate level. A principal rationale behind the concept of the diversified corporation is that the benefits of a portfolio transcend financial strength; a portfolio of related businesses defines an integrated set of resources, core competencies that transcend business units, and the potential for developing a sustainable corporate advantage that must be considered along with competitive considerations at the business unit level.

To analyze *immediate competitors,* the following five key questions are useful: (1) Who are our direct competitors, now and in the future? (2) What are their major strengths and weaknesses? (3) How have they behaved in the past? (4) How might they behave in the future? and (5) How will this affect our industry and company? In many markets it is possible to identify a *leader,* one or more *challengers,* and a number of *followers* and *nichers.* While labeling competitors has obvious drawbacks and risks erring on the side of simplicity, it provides further insight into the competitive dynamics of the industry.

Leaders, for example, tend to focus on expanding total demand by attracting new users, developing new uses for their product or service, or by encouraging more use of existing products and services. Defending market share is important to them but they may not wish to aggressively take more share from their immediate rivals because this can be more costly than expanding the market, or because they wish to avoid scrutiny by regulatory agencies. Coca-Cola, for example, is more focused on developing new markets overseas than it is on taking market share from Pepsi Cola in the domestic market.

Challengers typically concentrate on a single target—attacking the leader. Sometimes they do so directly, as in the case of Fuji's challenge to Kodak. At other times, they use indirect strategies such as first attacking competitors of a similar size before taking on the industry leader. Computer Associates, for example, used this strategy successfully in the software industry.

Followers and *nichers,* by definition, compete with a more modest strategic objective. Some followers use a strategy of innovative imitation, whereas others elect to compete selectively in a few segments or with a more limited product or service offering. Nichers typically focus on a narrow slice of the market by concentrating, for example, on specific end users either geographically or by offering specialty products or services.

The identification of *potential* competitors is more difficult. Firms that are currently not in the industry but can enter at relatively low cost should be considered. So should companies for whom there is obvious synergy from being in the industry or whose portfolio suggests future acquisitions in the industry. Customers or suppliers who can integrate backward or forward comprise another category of potential competitors.[18]

Product Life Cycle Analysis

In chapter 2 we introduced the product life cycle concept in the context of analyzing how industries evolve. It is also useful as a benchmark for strategy development. As noted, the evolution of an industry or product class depends on the interaction of a number of factors including the competitive strategies of rival firms, changes in customer behavior, and legal and social influences. Because companies can affect the shape of the product life cycle, simple extrapolations of current growth trends are of limited value. What is useful, however, is to consider typical competitive responses to the predictable changes that accompany the transition from a market's embryonic state to growth to maturity and, ultimately, decline (Figure 4-6).

The *introductory* or embryonic stage of a product or industry life cycle is frequently characterized by a high level of uncertainty; competitors may be unsure which segments to target and how; potential customers may be unfamiliar with the new product or service, the benefits it offers, where to buy it, or how much to pay. As a result, a substantial amount of strategic experimentation is a hallmark of embryonic industries. *Growth* environments are less uncertain but competitively more intense. At this stage of an industry's evolution, the number of rivals is usually largest. As a consequence, competitive shakeouts are common toward the end of the growth phase. *Mature* industries, while the most stable, do not have to be stagnant. Constant innovation can give rise to new spurts of growth in specific segments, technological breakthroughs can alter the course of market development and upset the competitive order, and global opportunities can open avenues for further growth. *Declining* industries have typically been regarded as unattractive. Even here, however, there can be attractive strategic options. We will return to these different scenarios later in this chapter when we consider specific strategies for each environment.

Critical Success Factors

In every business, certain activities or issues are critical to attaining a position of long-term competitive advantage. They can differ substantially among, or even within, industries. The requirements for success in the bulk chemicals segment are different, for example, from those in the specialty chemicals segment. Identifying and confirming *critical*

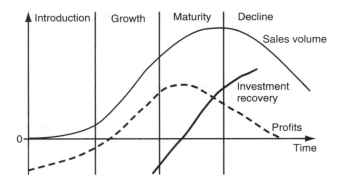

Characteristic	Introduction	Growth	Maturity	Decline
Concentration of competitors	High; few pioneers	Declining as more competition enters	Increasing after shakeout	High; few remaining harvesters
Product differentiation	Low, if any	Increasing; imitations and variations	High; increasing market segmentation	Decreasing as competitors leave market
Barriers to entry	High, if product can be protected	Decreasing; growing technology transfer	Increasing as capital intensity increases	High capital intensity, low returns
Barriers to exit	Low; little investment	Low, but increasing	High for large company	Decreasing; endgame
Price elasticity of demand	Inelastic, few customers	Increasingly elastic	Inelastic only in segments	Very elastic; bargaining power of buyers high
Ratio of fixed to variable cost	Generally low	Increasing	High	Decreasing
Economies of scale	Few, generally unimportant	Increasing capital intensity	High	High
Experience curve effects	Large early gains	Very high; large production volume	Decreasing magnitude	Few
Vertical integration of competitors	Low	Increasing	High	High
Risk involved in business	Low	Increasing	Increasing	Declining exit barriers

FIGURE 4-6 Strategic Choices over the Product Life Cycle

Source: A. J. Rowe, R. O. Mason, K. E. Dickel, and N. A. Snyder, *Strategic Management: A Methodological Approach,* 3rd edition, 1989, Addison-Wesley Longman, Glenview, IL. Reprinted by permission.

success factors are important for several reasons. First, it helps in identifying capability gaps and opportunities for improvement. Second, it is important in identifying possible synergies with other business units and between the business and the activities of the parent corporation.

STRATEGY AND CONTEXT*

Generic strategy descriptions are useful for identifying broad dimensions for developing a competitive advantage. We can be more specific about the relative effectiveness of different strategic options by considering the *context* in which a strategy is developed. To do this, we examine a number of generic industry settings. The first three relate to the different evolutionary stages an industry typically moves through: *emerging* or *embryonic* industries, *growth* industries, and *mature* or *declining* industries. Their definitions are related to the product life cycle concept introduced in chapter 3. Three additional generic industry scenarios are discussed, which pose unique strategic challenges: *fragmented* industries, a *deregulating* industry environment, and *global* industries.[19]

Strategy in Emerging or Embryonic Industries

New industries or segments can emerge in a variety of ways. Technological breakthroughs can launch entirely new industries or reform old ones—consider the changes to the telephone industry with the advent of cellular technology. Sometimes changes in the broader strategic environment can spawn new industries. An example is solar energy. Also changes in customer behavior and expectations can lead to the birth or rebirth of markets. On-line services became popular after customers had accepted the new Internet technology.

From a strategy development perspective, new industries represent a blank canvas—there are no rules of the game. This can be a great advantage. First movers have the opportunity to shape customer expectations and define the competitive rules of the game. The absence of rules, however, also poses enormous risks. Technologies are typically immature. This means competitors will actively try to improve upon existing designs and processes, or leapfrog them altogether with next-generation technology. As a consequence, a battle for standards may ensue. Costs may be high and unpredictable, entry barriers low, supplier relationships underdeveloped, and distribution channels just emerging. Strategically it is important, therefore, to assess what opportunity a company has to exercise leadership in the market as a way to reduce risk. Leadership opportunities include (1) the ability to shape the industry structure based on timing and method of entry and experience in similar situations, (2) the ability to control product and process development through superior technology, quality, or customer knowledge, (3) the ability to leverage existing relationships with suppliers and distributors, or (4) the ability to leverage access to a core group of early, loyal customers.

Strategy in Growth Industries

Growth and later the onset of maturity present a host of different challenges. Rather than worrying about whether the industry will take off, competitors are now totally focused on the battle for market share. Over time, buyers have become more knowledgeable and now carefully distinguish between competitive offerings. As a result, increased segmentation often accompanies the transition to market maturity. Cost control becomes an important element of strategy as unit margins shrink, and new products and applications are harder to find. In industries with a global potential, international markets become more important to the major players. The globalization of competition also introduces new uncertainties as a second wave of global competitors enters the race.

---

*Based on material in Michael E. Porter, 1980, op. cit. and from John A Pearce II and Richard B. Robinson, Jr,. *Strategic Management,* 6th edition, 1997; Irwin. Reproduced with permission of McGraw-Hill Companies.

Strategically, there are a number of factors to watch: (1) during the early growth phase companies tend to add more products, models, sizes, and flavors to appeal to an increasingly segmented market. Toward the end of the growth phase cost considerations often force a certain amount of pruning, (2) process innovation becomes an important dimension of cost control, as does the redefinition of supplier and distributor relations, and (3) horizontal integration, for example, buying a weaker competitor, may become attractive as a way of consolidating a company's market position or increasing a firm's international presence.

Strategy in Mature and Declining Industries

Carefully choosing between a differentiation and low-cost posture, and deciding whether to compete in multiple segments or whether to focus on a narrower target, is always important. As maturity sets in and ultimate decline becomes inevitable, however, such choices become a matter of survival. Growth tends to mask a host of strategic errors and lets companies survive; a low- or no-growth environment is far less benevolent.

From a strategic perspective, mature environments can be profitable; declining industries are rarely attractive. Some of the challenges at these stages of an industry's development include (1) concentrating on segments that offer chances for higher growth or higher return, (2) managing product and process innovation aimed at further differentiation, cost reduction, or at rejuvenating segment growth, (3) streamlining production and delivery to cut costs, and (4) gradually "harvesting" the business in preparation for a strategic shift to more promising products, industries, or segments.

Along with these challenges, mature and declining industries are characterized by a number of strategic pitfalls that companies should avoid: (1) an overly optimistic view of the industry or of the company's position within it, (2) a lack of strategic clarity due to a failure to choose between a differentiated and low-cost focus or between a broad-based or focused competitive approach, (3) investing too much for too little return—the so-called "cash trap," (4) trading market share for profitability in response to short-term performance pressures, (5) unwillingness to compete on price, (6) resistance to industry structural changes or new practices, (7) too much emphasis on new product development compared to improving existing ones, and (8) getting caught with excess capacity.[20]

Strategy in Fragmented Industries

Fragmented industries—industries in which no single company or small group of firms has a large enough market share to strongly affect the industry structure or outcomes—are all around us. Many areas of the economy such as retail sectors, distribution businesses, professional services, and small manufacturing share this trait. Fragmentation can occur for a variety of reasons, some simply historical. Nevertheless, fragmentation seems to be most prevalent when (1) entry and exit barriers are low, (2) there are no economies of scale or scope, (3) cost structures make consolidation unattractive, (4) close local control is essential, and (5) products or services are highly diverse or need to be customized.

Overcoming fragmentation can provide significant strategic opportunities. Sometimes, scale and scope economies are hidden, or await new technological breakthroughs, or are not well recognized because the attention of the players has been elsewhere. In such instances, creative strategy can unlock these hidden sources of advantage and dramatically change the dynamics of the industry. Wall Street was distinctly skeptical when H. Wayne Huizinga, a third generation garbageman of Dutch descent, took Waste Management public in 1971 and explained how he, using stock as his principal currency, would acquire hundreds of mom-and-pop garbage companies and by exploiting differences in public and private valuation and placing these smaller entities under single management would unlock hidden value. At the time of its initial public offering, Waste Management had a capitalization of $5 million. When Huizinga departed in 1984, its market value was $3 billion. Though hard to understand today, Huizinga got the same initial reception when he took control of Blockbuster in 1987. Guess what happened. Blockbuster's market capitalization climbed from $32 million to $8.4 billion in September of 1994, when he sold the company to cable giant Viacom.

In the theater, third acts are often marked by some sort of comeuppance or denouement. Life, however, does not necessarily imitate art. Huizinga's third production, a conglomerate called Republic Industries, through its AutoNation U.S.A. subsidiary, has already changed how Americans buy and sell cars. Seeking to create a cradle-to-grave auto distributor that will sell, finance, lease, rent, repair, and recondition cars nationwide, Huizinga has rewritten the rule book for competing in the industry. The business is soon expected to hit $1 billion in annual revenues.[21]

If consolidation is not an option, focus strategies that creatively segment the market based on product, customer, type of order/service, or geographic area, combined with a "no frills" posture—low overhead, tight cost control—may be effective.

Strategy in a Deregulating Environment

Deregulation has reshaped a number of industries in recent years. There are some interesting competitive dynamics that take place when artificial constraints are lifted and new entrants are allowed to rush in. Perhaps the most important has to do with the timing of strategic moves. U.S. experience shows that deregulating environments tend to undergo significant change twice—once when the market is opened up and again about five years later.[22]

Deregulation in the United States became a major issue in 1975 when the Securities and Exchange Commission abolished fixed rates for U.S. securities brokers. Other deregulatory actions quickly followed—in airlines, trucking, railroads, banking and telecommunications. In each instance, a more or less similar pattern developed. Immediately following the opening up of the market, a large number of new entrants rushed in—most failed within a relatively short period of time; industry profitability deteriorated rapidly as new entrants, often operating from a lower-cost basis, destroyed industry pricing for all competitors; the pattern of segment profitability altered significantly—segments that once were attractive became unattractive because too many competitors entered, while previously unattractive segments suddenly became more interesting from a strategic perspective; the variance in profitability between the best and worst players increased substantially reflecting a wider quality range of competitors; two waves of merger and acquisition activity ensued—a first wave focused on consolidating weaker players, a second wave among larger players aimed at market dominance; and after consolidation, only a few players remained broad-based competitors; most were forced to narrow their focus to specific segments or products in a much more segmented industry.

Strategically, deregulation poses a host of challenges for companies. Bleeke identified four distinct strategic postures that proved successful in coping with the turmoil associated with deregulation: (1) broad-based distribution companies that were successful in offering a wide range of products and services over a large geographic area, (2) low-cost entrants that developed into niche players, (3) focused segment marketers that emphasized value added to specific loyal customer groups, and (4) shared utilities that focused on making economies of scale available to smaller competitors.[23]

Broad-based distribution companies that understood the challenges associated with fending off a flood of low-cost upstarts took early pricing actions, eliminated cross subsidies between products or segments, and conserved resources for a protracted battle in a deteriorating environment. Following deregulation AT&T, for example, quickly reduced prices to high-volume business customers to counter MCI's and Sprint's aggressive marketing efforts. It also cut about 20 percent of its workforce in an effort to match the cost structure of the new entrants. And it conserved capital by cutting back on new market development and acquisitions to prepare for the inevitable rainy day.

Low-cost entrants typically are the catalysts for change in a deregulating environment. Few low-cost entrants, however, can successfully stake out a sustainable position based on low cost alone. Most survivors therefore tend to become specialty or niche players over time. The key strategic choices they have to make are what segments to target—taking on broad-based competitors in their core markets may not be the best choice—and deciding on a migration route toward their specialty or niche status.

Focused segment marketers target value-added segments from the outset. Their staying power often depends on the strength of their relationship to their customers. Accordingly, the principal strategic challenges facing focused segment marketers include (1) identifying new approaches for strengthening relationships with customers, for example, by developing customer information systems and databases, (2) leveraging segment strength into entry-related segments or product categories, and (3) upgrading products and services to lock in existing customers. Frequent flyer plans, extended warranties, and selected insurance services all fall into this category.

Shared utilities define a fourth strategic group in a deregulated environment. Their role is to provide low-cost entrants with economies of scale by sharing costs among many companies. Telerate, for example, provides worldwide instant government bond and foreign exchange quotations to a whole range of small- and medium-size traders allowing them to compete more effectively with their larger rivals. As such, shared utilities are essential to the evolution of the industry. They also are natural monopolies. Thus, a shakeout among competing utilities is often unavoidable. The battle among different airline reservations systems is a good illustration. At most a few will ultimately survive. More often, one will become the de facto industry standard.

Strategy in Global Industries

As the globalization of the competitive landscape intensifies, global issues will increasingly occupy the minds of strategists. Once mainly a challenge for large multinationals, a global strategic outlook has become important to large and midsize companies alike. Conventional wisdom has it that large corporations have a better chance of competing successfully in the global arena. Recent evidence, however, indicates that midsize companies often have a distinct advantage. This advantage is rooted in precisely those characteristics once thought to be detrimental to success: size—smaller can mean nimbler, not less capable; pressure to succeed—for smaller companies international sales are a must, not a luxury; and an entrepreneurial culture that more easily accommodates a global vision and creative implementation.

The increasing importance of global strategic thinking justifies a more detailed treatment than a single section can accommodate. Accordingly, we devote an entire chapter to this subject. In chapter 6 we take a closer look at the opportunities and risks associated with staking out a global competitive position and identify the principal dimensions of a global strategy. The chapter begins by taking a look at the forces that drive the globalization of the world economy and characterize globalization as an economic, political, social, and technological phenomenon. Industry globalization is discussed next. This discussion focuses on such questions as "What is a global industry?"; "What are the driving forces behind the globalization of industries?"; and "What explains the dominance of particular countries or regions in global industries?" The third major topic covered is global strategic thinking. Here, we identify the principal dimensions of global strategy and introduce a framework for global strategic thinking that links global strategy options to the nature of the global industry environment. A major tenet of this discussion is that global strategy, more than strategy at the corporate or business unit levels, increasingly is played out in two arenas—a market and a nonmarket arena. Market dimensions of global strategic thinking concern questions such as "Which markets should we participate in?"; "Why?"; "In what form?"; "To what extent should we standardize products and services?"; "Where should we locate key value-added activities?"; "Should we have a uniform market positioning worldwide?"; and "How do we coordinate competitive moves across the globe?" They are aimed at creating value through economic performance in a global context. Nonmarket dimensions of global strategy deal with shaping the global competitive environment. As many executives will attest, the rules of global competition are critical to performance. As a consequence, to enhance their global competitiveness, an increasing number of companies have concluded that they need to participate in the political process of shaping those rules. An integrated global strategy therefore consists of market and nonmarket components that act synergistically to create a sustained competitive advantage on a global scale. Chapter 6 concludes with a consideration of the various strategic risk factors associated with a global posture.

OTHER DIMENSIONS OF BUSINESS UNIT STRATEGY

Creating Value Through Innovation

Value creation often depends on innovation. Many companies are finding that in today's competitive environment sustainable profitable growth requires more than a focus on judicious acquisitions on one hand or careful "subtraction"—shedding unprofitable operations, downsizing, and the like—on the other. They realize that one answer is to create more value from core businesses and to leverage core competencies into new market opportunities. This, in turn, demands a greater focus on innovation.[24]

True innovativeness is a strategic quality that has eluded many companies, however. One reason is that creating a culture of innovation transcends traditional strategic planning practices and techniques. Strategic planning too often tends to focus on existing or closely related products and services rather than on opportunities that drive future demand. Innovation is about anticipating, assessing, and fulfilling potential customer needs in a creative manner. Sometimes it is technology-based; more often it springs from explicit or latent customer needs and is market-driven. Innovation also encompasses far more than product development. It can be directed at any point in the customer's or in the company's value chain, from sourcing raw materials to value-added after-sale services.

Effective innovation strategies are developed in the context of an overall business strategy. The process involves (1) setting growth targets for the company as a whole; (2) identifying how much growth can be realized by strengthening core businesses and acting on planned acquisitions and other external opportunities; (3) determining how much can be achieved through internal growth; (4) screening promising market opportunities against market potential, current and potential competition, and any synergies that may exist with current product lines, customer applications, distribution, manufacturing processes, and technologies; and (5) assessing competitive opportunities in terms of risk, return, and timing, to arrive at a small number of high-potential ventures that meet explicitly stated goals.

Fostering a culture of innovation takes time and lots of effort. Although there is no universal model for creating such an environment, a look at successful companies reveals certain common characteristics: (1) *A top-level commitment to innovation*. In companies such as 3M, commitment to innovation is evident in the attitudes of top executives, the communication of these beliefs to all levels of the organization, and in a willingness to sponsor and guide new product activity. (2) *A long-term focus.* "Quarteritis"—a preoccupation with the next quarter's results—is one of the most common stumbling blocks to innovation. Innovation is an investment in the future, not a rescue mission for current top- or bottom-line problems. (3) *Flexible organization*. Innovation rarely flourishes in a rigid structure, with complicated approval processes, or bureaucratic delays and bottlenecks. (4) *Loose/tight planning and control.* Allocating all direct, indirect, overhead, and other costs to a development project virtually guarantees its demise. Very few innovative ideas can immediately be translated into commercial ventures that meet their own costs or meet conventional payback requirements. (5) *Appropriate incentives.* Reward systems in many companies are oriented toward existing businesses, with short-term considerations outweighing longer-term innovation and market development objectives. Innovation can flourish only when risk taking is encouraged, occasional failure accepted, and managers are held accountable for missing opportunities as well as exploiting them.

Timing: Key to Strategic Effectiveness

In addition to having the right value proposition, timing can be crucial. The first company to come out with a new product or service often has what is called a *first mover advantage*. In high-tech industries, for example, first movers can sometimes set standards for all subsequent products. Microsoft was able to accomplish this with its Windows operating system. In general, first movers have a window of opportunity to establish themselves as industry leaders in terms of technology, cost, or service.

Being a first mover can also be risky, however. Later entrants have the opportunity to evaluate alternative technologies, delay investment in risky projects or plant capacity, imitate or leapfrog superior product or technology offerings, and tap into proven market segments rather than take risks associated with developing latent market demand into an ongoing revenue stream.

Entry and Exit Decisions

Sooner or later every company faces the strategic decision whether or not—through internal development or by acquisition—to enter a new business or to withdraw from a market it currently serves. While all of the principles and analytic techniques discussed earlier apply to these decisions, the discontinuity they bring to a company's overall strategic posture justifies their special consideration.

Entry into a new segment or industry through *internal development* is akin to a start-up—it involves creating a new business from scratch, often in a somewhat unfamiliar competitive environment—and therefore carries a substantially higher level of risk than other product/market choices. It is also likely to be much slower and often more expensive than anticipated. Developing new products, processes, partnerships, and systems from scratch takes time and requires substantial learning. For these reasons companies increasingly are turning to *joint ventures* and *alliances* or, if control is important, to *acquisition* of existing players.

Two major issues must be analyzed as part of the decision process to enter a new market: (1) What structural barriers to entry are there? and (2) How will incumbent firms react? Some of the most important structural impediments were discussed in chapter 2—the level of investment required, access to production or distribution facilities, the threat of overcapacity, and so forth. Potential retaliation is harder to analyze. Incumbents will counter if resistance is likely to pay off. And, as many companies know, retaliation is not always exclusively based on economic considerations. Porter's five forces model once again is helpful in identifying when vigorous opposition is most likely to occur. If market growth is low, products or services are not highly differentiated, fixed costs are high, capacity ample, and the market in question is of great strategic importance to incumbents, then strong retaliation is likely.[25]

This suggests that the search for new markets to enter should focus on industries that are experiencing some disequilibrium, where incumbents may be slow to retaliate, where the firm can influence the industry structure, and where the benefits of entry exceed the costs, including the costs of dealing with possible retaliation by incumbents.[26]

Exit decisions are often even more difficult. First, exiting may not be a realistic option. Possible exit barriers include government restrictions, labor and pension obligations, synergies with other businesses, or simply a lack of buyers for specialized assets with a low residual value. Even if a business can be spun off or sold in part or as a whole, there are a host of issues to address before a company can make a clean cut. The impact of an exit on customer, supplier, and distributor relations, for example, can be devastating; shared cost arrangements can produce cost increases in other parts of the business, and labor relations may become strained affecting the strategic outlook for the company as a whole.

Vertical Integration

Decisions about "vertical scope" are of key strategic importance in many businesses. Should Nike enter retailing? Why did Disney purchase a television network? When does backward integration to secure access to raw materials or other supplies pay off?

The issue of vertical integration is fundamental to strategic choice. It defines to what extent and how companies participate in an industry's value chain and therefore affects industry structure and competitive intensity. In the oil industry, for example, there are companies that are fully integrated from exploration to refining and marketing, while others specialize in one or more "upstream" or "downstream" stages of the value chain. Which is strategically better? Do we know?

Such questions were addressed in the PIMS study discussed earlier. Specifically, a comparative analysis of a large number of businesses in a variety of industries helped answer three important questions: (1) Are highly integrated businesses in general more or less profitable than less integrated ones? (2) Under what circumstances is a high level of vertical integration likely to be most profitable? and (3) Apart from their influence on overall profitability, what are the principal benefits and risks associated with vertical integration strategies?[27]

The answers are intriguing. With respect to the first question—"How profitable is vertical integration?"—the study found that for both industrial and consumer manufacturing businesses *backward* integration generally raised ROI but *forward* integration did not, and that partway integration generally hurt ROI. The results also indicate that the impact of vertical integration on profitability varies with the size of the business; larger businesses tend to benefit to a greater extent than smaller ones. This suggests—in answer to the second question—that vertical integration may be a particularly attractive option for businesses with a substantial market share in which further backward integration has the potential of enhancing competitive advantage and increasing barriers to entry. Finally, with respect to question three—"Apart from their influence on profitability, what are the principal benefits and risks associated with vertical integration strategies?"—the PIMS study suggests that alternatives to ownership—long-term contracts, alliances—should actively be considered, vertical integration almost always requires substantial increases in investment, projected cost reductions do not always materialize, but vertical integration sometimes results in increased product innovation. As a final observation, we note that the higher the level of vertical integration, the more difficult it may be to exit a business. As a consequence, integration decisions should be made with great care.

Links with Corporate Strategy

Whereas business unit strategy focuses on *how* to compete in a particular business/industry, corporate strategy is about selecting *which* industries a corporation should compete in. Clearly, the two are related. In fact, the boundaries between the two have become increasingly permeable, reflecting the growing realization that the relationships among strategic business units and between different SBUs and corporate headquarters are important determinants of corporate and competitive advantage. The term *horizontal strategy* is often used to describe coordinating mechanisms aimed at unlocking value based on synergies between different parts of the corporate portfolio.

Horizontal strategic thinking gained prominence as corporate attitudes toward diversification changed in the 1970s. Before that time, many corporate portfolios had few synergies. Disappointing performance, however, led companies to focus more on *related* diversification, which meant that more attention needed to be paid to issues of "fit" between different components of the portfolio and between the businesses and corporate headquarters. Horizontal strategic thinking also received a push when the emphasis further shifted from growth to performance. Consequently, the technology revolution has both increased the potential for synergies and made them more achievable. Finally, as markets became more global, companies increasingly compete as much at the corporate level as they do at the business unit level, often in multiple businesses. Procter &

Gamble, Kimberly Clark, Scott Paper and Johnson & Johnson compete with each other in multiple lines of business. In some industries corporations compete in one business unit, are each other's customers in another, and have alliances in a third. In short, business unit strategy and corporate strategy are more closely related than ever before.

This close relationship is reflected in the planning processes used in most large, diversified corporations. While we can speak of separate strategies at the corporate and the business unit level, the process by which these strategies are generated increasingly reflects their interdependence. Strategy development at the corporate level focuses typically on two main issues—the composition of the corporate portfolio and the management of that portfolio—while business unit strategy centers on attaining a sustainable competitive advantage at the business unit level.

SUMMARY

In this chapter we looked at strategy formulation at the business unit level—the question of *how* to compete in an industry. We began with a description of the strategic logic behind competitive strategy—the importance of choosing an industry first, the influence of relative position, and how such a position can be developed and sustained using principles of competitive advantage. We identified a number of techniques that are useful in answering the three fundamental questions in the strategy formulation process: (1) "Where are we now?" (2) "Where do we want to go?" and (3) "How do we get there?" We then refined our analysis by considering several industry scenarios, which pose unique challenges such as embryonic, growth, and mature industry settings, and industries that are highly fragmented, or changing rapidly because of deregulation or globalization. We concluded by considering three special issues: entry into new markets, vertical integration, and how strategy development at the business unit level is linked to corporate strategy.

Notes

1. See e.g., Michael E. Porter, *Competitive Strategy: Techniques for Analyzing Industries and Competitors* (New York: Free Press, 1980) and Michael E. Porter, *Competitive Advantage: Creating and Sustaining Superior Performance* (New York: Free Press, 1985).
2. Michael E. Porter, in Richard P. Rumelt, Dan E. Schendel, and David J. Teece (eds.), *Fundamental Issues in Strategy* (Boston: Harvard Business School Press, 1994), 431.
3. Anita M. McGahan and Michael E. Porter, "How Much Does Industry Matter, Really?" *Strategic Management Journal* 18 (summer special issue, 1997): 15–30.
4. Recall that *industry attractiveness*—defined in terms of its profit potential—is largely determined by the intensity of the *competitive rivalry* within that industry. In chapter 2 we in-
troduced Porter's so-called *five forces model* to analyze rivalry in terms of five forces: the *threat of new entrants*, the *bargaining power of customers*, the *bargaining power of suppliers*, the *threat of substitute products* or *services* and the *jockeying among current rivals*.
5. Porter, in Rumelt et al., *Fundamental Issues in Strategy,* 431.
6. Porter, in Rumelt et al., *Fundamental Issues in Strategy,* 434.
7. Adrian J. Slywotzky and David J. Morrison, *The Profit Zone: How Strategic Business Design Will Lead You to Tomorrow's Profits* (New York: Random House, 1997).
8. Ibid., chap. 1.
9. Bradley T. Gale and Robert D. Buzzell, "Market Position and Competitive Strategy," in *The Interface of Marketing and Strategy,*

George Day, Barton Weitz, and Robin Wensley (eds.), 1993, JAI Press, Inc. 137-145

10. Sidney Schoeffler, Robert D. Buzzell, and Donald F. Heany, "Impact of Strategic Planning on Profit Performance," *Harvard Business Review* (March–April 1974); vol. 62, no. 3 see also Robert D. Buzzell and Bradley T. Gale, *The PIMS Principles: Linking Strategy to Performance* (New York: Free Press, 1987).

11. "Michael Dell: Whirlwind on the Web," *Business Week* (April 7, 1997).

12. Ibid.

13. Michael Treacy and Fred Wiersema, "Customer Intimacy and Other Value Disciplines," *Harvard Business Review* (Jan.–Feb. 1993): vol. 71, no. 1 84–93.

14. This characterization is based on George S. Day and David J. Reibstein (eds.), *Wharton on Dynamic Competitive Strategy* (John Wiley & Sons, 1997), 14–18.

15. This section is based on Orit Gadiesh and James L. Gilbert, "Profit Pools: A Fresh Look at Strategy," *Harvard Business Review* (May–June 1998): vol. 76, no. 3 139–147, and Orit Gadiesh and James L. Gilbert, "How to Map Your Industry's Profit Pool," *Harvard Business Review* (May–June 1998): vol. 76, no. 3 149–162.

16. William L. Moore and Edgar A. Pessemier, *Product Planning and Management: Designing and Delivering Value* (New York: McGraw-Hill, 1993), chap. 2.

17. Richard Rumelt, *Strategy, Structure, and Economic Performance,* Division of Research (Boston: Harvard Business School, 1974).

18. Michael E. Porter, *Competitive Strategy,* 50.

19. The discussion of the first three contextual environments draws on material in Michael E. Porter, *Competitive Strategy,* and John A. Pearce II and Richard B. Robinson Jr., *Strategic Management: Formulation, Implementation and Control,* 6th ed. (Chicago: Irwin, 1997), chap. 8.

20. Michael E. Porter, *Competitive Strategy,* chaps. 11, 12.

21. See Andrew E. Serwer, "Huizinga's Third Act," *Fortune Magazine* (August 5, 1996); "Waste Management, Inc.," notable corporate chronologies (Gale Research, 1996); and "Off-the-Shelf Autos," a chat with J. David Power III by Tim Ferguson, *Forbes Magazine* (February 10, 1997).

22. Joel E. Bleeke, "Strategic Choices for Newly Opened Markets," *Harvard Business Review* (Sept.–Oct. 1990) vol. 68, no. 5 158–167.

23. Ibid.

24. This section is based on C. A. de Kluyver, "Innovation: The Strategic Thrust of the Nineties," *A Cresap Insight* (July 1988).

25. Michael E. Porter, *Competitive Strategy,* chap. 16.

26. Ibid.

27. Robert D. Buzzell and Bradley T. Gale, *The PIMS Principles,* 164.

CHAPTER

Corporate Strategy

*For me all is in the conception—I must have a clear vision of the whole
composition from the very beginning. I could mention the name of a
great sculptor who produces some admirable pieces but for him a
composition is nothing but the grouping of fragments and the result is a
confusion of expression. Look instead at one of Cézanne's pictures: all is
so well arranged in them that no matter how figures are represented and
no matter at what distance you stand, you will be able always to
distinguish each figure clearly and you will always know which limb
belongs to which body. If in the picture there is order and clarity it means
that this same order and clarity existed in the mind of the painter and that
the painter was conscious of their necessity.**

—HENRI MATISSE

INTRODUCTION

Corporate strategy, which is concerned with creating a blueprint for the long-term direction for a diversified company, is an important and complex subject. It is important because it directly affects our economic well-being. A number of today's global 1,000 companies are larger than the economies of entire nations; they typically are engaged in several different businesses and have a global reach. Their strategic choices regarding which businesses or markets to enter affect not only their own financial performance but also the fate of entire economies, and with it, the fate of citizens around the world. Corporate strategy is also an exceedingly difficult subject. In contrast to business unit strategy, strategy at the corporate level is much less understood. The lack of a fully developed framework is evident in the statistics. The economic half-life of a typical multinational corporation is 40 years or less. And a number of studies have shown that the majority of mergers and acquisitions fail and result in breakups or divestitures within ten years.[1] What is not known with any degree of certainty, however, is what proportion of these failures can be blamed on flaws in strategy or missteps in execution.

An appreciation of history is important to understanding strategic thinking at the corporate level. The corporate strategy framework we use today has its roots in the mistakes of the past. It reflects the now much discredited conglomerate deals of the 1960s and 1970s that gave rise to such unwieldy companies as ITT Corporation and Litton Industries and destroyed more shareholder value than they created. It takes into account the lessons learned from the debt-laden leveraged buyouts and breakups of the 1980s,

---

*From "Notes of a Painter," *La Grande Revue* 25 (1908): 731–745, as quoted in Herschell B. Chipp, *Theories of Modern Art: A Source Book by Artists and Critics* (Berkeley, Calif.: University of California Press, 1968), 134.

and it explains why senior executives in many industries are once again preoccupied with growth by acquisition and have unleashed a new global wave of mergers in the 1990s.

Indeed, if there is one constant in the history of corporate strategy, it is the quest for size. Grow bigger or be swallowed has in reality become the corporate mantra in many boardrooms. As we approach the turn of the century, the value of all announced mergers and acquisitions continues to increase steadily each year. And while high profile deals such as the combination of AT&T and NCR and of Matsushita and MCA have already unraveled, banks, healthcare providers, computer software companies, and media, telecommunications, and entertainment giants are leading the next wave of consolidation.[2]

We begin our discussion by taking a look at the concept of *economics of scale and scope*—a fundamental underpinning of corporate strategy—and try to answer the question: Is bigger always better? Next, we turn to the context in which corporate strategy is developed and executed. In particular, we note the importance of dispersion in the ownership of large corporations in the last 30 years and emergence *of the market for corporate control*. With this background, we trace the *evolution of strategic thinking* at the corporate level. Four perspectives are identified—the *portfolio, value-based, generic strategy,* and *resource-based* points of view—and their relative merits assessed. This discussion leads us to the consideration of *strategy choices* at the corporate level. In this section we look at *concentrated growth strategies, diversification issues, merger and acquisition activities, and cooperative strategies* including joint ventures and alliances, and *sell-offs, spin-offs, and liquidations*. Next, we look at the issue of *corporate parenting* and how a parenting style affects portfolio composition and management. We conclude the chapter with a discussion of *how to evaluate* strategy choices at the corporate level.

THE ECONOMICS OF SCALE AND SCOPE

The "Logic of Managerial Enterprise"

Alfred D. Chandler, the well-known business historian, in a seminal article in the *Harvard Business Review* entitled "The Enduring Logic of Industrial Success," argued that "to compete globally, you have to be big. History explains why."[3] Looking back over a century of corporate history, he noted that the "logic of managerial enterprise" begins with economics and the cost advantages that come with scale and scope in technologically advanced capital-intensive industries. Large plants frequently can produce products at a much lower cost than small ones because the cost per unit decreases as volume goes up (*economies of scale*). In addition, larger plants can use many of the same raw and semifinished materials and production processes to make a variety of different products (*economies of scope*). What is more, these principles are not limited to the manufacturing sector. Procter & Gamble, through its multibrand strategies, has considerable influence at the retail level. And 20 or 30 years ago, large companies had their books audited by any one of a number of respectable accounting firms; today we talk about the "Big Four."

The underlying scale and scope economies in a particular industry are usually well understood. Oil refining is a good example. As far back as 1881, John D. Rockefeller combined Standard Oil and 39 allied companies to form the Standard Oil Trust. His goal was not to create a monopoly even though the companies in the trust already controlled almost 90 percent of the kerosene produced in the United States. Rather, Rockefeller wanted to capitalize on the potential cost advantages that could only be realized by placing the companies under a single management.[4]

Size alone, Chandler noted, is not enough to guarantee competitive success. To capitalize on the advantages scale and scope can bring, companies must make related investments to create global marketing and distribution organizations, and the right management infrastructure to effectively coordinate the myriad of activities that make up today's multinational corporation.[5]

Timing Is Key

The timing of such moves is critical. It is no accident that IBM, Intel, Microsoft, Hoechst, and Sony—all dominant in their industries—were *first movers.* First mover advantage explains why American hardware and software companies were successful in building a global presence, and why Japanese corporations seized the advantage in many electronics industries. Challengers face a formidable challenge. They must build productive capacity while first movers are perfecting their production processes, develop marketing and distribution organizations to compete for market share in already established markets, and attract managerial talent capable of beating entrenched competitors.

The Diversification Movement of the 1960s

This "logic of managerial enterprise," the right combination of scale and scope economics, marketing and distribution power, and management structure and first mover advantage still guides corporate strategy today. Its indiscriminate application, however, has cost shareholders dearly. When misapplied, the logic of corporate growth can turn size from a competitive asset into a liability. The misguided diversification movement of the 1960s provides ample evidence. Facing stronger competition from abroad and diminished growth prospects in a number of traditional industries, many U.S. companies began moving into industries in which they had no particular competitive advantage. Believing that management was a general skill rather than an industry-specific talent, executives thought that since they were successful in their own industries they could be just as successful in others. In effect they were ignoring the fundamentals of the logic of managerial enterprise. Under these circumstances, bigger was worse, not better.

Research by the Ashridge Strategic Management Center shows that while a few multibusiness corporations have created substantial net value, most continue to destroy shareholder value in at least part of their portfolio.[6] Four kinds of value destruction are cited: (1) potential negative effects of central executive influence on the companies it is in charge of, (2) the pursuit of elusive synergies in constructing a portfolio of businesses, (3) the constraining behavior of corporate staffs, and (4) inopportune acquisition. This does not mean that opportunities to realize economies of scale and scope should be ignored. Rather, these findings speak to the fact that "big is not always better" and that a trade-off exists between size and the organizational complexity of running a global multibusiness corporation.[7]

The Decade of Restructuring

The diversification movement reached its peak at the end of the 1960s. Of the nearly 6,000 mergers and acquisitions concluded in 1969, almost three-quarters involved product diversification, and approximately one-half were in unrelated businesses. With such unprecedented levels of growth, a separation between top management at the corporate office and middle management responsible for the running of the different operating divisions became inevitable. Top management was too busy to be concerned with everyday operations. Besides, they often had little if any specific knowledge of or experience with the products, markets, and technologies of the divisions they had acquired. This lack of understanding by top management of the operating characteristics of the different divisions and the enormous differences among operating units contributed to a greater reliance on financial data at the corporate level. Such data, however, were of little use in diagnosing the complexities of the competitive battles at the business unit level. As a consequence, performance in many conglomerates started to suffer, and by the mid-1970s, operating companies were being divested in record numbers in an effort to shore up lagging results. Changes in the ownership of U.S. companies abetted this trend. An institutional market for corporate control had begun to emerge that facilitated the buying, selling, splitting up, and recombining of industrial companies in ways that would have been impossible before the acquisition wave of the 1960s. In the process, household names such as International Harvester and B.F. Goodrich disappeared, and many industries—from chemicals to steel to pharmaceuticals—were fundamentally restructured.

The 1990s: Consolidation in the Face of Globalization

As we approach the turn of the century, we are once again witnessing a global wave of consolidation. The drivers are different this time; deregulation and globalization have put the quest for scale and scope at the top of many corporate strategic agendas in many industries. This time also, corporate executives, directors, and the financial community tell us they are heeding the lessons of the past and will stick closer to the "logic of managerial enterprise." Early combinations such as the 1991 merger of Chemical Bank Corporation and Manufacturers Hanover Corporation seemed to signal that "the Age of Reason in mergers and acquisitions had begun."[8] The WorldCom-MCI combination also was a trendsetter; the combined entity is the first major company since AT&T capable of offering long distance and local service across the United States.[9] Other notable combinations include the union between Compaq Computer and Digital Equipment Corporation and the Daimler-Chrysler merger. By taking over Digital, Compaq instantly transformed itself from a PC maker into a full-line information systems and service company capable of competing with the likes of IBM, H-P, and Sun in the higher-end markets that it could not serve before. Similarly, the Daimler-Chrysler combination has changed the competitive dynamics of the global auto industry. By combining forces, Daimler, Germany's biggest industrial concern, and Chrysler, America's number 3 carmaker, can offer a full product line around the globe. But this merger is about more than cutting costs and filling product and geographic gaps. It is about the emergence of a new category of global carmaker at a critical moment in the industry—when there is plant capacity to build at least 15 million more vehicles each year than will be sold. Other automakers will have to respond, forestalling further industry consolidation.

History shows that big mergers in general, and high-tech combinations in particular, have a tendency to derail. Fusing the different cultures and product lines may take years, and any period longer than a year is an eternity in the high-tech world.[10] At first glance, the deals of this decade appear to reflect a more strategic perspective focused more on synergies of operation, economies of scale, and global market clout and not burdened by the same debt levels that characterized the doomed combinations of the seventies. It would be premature, however, to conclude that Corporate America has learned all there is to learn. The takeover of Turner Broadcasting by Time-Warner, for example, and the acquisition of Capital Cities/ABC by Disney left many analysts wondering where the shareholder value will come from. And with each bigger deal and richer offer, we may once again see a test of the limits of financial leverage.

One thing is clear, like it or not, size has once again become an imperative in corporate strategy. And because few companies can rely on internal sources of growth alone, mergers, acquisitions, joint ventures, and alliances, despite their uneven track record, have emerged as major instruments of corporate strategy.

STRATEGY AND CORPORATE GOVERNANCE

Ownership Patterns

At the end of the last century and in the beginning of the twentieth century most large U.S. corporations were controlled by "captains of industry." Wealthy entrepreneurs—Morgan, Rockefeller, Carnegie, and Du Pont—not only owned the majority of the stock in companies such as Standard Oil and U.S. Steel, they also exercised their rights to run these companies.[11]

By the 1930s, however, the ownership of U.S. corporations had become much more widespread. In analyzing this trend, Berle and Means concluded that capitalism in the United States had made a transition from the *entrepreneurial model* to *managerial capitalism,* a model in which ownership and control had become substantially divorced.[12] In effect, effective control of the corporation was no longer exercised by the legal owners of equity—the shareholders—but by hired professional managers.

With the rise of institutional investing in the seventies, primarily through private and public pension funds, the responsibility of ownership once again reconcentrated in the hands of a relatively small number of institutional investors acting as fiduciaries on behalf of individuals. This large-scale institutionalization of equity brought further changes to the corporate governance landscape. Because of their size, institutional investors today effectively own a major fraction of most major companies. This makes it difficult for them to trade. Because their liquidity is restricted they have little choice but to protect and enhance their investments through active monitoring of the companies in which they invest. This current model of corporate governance, which emphasizes monitoring over trading, is often described as *fiduciary capitalism.*[13]

Relationship of Corporate Governance to Strategy

For the greater part of this century—when managerial capitalism prevailed—managers had relatively free rein in interpreting their responsibilities toward the various corporate stakeholders and, as long as the corporation made money and its operations were conducted within the confines of the law, they were pretty much left alone. Executives were expected to be competent at running their business, behave ethically at all times, and were trusted to balance the needs of shareholders with those of society at large. Boards of directors, mostly selected and controlled by management, intervened only infrequently, if at all. Indeed, for the first half of this century, corporate executives of many publicly held companies managed with little or no outside control.

The turbulent sixties and seventies changed all that. As institutional shareholding gained momentum senior executives and corporate boards came under greater scrutiny. Pension fund managers, in particular, experienced growing pressure in their capacity as fiduciaries to realize better returns for their beneficiaries. Shareholders disillusioned by unimpressive corporate earnings, and upset that CEOs paid themselves royally, that ill-considered acquisitions had depressed shareholder value and amounted to little more than empire building on a broad scale; and that boards appeared incapable of standing up to management; began to exercise their newfound powers. Terms such as leveraged buyout, dawn raids, poison pills, and junk bonds became household words and individuals such as Carl Icahn, Irwin Jacobs, and T. Boone Pickens became well known. The resulting takeover boom of the eighties woke up sleepy boards, exposed underperforming companies, unlocked shareholder value and, in the process, helped to more closely align the incentives of management with those of shareholders.

The 1980s, however, will also be remembered as a period of excess in the form of ill-considered adventures in leverage. As explosively as it started, the takeover era ended in a more quiet fashion as capital dried up and junk-bond financed, highly leveraged hostile takeovers faded from the stage. Of lasting importance in this era was the rise of institutional investors who knew the value of ownership rights, had fiduciary responsibilities to use them, and were big enough to make a difference.[14]

The nineties, while no less dynamic, saw more gradual change. As boards found themselves under much closer scrutiny, directors started to take their oversight roles more seriously. Major shareholders, particularly a small group of public sector pension funds, using their growing leverage began to play a more active role in the governance process.[15] The result was a wave of structural and procedural reforms aimed at making boards more responsive, more proactive, and more accountable.

There can be no question that the turmoil of the seventies and eighties, the rise of global competition, the emergence of the market for corporate control, and the changes in corporate governance that accompanied them have redefined the way senior executives approach corporate strategy. CEOs around the world have adopted greater discipline in shaping corporate strategy and are reminded on a daily basis of the need to be more accountable to boards of directors, shareholders, and other stakeholders. It is no coincidence that turnover among CEOs at major public corporations has reached an all-time high. At the same time, the competitive environment of today demands greater strategic focus, a global perspective, and superb leadership skills. These events have left a lasting imprint on corporate strategy.

THE EVOLUTION OF STRATEGIC THINKING AT THE CORPORATE LEVEL

Early Perspectives

The view of the modern corporation as a *portfolio of businesses* and the related *portfolio management concept* date back to the early seventies. Earlier work on corporate strategy had focused on the importance of building a *distinctive competence* that would provide the corporation with a competitive advantage in its various businesses, on the evolution of the *multidivisional* organizational structure that accompanied the conglomerate boom of the sixties, and on the need to create a *fit* between structure and strategy so that "structure followed strategy."[16]

These early perspectives did not provide much guidance regarding which businesses a corporation should participate in. As corporate America continued to diversify, however, this issue became more pressing. One well-known study examined the relation between corporate performance and the degree of *relatedness* among the various businesses the company participated in.[17] It identified three categories of relatedness based on their *specialization ratio,* the proportion of revenues derived from the largest single group of related businesses: *dominant business companies, related business companies, and unrelated business companies.* Dominant business companies such as General Motors and IBM derive a majority of their revenues from a single line of business. Related business companies such as General Foods, Eastman Kodak, and DuPont are diversified beyond a single type of business but maintain a common thread of relatedness—usually in the form of core strengths and skills—throughout the portfolio while the components of the portfolios of unrelated business companies, or conglomerates, have little in common. Rockwell International and Textron are examples of companies in which the principal link between businesses was financial. The study concluded that closely related portfolios outperformed widely diversified corporations. This finding was welcomed because it explained performance in terms of *synergy* among related businesses, an intuitive notion for many executives.[18]

The BCG Approach to Portfolio Analysis

By the mid-1970s most large corporations had diversified, primarily through acquisition. Corporate executives struggled with formulating a coherent strategy for their diverse array of semiautonomous divisions of which they often knew little. The well-known *growth/share matrix,* introduced in the seventies by the Boston Consulting Group, helped them confront these issues.[19]

The Boston Consulting Group's approach to portfolio analysis is based on the observation that multidivisional, multiproduct companies have a distinct advantage over nondiversified companies: the ability to channel resources into the most productive units. A diversified company can slow the growth of one division to fuel the expansion of another. This ability to integrate investment patterns between different businesses makes it possible to optimize the performance of the portfolio as a whole rather than focus on the performance of individual units. To achieve this optimal allocation of resources, the BCG approach assigns a role to each strategic business unit and integrates these roles into one overall portfolio strategy. Product roles are assigned on the basis of a unit's cash flow potential and cost position relative to its principal competitors. Differences in growth and cash flow potential determine how funds are allocated across the portfolio.

The analysis begins with the construction of a so-called *growth/share matrix* for the company and for its major competitors. Each business unit is plotted on a two-dimensional graph according to the relative market share it commands and the growth rate that characterizes its market (Figure 5-1). The size of the circle is proportional to the unit's annual dollar sales. Relative market share is defined as ratio of the unit's sales to that of the industry's largest competitor.

The product portfolio matrix is usually divided into four quadrants each defining a different growth/share position. High-growth markets typically show growth rates of more than 10 percent per year, and high share products occupy a leadership position in their markets, that is, they have a relative market share of at least 1.0. *Cash cows* are high share/low-growth products that generate large amounts of cash—far more than

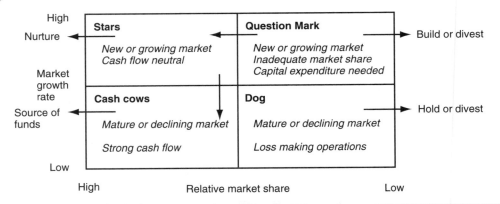

FIGURE 5-1 The Boston Consulting Group's Approach to Portfolio Analysis—1

Source: © The Boston Consulting Group. Reprinted by permission.

they can profitably reinvest and therefore a source of funds. *Dogs* are low share/low-growth products; they neither generate nor require much cash. Because some level of reinvestment is needed and returns are usually modest at best, they are also referred to as "cash traps." *Question marks,* also known as *problem children,* are low share/high-growth products. Substantial cash investments are needed to improve their share position from being a me-too entry to a position of market leadership. *Stars* are high-growth/high share products that may or may not be self-sufficient in terms of their cash needs. If handled right, they are the company's future cash cows.

As conceptualized by the Boston Consulting Group, the way products move across the chart over time reflects the strategic moves by the company and the evolutionary forces acting on the industry. For example, if only share-maintenance level investments are made, natural market forces will cause all products to move downward and to eventually end up as cash cows or dogs depending upon their share position when market growth begins to slow. The major strategic issue therefore becomes one of using excess cash generated by cash cows to fund market share increases for the most promising products in the portfolio—selected question marks whose position is strong enough to become stars. Under this philosophy, question marks with a relatively weak competitive position should be "starved" from further investment and either divested or continued under a "no cash in" doctrine. Dogs can remain in the portfolio as long as they contribute to cash flow and do not tie up disproportionate amounts of working capital that can be put to better use. These basic movements are illustrated in Figure 5-2.

These generic strategies are based on the finding that in many stable market situations high market share and profitability are strongly correlated. Market dominance, therefore, becomes an appropriate strategic goal in high-growth markets, and maximizing cash generation is desirable in low-growth markets where market share gains are more costly to obtain. How many and which products to select for growth depends on their relative competitive strength, the cost of gaining market leadership, and the cash flow generated by other products in the portfolio.

Experience curve effects are an important factor in explaining the correlation between market share and profitability in many businesses. For many manufacturing businesses, for example, a large percentage of the variances in profitability can be explained

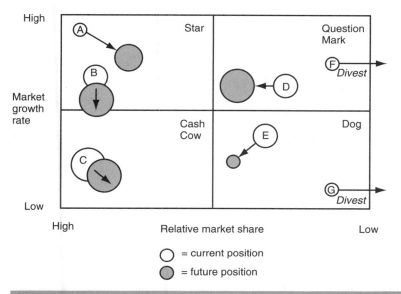

FIGURE 5-2 **The Boston Consulting Group's Approach to Portfolio Analysis—2**

Source: © The Boston Consulting Group. Reprinted by permission.

by competitive cost differentials, which reflect differences in competitors' experience: the company with the largest cumulative volume of production often has the lowest unit cost, which translates into higher cash flow. The assumption of a strong correlation between market share and profitability is not always justified, however, and therefore must be treated with care. Poor investment decisions can erode a market leader's capacity to generate cash. Experience in related products or technologies—so-called shared experience—is sometimes as important as direct experience. And for some types of businesses such as service companies experience effects may be less pronounced.

Variants of the BCG Approach

Shortly after the Boston Consulting Group pioneered its portfolio approach, General Electric, with the assistance of McKinsey & Company, developed a slightly more complex matrix approach. Shown in Figure 5-3, the *General Electric Business Screen* uses nine cells to describe a company's portfolio. Its dimensions are broader; instead of classifying markets based on their growth rate alone, it uses *long-term industry attractiveness* defined to include such factors as the industry's growth rate, its investment intensity, its technological intensity, and the presence or absence of governmental influences and other regulatory factors. Similarly, instead of characterizing a business's position in terms of market share alone, it defines *business strength* in terms of market share, technical strength, management cohesiveness and depth, and access to financial resources. Despite these differences, its prescriptions show considerable similarity; based on their classification businesses are targeted for growth/investment, selective investment/earnings, or harvesting/divestment.[20]

Another variant of the portfolio methodology that has gained some currency was developed at Arthur D. Little, Inc. This so-called *life-cycle matrix approach* plots businesses

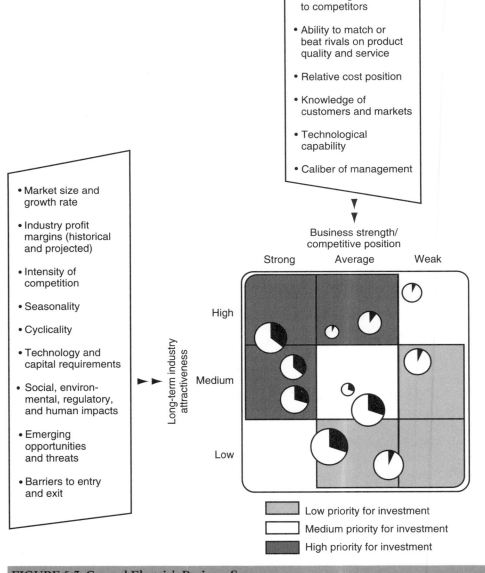

- Market size and growth rate
- Industry profit margins (historical and projected)
- Intensity of competition
- Seasonality
- Cyclicality
- Technology and capital requirements
- Social, environmental, regulatory, and human impacts
- Emerging opportunities and threats
- Barriers to entry and exit

- Relative market share
- Possession of desirable core competencies
- Profit margins relative to competitors
- Ability to match or beat rivals on product quality and service
- Relative cost position
- Knowledge of customers and markets
- Technological capability
- Caliber of management

Business strength/
competitive position

Strong   Average   Weak

Long-term industry attractiveness

High

Medium

Low

Low priority for investment

Medium priority for investment

High priority for investment

FIGURE 5-3 General Electric's Business Screen

Source: From Arthur A. Thompson, Jr., and A. J. Strickland, III, *Strategic Management,* 9th edition, 1990. Reprinted by permission of McGraw-Hill Company, Inc., New York, NY.

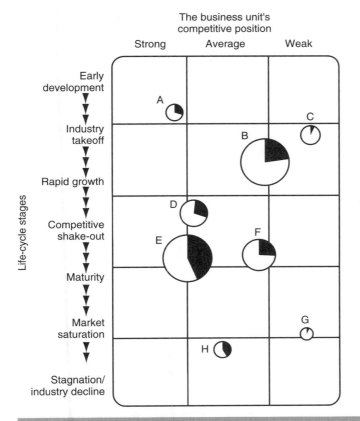

The business unit's
competitive position

Strong   Average   Weak

Early
development

A

C

Industry
takeoff

B

Rapid growth

D

Competitive
shake-out

E   F

Maturity

Market
saturation

G

H

Stagnation/
industry decline

Life-cycle stages

FIGURE 5-4 Arthur D. Little's Life-Cycle Approach to Portfolio Analysis

Source: From Arthur A. Thompson, Jr., and A. J. Strickland, III, *Strategic Management,* 9th edition, 1990.
Reprinted by permission of McGraw-Hill Company, Inc., New York, NY.

based on the stage of their industry's evolution and the strength of their competitive position (Figure 5-4).[21]

Limitations of Portfolio Analysis

While portfolio analysis is useful in describing the breadth and depth of the current portfolio of a corporation, it has a number of serious limitations. First, it tends to encourage evaluation of businesses as freestanding units. This may prevent a focus on core competency building across businesses and fragment resource allocation. Second, labeling businesses as cash cows or dogs may lead to self-fulfilling prophecies; milking a cash cow business will almost certainly limit its growth, classifying a business as a dog does not encourage creativity in charting its future. Third, portfolio has prescriptive limitations. It does not answer such questions as "How do we grow overall revenues?" and "What new businesses should be added to the portfolio?" Finally, as ownership of large corporations dispersed and shares were traded more freely, the assumption that companies had to be self-sufficient in capital, a central premise of the BCG approach, began to lose its validity. Options such as paying out "excess" free cash flow to shareholders in the form of dividends and raising additional investment funds in the capital markets now had to be considered.

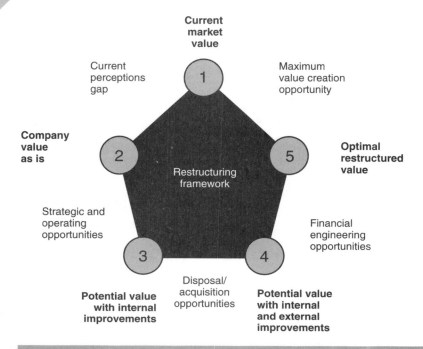

FIGURE 5-5 The Pentagon of Value-Based Management

Source: Tom Copeland, Tim Keller, and Jack Murrin, *Valuation: Measuring and Managing the Value of Companies*, 2nd edition. Copyright © John Wiley & Sons, New York, NY. Reprinted by permission of John Wiley & Sons, Inc.

At the same time, the rapid growth in the corporate headquarters' staffs at many corporations prompted investors to begin asking what value, if any, these corporate resources contributed to the semiautonomous operations of the divisions.

The Value-Based Approach

These changes in the strategic environment set the stage for the emergence of the so-called *value-based approach* to corporate strategy with its focus on maximizing shareholder value.[22] This approach also treats strategic business units as separate entities that are valued according to their cash flow, and allows analysis of such questions as "How much economic value is created by different divisions?" and "What is the optimal structure of the corporation?" In effect, it imputes a *share price* for each business unit. If the market value of the corporation as a whole is less than the sum of the valuations of the different business units, action is called for, often in the form of a sell-off of those business units that are implicitly undervalued.

Figure 5-5 shows the so-called "pentagon" framework that defines the value-based approach.[23] It depicts several levels of analysis; starting with internally available data and restructuring options within the current portfolio. In the first step, the current market valuation of the company is compared with an objective assessment of the value of the company generated with its current corporate strategy. If the "as is" discounted cash flow analysis of the current portfolio produces a higher value than shareholders are willing to pay, management needs to improve its communications with shareholders and, to show its confidence in its corporate strategy, consider moves such as a share repurchase program. If the internally developed cash flow analysis shows the company is overvalued by the market, it may mean shareholders are anticipating a possible takeover or breakup of the company. This outcome is a clear warning signal that management needs to revisit its corporate strategy and improve shareholder value.

Depending on the outcome of the overall valuation of the company, it is logical to consider strategic and operating improvements within the current portfolio as the second step. Such improvements can be targeted at the business unit level, for example, by focusing on increasing sales growth and operating margins, or decreasing working capital requirements (*business unit strategy*), or at the corporate level, for example, by reducing overhead, or by reexamining the strategies for managing the portfolio (*parenting strategies*). If the problems uncovered at this stage are manageable, simple improvement strategies or a turnaround strategy involving one or more business units are called for. If the problems are pervasive, or if they can be dealt with better by another corporate parent, more drastic action may be needed.

If simple improvements or a turnaround strategy are not likely to improve shareholder value sufficiently, portfolio adjustments must be considered. As part of this process, management must revisit the rationale for the corporation's diversified posture and its fit with its parenting philosophy. Portfolio strategies include moves to shrink the scope of the company's activities through sell-offs, spin-offs, or liquidation, as well as expansion strategies. Expansion strategies can take various forms. *Concentrated* growth strategies are aimed at strengthening the current businesses in the portfolio through *vertical* or *horizontal* integration. *Diversification* strategies are designed to expand the portfolio of activities in new directions. In choosing which industries to diversify into, the two basic options are to select businesses *related* or *unrelated* to the company's current core activities. Today, expansion increasingly involves *cooperative* choices—joint ventures and alliances—either as stepping stones toward acquisition or as a deliberate strategy to increase scope at a lower cost.

The fourth and final step involves *financial engineering* of the reconfigured corporate portfolio. Changes in configuration or parenting style sometimes afford opportunities to increase shareholder value through recapitalization, changing the company's global ownership structure to minimize its tax liability, or changing its debt-to-equity ratio. While more tactical in nature, such moves are important in the total effort to maximize shareholder value.

In recent years, the original shareholder value approach to strategy has been expanded into a total value-based management discipline. Disney, Marriott, and Pepsico are among the many companies that use value-based planning and concepts such as *economic value added* (EVA) at both the corporate and business unit level today.

Generic Strategies at the Corporate Level

Taking a slightly different perspective, Michael Porter identified four *generic strategies* by which value can be realized in a diversified portfolio based on the degree of corporate involvement in the operation of the different business units.[24] The first two, *portfolio management* and *restructuring,* apply primarily to companies whose businesses are essentially unrelated. Both focus more on *capturing* than *creating* value, on spotting undervalued businesses, buying them for less than they are worth and restructuring them if necessary, and on realizing onetime benefits at the time of their sale. The third and fourth, in contrast, focus on value *creation* through the *transfer of skills* or *activity shar-ing*. These strategies are primarily applicable to companies in which the different businesses are related in some way and invest for the long term to realize synergies and shared benefits.

Core Competencies and the Resource-Based View of Strategy

With the publication of their enormously influential article "The Core Competence of the Corporation," Hamel and Prahalad shifted the focus of strategy to the building of core capabilities that transcend the boundaries of traditional business units, and urged companies to center their portfolio around *core businesses* and adopt goals and processes aimed at enhancing *core competencies.*[25] This perspective was later extended to what is known today as the *resource-based view of the firm*. Its central thesis is that a corporation is a collection of tangible and intangible assets, which collectively define its distinctive competence, and that corporate strategy should be focused on the creation of value through the configuration and coordination of a set of multimarket activities.

Figure 5-6 depicts the resource-based point of view. Instead of focusing on synergies between component businesses it emphasizes the importance of a fit between corporate resources and product markets. The three sides of the triangle—*resources; businesses;* and *structure, systems,* and *processes*—represent the foundations of a strategy. When aligned in pursuit of a *vision,* and motivated by the right *goals* and *objectives,* a *corporate advantage* can be created that justifies the corporation's existence as a multi-business entity.[26] More recently, a related perspective focusing on the fit between the capabilities of the corporate parent and the needs of the various businesses in the portfolio has been added.[27] This *parenting framework* focuses on the competencies of the parent organization and on the value created from the relationship between the parent company and its component businesses.

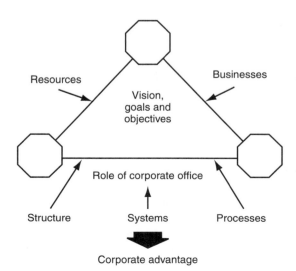

FIGURE 5-6 The Resource-Based View of Corporate Strategy

Source: From David J. Collis and Cynthia A. Montgomery, *Corporate Strategy: Resources and the Scope of the Firm,* 1997. Copyright © 1997 McGraw-Hill Company, Inc., New York, NY. Reproduced with permission.

While there are significant differences among all these perspectives they should not be viewed as mutually exclusive. It is difficult if not impossible to construct a cohesive corporate portfolio without paying attention to synergy among the various businesses. Shareholder value should be a primary objective. And to be sustainable, competitive advantage at the corporate level must reflect a fit between the shared resources and competencies the company is developing and the product markets it competes in as well as a congruence between the critical success factors in the various businesses and the ability of the parent corporation to exploit these factors.

Today's Perspective

Current thinking about corporate strategy, while dominated by the resource-based point of view, also borrows from other approaches. It holds that companies should focus on how to create *value* through the *configuration* and *coordination* of its multimarket activities.[28] The basic premise is that value creation is the fundamental purpose of corporate strategy and the value of a multibusiness corporation should be greater than the sum of its component parts. To justify its existence as a multibusiness entity, a corporation must contribute to the competitive advantage of its individual businesses by shaping its portfolio and by coordinating its multimarket activities; by deciding which businesses the company, rather than some other company, should own and why; and by developing an organizational structure and the supporting management philosophy and processes that generate a superior performance in its individual businesses.

Analysis of Strategic Fit Among Businesses

The fit or degree of synergy among businesses in a portfolio can take a variety of forms. In the Boston Consulting Group's approach to portfolio planning, *strategic fit* was primarily defined in terms of financial characteristics—the ability of business units to generate or productively use cash. Other approaches to portfolio analysis recognize that generic functional skills such as distribution or manufacturing can be important factors of synergy. Complementary asset structures or skill sets can also define attractive opportunities, for example, when a transaction intensive business such as claim processing is paired with information technology skills. For convenience, we classify different types of "fit" into three categories.

Operating or Resource Fit   Sustained competitive advantage can often be traced to a fit among unique skills, resources, and the product markets in which they are applied. They can reside within specific businesses as in the case of R&D capabilities or take the form of core competencies that transcend the boundaries of business units such as Sony's ability to miniaturize anything or Honda's core competency in small engines. A related form of operating fit is found when the business models for different business units have common characteristics, for example, when there is a high degree of similarity in critical success factors. Some companies specialize in businesses in which brand development and management skills are key to success while others concentrate on manufacturing synergies.

Market-Related Fit   Similarity in served markets, in customers, buying behavior, distribution patterns, and so forth, can enhance competitiveness when such synergies translate into economies of scale or scope, or strengthen a company's position with suppliers, partners, distributors or customers.

Management or Parenting Fit   The existence of potential synergies among markets, resources, or operations may not be enough. The realization of potential synergies depends in important ways on the presence or absence of management or parenting fit—the fit between the corporate parent and the different businesses. Assessing management fit involves three steps: (1) an identification of the critical success factors associated with each of the businesses in the portfolio, (2) an assessment of what the focus of improvement should be in each of the businesses, and (3) an evaluation of how well the skills of the parent corporation fit with the value enhancement efforts targeted at the business unit level.[29]

Whatever the basis of the "fit" or "synergy" between different businesses and between the parent organization and its business units, complementarity of skills, resources, or practices is not enough. Value creation occurs when potential synergies are *realized* and translated into corporate advantage as evidenced by enhanced, sustained performance.

STRATEGY OPTIONS AT THE CORPORATE LEVEL

Concentrated Growth Strategies

If a company's current lines of business show real growth potential, it makes sense to concentrate corporate resources on existing opportunities. Two avenues for growth—*vertical* and *horizontal*—are available.

Vertical integration, or increasing the extent to which a company participates vertically in the industry's value chain, can be valuable if a company or business unit has a strong competitive position in a highly attractive industry, especially when technology is predictable and markets are growing rapidly. Although *backward* integration is usually more profitable than *forward* integration, such moves often involve an expensive investment in assets. This can reduce a company's strategic flexibility by creating an exit barrier; preventing the company from leaving the industry if its fortunes decline.

Horizontal growth involves increasing the range of products and services offered to current markets or expanding the firm's presence into a wider number of geographic locations. KLM's decision to purchase a controlling interest in Northwest Airlines, for example, was primarily made to obtain access to American and Asian markets. In recent years, strategic alliances have become an increasingly popular way to implement horizontal growth strategies.

Diversification Strategies

The word *diversification* is used in connection with many aspects of strategy. We talk about diversifying into new industries, technologies, supplier bases, customer segments, geographical regions, or sources of funds. The most common use of the term, however, involves product/market diversification—the spreading of business activity over a number of product/market combinations.[30]

Diversification decisions pose one of the greatest challenges in corporate strategy. While some companies including General Electric, Disney, and 3M have been very successful in diversifying their interests, failures such as Quaker Oats' unfortunate experience with Snapple, and RCA's experience with computers, carpets, and rental cars remind us that diversification decisions are fraught with risk.

Why do companies diversify? What options do we have? Edith Penrose talks about *internal and external inducements for growth* as primary drivers behind diversification. Internal inducements such as the need to counterbalance cyclical performance or the opportunity to use excess capacity originate from the company's current strategic positioning. External inducements are conditions in the firm's external strategic environment that draw it into new businesses. They can take the form of opportunities—leveraging a strong brand name, for example—or threats as in the case of declining demand in key segments.[31]

As noted earlier, unrelated (financial) diversification more often destroys rather than creates value for shareholders. (These options are shown in Figure 5-7.) Only when such diversification is undertaken as a defensive move, for example, to escape industries with inherently low levels of profitability or as a counter to highly cyclical businesses, does it raise profits from mediocre to average levels. The advantages of a diversified portfolio of businesses are confirmed in the case of related business companies (strategic diversification); they have outperformed dominant business companies on a number of dimensions in recent history.

To evaluate the strategic risks associated with diversification opportunities, Markides suggests senior executives ask themselves six critical questions:[32] (1) What can our company do better than any of its competitors in its current market(s)? This question is aimed at identifying a company's unique strategic assets. It forces the organization to think about how it can add value to an acquired company or in a new market. (2) What strategic assets are needed to succeed in the new market? Having *some* of the skills needed to successfully stake out a position in a new market is not enough. A company must have, or know where to get, *all* of them. (3) Can we catch up to or leapfrog competitors at their own game? If a company does not have all of the requisite skills to succeed in a new market, it must know how to buy them, develop them, or make them unnecessary by changing the rules of competition. Markides describes how Sharp Corporation decided to leverage its skills in manufacturing and retailing of radios by moving first into televisions and then into microwave ovens. Sharp licensed the television technology from RCA and acquired microwave knowledge from Litton. Later, Sharp invested heavily to build a large-scale integrated circuit manufacturing and R&D facility to prepare for entry into semiconductors. Sometimes unavailable skills can be made obsolete by rewriting the rules of competition. When Canon diversified from cameras into photocopiers, it lacked a strong direct salesforce capable of challenging Xerox in its customer base of large companies. Rather than investing in a salesforce, Canon decided to target small-size and midsize companies as well as the consumer market through established dealers. (4) Will diversification break up strategic assets that need to be kept together? This question suggests that strategic assets are often synergistic. Selecting one or more carefully developed skills from an integrated strategic set of competencies developed for one market for application in a new market environment is unlikely to be successful if such synergies exist. (5) Will we simply be a player in the new market or will we be a winner? Markides notes that diversifying companies are often quickly outmaneuvered by their new competitors, since they frequently fail to ask whether their strategic assets can be easily imitated, bought, or replaced. (6) What can our company learn by diversifying, and are we sufficiently organized to learn it? Ideally, diversification itself becomes a core competence and as experience is gained diversification decisions are made better and more efficiently.

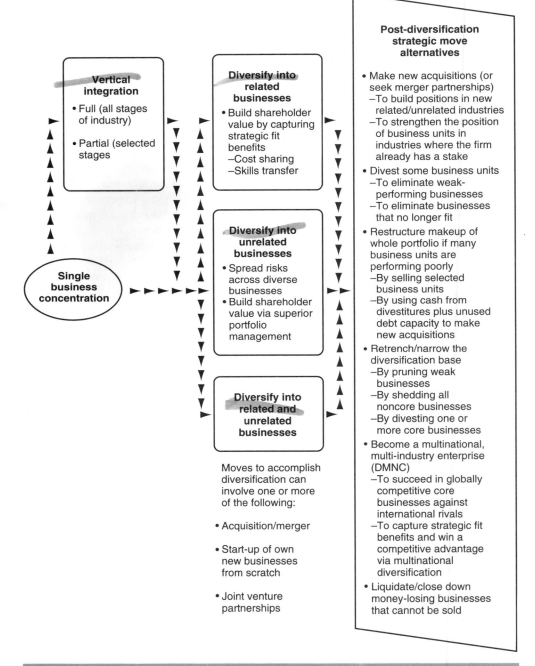

Vertical integration
- Full (all stages of industry)
- Partial (selected stages)

Single business concentration

Diversify into related businesses
- Build shareholder value by capturing strategic fit benefits
  - Cost sharing
  - Skills transfer

Diversify into unrelated businesses
- Spread risks across diverse businesses
- Build shareholder value via superior portfolio management

Diversify into related and unrelated businesses

Moves to accomplish diversification can involve one or more of the following:

- Acquisition/merger

- Start-up of own new businesses from scratch

- Joint venture partnerships

Post-diversification strategic move alternatives

- Make new acquisitions (or seek merger partnerships)
  - To build positions in new related/unrelated industries
  - To strengthen the position of business units in industries where the firm already has a stake
- Divest some business units
  - To eliminate weak-performing businesses
  - To eliminate businesses that no longer fit
- Restructure makeup of whole portfolio if many business units are performing poorly
  - By selling selected business units
  - By using cash from divestitures plus unused debt capacity to make new acquisitions
- Retrench/narrow the diversification base
  - By pruning weak businesses
  - By shedding all noncore businesses
  - By divesting one or more core businesses
- Become a multinational, multi-industry enterprise (DMNC)
  - To succeed in globally competitive core businesses against international rivals
  - To capture strategic fit benefits and win a competitive advantage via multinational diversification
- Liquidate/close down money-losing businesses that cannot be sold

---

FIGURE 5-7 Diversification Options

Source: Arthur A. Thompson, Jr., and A. J. Strickland, III, *Strategic Management,* 9th edition, 1990.
Reprinted by permission of McGraw-Hill Company, Inc., New York, NY.

Answering these kinds of questions can reduce uncertainty but not eliminate it. It is also clear that diversification is not a panacea for rescuing mediocre performance. It can improve shareholder value but needs to be carefully planned in the context of an overall strategy for the corporation.

Mergers and Acquisitions

Companies can implement diversification strategies through internal development, mergers, and acquisitions, or through cooperative ventures such as alliances. Internal development can be slow and expensive. As a result, buying another company is often seen as the easiest way to diversify.[33] The advantages of buying an existing player are compelling. An acquisition can quickly position a firm in a new business or market. It also eliminates a potential competitor and therefore does not contribute to the development of excess capacity.

Acquisitions, however, also are generally expensive. Premiums of 30 percent or more over the current value of the stock are not unheard of. This means that while sellers often pocket handsome profits acquiring companies they frequently lose shareholder value. The process by which merger and acquisition decisions are made contributes to this problem. In theory, acquisitions are part of a well-thought-out diversification strategy, which explicitly identifies the most attractive industries to diversify into and the most suitable players in those industries. It also should specify a comprehensive framework for the due diligence of potential partners, plans for integrating acquired companies into the corporate portfolio, and a careful determination of "how much is too much" to pay. In practice, the process is far more complex. Once a potential target company comes on the market, or the board has approved plans to expand into new businesses or markets, time is short. The ensuing pressure to "do a deal," emanating from within the corporation—senior executives, directors—and from external sources—investment bankers who stand to gain from *any* deal and shareholder groups or competitors bidding against the firm—can become so intense that shortcuts are often made. Valuations rise as companies become overconfident in their ability to add value to the prospect company and as expectations regarding synergies reach unrealistic levels; due diligence is done more quickly than is desirable and is almost exclusively confined to financial considerations; integration planning takes a back seat; and differences in corporate cultures are often ignored. In this climate, even the best-laid strategies cannot guarantee a successful outcome as many companies or, more precisely, their shareholders have learned.

What can be done to increase the effectiveness of the merger and acquisition process? Although there are no hard and fast rules of success, several themes have emerged: (1) Successful acquisitions are usually part of a well-developed corporate strategy. (2) Diversification through acquisition is an ongoing, long-term process and patience is a virtue. (3) Successful acquisitions usually result from disciplined strategic analysis, which looks at industries first before it targets companies, but recognizes good deals are firm-specific. (4) There are only a few ways by which an acquirer can add value, and before proceeding with an acquisition the buying company should be able to specify how synergies will be achieved and value created. (5) Objectivity is essential but hard to achieve once the acquisition chase ensues. (6) Most acquisitions flounder on implementation—strategies for implementation should be formulated before the acquisition is completed and executed quickly after the acquisition deal is closed.

Cooperative Strategies

Cooperative strategies—joint ventures, alliances, and other partnering arrangements—have become more important in recent years. To many executives, they capture the benefits of internal development and acquisition while avoiding the drawbacks of both. Globalization is an important factor in the rise of cooperative ventures. In a global competitive environment, going it alone often means taking unprecedented risk. Escalating fixed costs associated with achieving global market coverage, keeping up with the latest technology, and increased exposure to currency and political risk all make risk sharing a necessity in many industries. Today, a global strategic posture without alliances would be unthinkable for many companies.

Cooperative strategies take many forms and are forged for many different reasons. The following sections discuss some of the key drivers.[34]

Risk Sharing   Many companies cannot afford "bet the company" moves to participate in all product markets of strategic interest. Whether we consider possible entry into China or investments in new promising technologies, the dominant logic dictates that companies prioritize their strategic interests and balance them according to risk.

Funding Limitations and the Need for Economies of Scale   In the past many companies focused on building sustainable advantage by establishing dominance in *all* of the businesses' value-creating activities. Through cumulative investment and vertical integration they built barriers to entry that were hard to penetrate. As the globalization of the business environment accelerates and the technology race intensifies such a strategic posture becomes increasingly hard to sustain. Going it alone is not practical anymore in many industries. To compete in the global arena today companies must incur immense fixed costs with a shorter payback period and at a higher level of risk.

Market Access and Geographical Representation   No company can afford to enter all markets of strategic interest. In addition, many lack the knowledge needed to compete effectively at the local level or the infrastructure and critical relationships necessary for the distribution of their products to customers. Hitachi has an alliance with Deere & Company in North America and with Fiat Allis in Europe to distribute its hydraulic excavators. This arrangement makes sense because Hitachi's product line is too narrow to justify a separate distribution network. What is more, customers benefit because the gaps in Hitachi's product line are filled with quality products such as bulldozers and wheel loaders from its alliance partners.

Technology Access   Today, a large number of products rely on so many different technologies that few companies can afford to remain at the forefront of all of them. Carmakers increasingly rely on advances in the electronics industry, application software developers depend on new features delivered by Microsoft in its next generation operating platform, and *advertising agencies* need more and more sophisticated tracking data to formulate schedules for clients. At the same time, the pace at which technology is spreading globally is increasing, making time an even more critical variable in developing and sustaining competitive advantage. Partnering therefore becomes essential. This, in turn, increases the speed by which technology diffuses around the world.

Other reasons to pursue a cooperative strategy include a lack of particular *management skills,* an *inability to add value* in-house, or a *lack of acquisition opportunities*

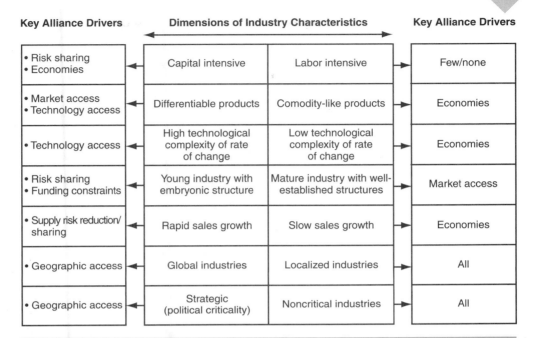

Key Alliance Drivers	Dimensions of Industry Characteristics		Key Alliance Drivers
• Risk sharing • Economies	Capital intensive	Labor intensive	Few/none
• Market access • Technology access	Differentiable products	Comodity-like products	Economies
• Technology access	High technological complexity of rate of change	Low technological complexity of rate of change	Economies
• Risk sharing • Funding constraints	Young industry with embryonic structure	Mature industry with well-established structures	Market access
• Supply risk reduction/ sharing	Rapid sales growth	Slow sales growth	Economies
• Geographic access	Global industries	Localized industries	All
• Geographic access	Strategic (political criticality)	Noncritical industries	All

FIGURE 5-8 Drivers of Cooperative Strategy

Source: From John Harbison and Peter Pekar, *A Practical Guide to Alliances: Leapfrogging the Learning Curve Viewpoint.* Copyright © 1993 Booz-Allen and Hamilton, New York, NY. Reprinted by permission.

due to size and geographical or ownership restrictions. The relevance of particular drivers varies by industry and by company within an industry (Figure 5-8).

Cooperative strategies cover a wide spectrum of nonequity, cross-equity, and shared-equity arrangements (Figure 5-9). Selecting the most appropriate arrangement involves analyzing the nature of the opportunity, the mutual strategic interests in the cooperative venture, and prior experience with joint ventures of both partners. The essential question is "How can we structure this opportunity to maximize benefit to both parties?"

The airline industry provides a good example of some drivers behind and issues involved in forging strategic alliances. Although the U.S. industry has been deregulated for some time, international aviation remains controlled by a host of bilateral agreements that smack of protectionism. Outdated limits on foreign ownership further distort natural market forces toward a more global industry posture. As a consequence, airline companies have been forced to confront the challenges of global competition in other ways. With takeovers and mergers blocked, they have formed all kinds of alliances, from code sharing to aircraft maintenance to frequent flyer plans.

It is widely expected that four major groups will dominate the airline industry before long. The "Oneworld" alliance, announced in 1998, includes British Airways, American Airlines, Qantas, Canadian Airways, and Cathay Pacific. The "Star" alliance is led by United Airlines and Lufthansa and includes a number of smaller carriers including Thai, SAS, Air Canada, Varig, SAA, Singapore, ANA, ANX, and Ansett. A third group, headed by KLM and Northwest, has signed up Continental and Alitalia. Finally, Delta, Swissair, Sabena, and Austrian have gotten together as the fourth group.

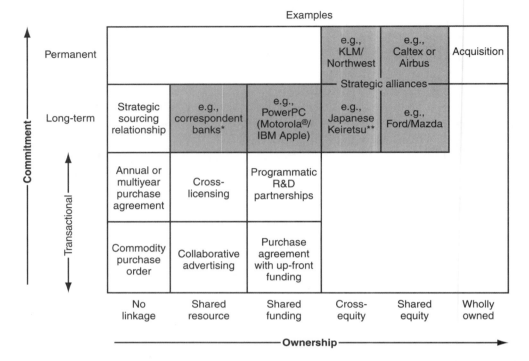

Extended Enterprise Segmentation

Examples

	No linkage	Shared resource	Shared funding	Cross-equity	Shared equity	Wholly owned
Permanent				e.g., KLM/ Northwest	e.g., Caltex or Airbus	Acquisition
Long-term	Strategic sourcing relationship	e.g., correspondent banks*	e.g., PowerPC (Motorola®/ IBM Apple)	e.g., Japanese Keiretsu**	e.g., Ford/Mazda	
Transactional	Annual or multiyear purchase agreement	Cross-licensing	Programmatic R&D partnerships			
	Commodity purchase order	Collaborative advertising	Purchase agreement with up-front funding			

Commitment ↑

Ownership →

*Agreement in which one bank works on behalf of another in a different geography on an ongoing basis.
**Companies are independently managed but own minority positions in each other's stock, and work together where possible.

FIGURE 5-9 Cooperative Strategies and Equity Arrangements

Source: From John Harbison and Peter Pekar, *A Practical Guide to Alliances: Leapfrogging the Learning Curve Viewpoint.* Copyright © 1993 Booz-Allen and Hamilton, New York, NY. Reprinted by permission.

Sell-Offs, Spin-Offs, and Liquidations

At times, management is faced with the prospect of having to retrench in one or more of its lines of business. A sell-off to a competitor or a spin-off into a separate company makes sense when analysis confirms the corporation is the wrong corporate parent for the business. In such circumstances, value can be realized by giving the markets the opportunity to decide the fate of the business. If there are no potential buyers, liquidation may have to be considered.

PARENTING OPTIONS: THE ROLE OF THE CORPORATE OFFICE

Outcome Control or Behavior Control?

The issue of "parenting" deals with such questions as "What is the role of corporate headquarters in shaping and executing divisional strategies?" "How do we control the activities of the various semiautonomous business units?" and "How do we provide coherence to the various corporate activities as a whole?" It addresses the third side of the triangle in the resource-based approach to corporate strategy—the organizational structure, systems, and processes that are used to implement corporate strategy.[35]

Through evolution or by design companies differ in important ways in how they organize and implement their decision making. Some, like Textron or ABB Brown Bovary, operate with a small headquarters staff, give substantial autonomy to their operating units, and exercise control primarily by setting financial standards of performance. They primarily focus on *outcome control*. Others such as Cooper Industries take a much more active role in running divisional operations and effectively exercise *behavior control* by getting involved in "how to" decisions as well as strategy formulation.

Most companies employ a mixture of the two. For example, in many companies corporate executives primarily evaluate divisional performance based on financial measures but may become more involved in initiatives such as upgrading manufacturing processes or implementing total quality programs.

Outcome control is typically more appropriate when (1) a single measure of current financial performance, such as cash flow, is appropriate to assess a unit's strategic position, (2) when factors outside the business unit have only a minor impact on performance, and (3) when there is little need for coordination between the various business units. For these reasons, outcome control is typically more relevant to companies with a portfolio of unrelated businesses whereas parenting styles involving substantial behavior control are more likely to be found in related business companies.[36]

EVALUATING STRATEGY OPTIONS AT THE CORPORATE LEVEL

The number of potentially viable strategy options at the corporate level is often considerable. Evaluating which one is better is complicated by their enormous diversity. Is internal growth better than external growth? Is concentrated growth preferable over diversification? Are cooperative strategies the answer? How do these options affect our parenting strategies? Clearly, not all can be equally effective. In fact, as history has shown, many are likely to fail, either because of flaws in the underlying analysis or in their implementation.

Evaluating strategy options at the corporate level involves balancing quantitative analysis with qualitative assessments. Often, specific options such as acquiring an existing business can be valued quantitatively.

Issues of Valuation

Every major strategic decision involves a cost/benefit calculation, whether formal or informal, precise or approximate. Whether the issue is opening a new factory overseas, entering a strategic partnership, or restructuring the portfolio, how a company values its strategic alternatives is crucially important to how its corporate strategy evolves. What is more, as senior executives find themselves under increased pressure for performance and accountability by shareholders and other stakeholders, they are asked to share not only what decisions they have made but also how they arrived at their conclusions. As a consequence, valuation has become an increasingly important skill in developing and executing a corporate strategy.

Many companies still use a mix of approaches and concepts to deal with the issue of valuation. Some are formal, based on analytic models and financial theories; others are informal, often representing little more than ad hoc rules of thumb. Valuation is sometimes done explicitly; at other times it is implicit. And the methods and concepts used frequently reflect the skills, attitudes, and experiences of the executives who apply them.

With the push for greater accountability and better performance a trend toward more formal, explicit, and institutionalized valuation of strategic options has emerged. Terms such as shareholder value analysis (SVA), discounted cash flow analysis (DCF), and economic value added (EVA) are heard with greater frequency today at board meetings, shareholder gatherings, and in briefings to analysts. The greater emphasis on formal evaluation is laudable; it brings a much-needed rigor to the task of strategy assessment at the corporate level. The implementation of such advanced valuation methods, however, presents a host of challenges.

Techniques

The complexity of putting a numerical value on a corporate (or, for that matter, a business unit) strategy can be quite daunting. The simple fact is, many popular press accounts notwithstanding, there is no single, fully developed financial theory that can produce unambiguous estimates of value in highly dynamic, inherently uncertain strategic environments. Techniques such as discounted cash flow analysis (DCF) are helpful in valuing well-defined, relatively predictable alternatives for which reasonably accurate cash flow forecasts can be generated. Valuing strategic alternatives in situations characterized by higher levels of uncertainty, identified as level three and four environments in chapter 2, however, is another matter entirely. As a consequence, a one-size-fits-all approach to strategy evaluation is not likely to succeed.

Although valuation is always a function of three basic elements (money, timing, and risk), not all valuation problems are identical. In a highly readable overview of modern valuation methods, Timothy Luehrman distinguishes between three classes of valuation problems: (1) valuing *operations,* or assets-in-place, (2) valuing *opportunities,* and (3) valuing *ownership claims.* Valuing *operations* is the most common valuation issue. It involves putting a value on an ongoing business or deciding on a specific strategic investment. Here discounted cash flow methods can be used, although Luehrman recommends replacing traditional *discounted cash flow analysis using the weighted-average cost of capital* (WACC-based DCF) with the so-called *adjusted present value* (APV) approach to facilitate adjustments for items such as tax shields and changes in capital structure. Valuing opportunities—the second type of valuation problem—is akin to valuing options rather than an underlying stock. It applies to putting a value on possible future operations. Deciding on how much to spend on R&D and on what kind is an example; such a decision foreshadows future alternatives. Here *option pricing* methods are more appropriate than discounted cash flow schemes although their application is far from straightforward. Finally, valuing *ownership claims*—important in assessing such strategic options as joint ventures and alliances—involves assessing the value of the venture as well as the equity cash flows associated with it. *Equity cash flow* analysis (ECF) is the preferred technique under this scenario.[37]

It will be evident that deciding on an overall, theoretically consistent, quantitative evaluation methodology for a complex corporate strategy proposal involving multiple options is not a simple issue. And while enormous progress has been made with user-friendly computer models, specialized skills will always be needed to successfully implement these techniques. Luehrman goes one step further when he states: "For most companies, getting from where they are now to this vision of the future is not a corporate finance problem—the financial theories are ready and waiting—but an organizational development project."[38]

Qualitative Factors

In addition to struggling with the technical issues associated with evaluating strategy options at the corporate level, many executives feel a company's overall strategic posture cannot be evaluated in purely quantitative terms. Questions beyond "Does it create a sustainable corporate advantage, and result in substantial shareholder value?" such as (1) Is there a clear and well-articulated vision for the future? (2) Is there internal consistency to our strategy, that is, are the various elements aligned with one another, do they form a coherent whole? (3) Does the strategy fit with what is happening in the external environment? (4) Is it sustainable? and (5) Can we implement this strategy effectively at an acceptable level of risk? cannot be answered in quantitative terms.[39] As a consequence, strategy evaluation at the corporate level will always involve judgment, and a measure of intuition. And, as many executives will attest, courage, faith, and hope also play a role.

When all is said and done, there are only three important tests: (1) the "goodness of fit" test, (2) the competitive advantage test, and (3) the performance test.[40] A good strategy is attuned to its external and internal environments, helps create a sustainable competitive advantage, and generates value for stakeholders. Without these three characteristics, a strategy is suspect and should be reexamined.

SUMMARY

Developing a corporate strategy is one of the most challenging tasks facing senior managers. While the body of knowledge about what works and what does not work grows daily, there are still many unresolved issues. What is more, the rapid changes that are taking place in the global competitive environment will make much of today's knowledge obsolete tomorrow. As a result, formulating effective corporate strategies will always require more than in-depth analysis based on vast quantities of information. It will demand intuition, creativity, and a keen insight into managerial and organizational behavior.

Notes

1. See e.g., Michael E. Porter, "From Competitive Advantage to Corporate Advantage," *Harvard Business Review* 65 (May–June 1987): 43–59; or D. J. Ravenscraft and M. J. Scherer, "Mergers, Sell-offs, and Economic Efficiency" (Washington, D.C.: The Brookings Institution, 1987).

2. "The Case Against Mergers," *Business Week* (October 30, 1995).

3. Alfred D. Chandler, "The Enduring Logic of Industrial Success," *Harvard Business Review* 68 (March–April 1990): 130–140.

4. Alfred D. Chandler, "The Enduring Logic of Industrial Success," 130–140.

5. Alfred D. Chandler, "The Enduring Logic of Industrial Success," 130–140.

6. Andrew Campbell and David Sadtler, "Corporate Breakups," *Strategy & Business,*

Booz·Allen & Hamilton, no. 12 (third quarter 1998): 64–73.

7. Peter C. Davis and Atul Kamra, "The Value of Big in Banking," *Strategy & Business,* Booz.Allen & Hamilton, no. 12 (third quarter 1998): 7–9.

8. "The Case Against Mergers."

9. "The New World Order," *Business Week* (Oct. 13, 1997).

10. "Compaq's Power Play," *Business Week* (Feb. 9, 1998).

11. James P. Hawley and Andrew T. Williams, "Corporate Governance in the United States: The Rise of Fiduciary Capitalism—A Review of the Literature," working paper, Graduate Business Programs, Saint Mary's College of California, 1996.

12. Adolph A. Berle and Gardiner C. Means, *The Modern Corporation and Private Property* (New York: MacMillan, 1932).

13. James P. Hawley and Andrew T. Williams, "Corporate Governance in the United States."

14. Roberta Romano, "Politics and Pension Funds" (New York: The Manhattan Institute, 1994).

15. Robert A. G. Monks and Nell Minow, *Corporate Governance* (Cambridge, Mass.: Blackwell Publishers, 1995).

16. K. R. Andrews, *A Concept of Corporate Strategy* (Chicago: Richard D. Irwin, 1960); and A. Chandler, *Strategy and Structure* (Boston: MIT Press, 1960).

17. Richard P. Rumelt, *Strategy, Structure, and Economic Performance,* dissertation published by the Division of Research, Harvard Business School, Boston, 1974.

18. David Collis and Cynthia Montgomery, "Corporate Strategy: A Conceptual Framework," Harvard Business School, 1991 (9-391-284).

19. Note on the Boston Consulting Group Concept of Competitive Analysis and Corporate Strategy, Harvard Business School, 1975 (175-175).

20. G. G. Dess and A. Miller, *Strategic Management*, McGraw-Hill, New York, 1993, 110–11.

21. See Charles D. Hofer and Dan Schendel, *Strategy Formulation: Analytical Concepts* (St. Paul, Minn.: West Publishing, 1978), 34.

22. See e.g., Tom Copeland, Tim Koller, and Jack Murrin, *Valuation: Measuring and Managing the Value of Companies,* (New York: McKinsey & Company, Wiley, 1995).

23. Copeland, Koller, and Murrin, *Valuation,* Chap. 11.

24. Porter, "From Competitive Advantage," 43–59.

25. C. K. Prahalad and G. Hamel, "The Core Competence of the Corporation," *Harvard Business Review* 68 (May–June 1990): 79–91.

26. David Collis and Cynthia Montgomery, "Corporate Strategy: A Conceptual Framework," Harvard Business School, 1991 (9-391-284).

27. Andrew Campbell, Michael Gould, and Marcus Alexander, "Corporate Strategy: The Quest for Parenting Advantage," *Harvard Business Review,* 73 (March–April 1995): 120–132.

28. David J. Collis and Cynthia A. Montgomery, *Corporate Strategy: Resources and Scope of the Firm* (Chicago: Irwin, 1997), 5.

29. For more on parent fit, see Campbell, Gould, and Alexander, "Corporate Strategy," 120–132.

30. This section is based in part on the "Note On Diversification As A Strategy," Harvard Business School, rev. June 1986 (9-382-129).

31. Edith Penrose, *The Theory of the Growth of the Firm* (London: Basil Blackwell, 1959).

32. Constantinos C. Markides, "To Diversify or Not To Diversify?" *Harvard Business Review* (Nov.–Dec. 1997): 93–99.

33. Collis and Montgomery, *Corporate Strategy,* chap. 4.

34. "A Practical Guide to Alliances: Leapfrogging the Learning Curve," Booz·Allen&Hamilton, 1993.

35. Collis and Montgomery, *Corporate Strategy,* 127.

36. Collis and Montgomery, *Corporate Strategy,* 146.

37. Timothy A. Luehrman, "What's it Worth? A General Manager's Guide to Valuation," *Harvard Business Review* (May–June 1997): 132–142.

38. Luehrman, "What's it Worth," 142.

39. Collis and Montgomery, *Corporate Strategy,* 175.

40. Collis and Montgomery, *Corporate Strategy,* 54.

CHAPTER

Global Strategy

A picture is not thought out and settled beforehand. While it is being done it changes as one's thoughts change. And when it is finished, it still goes on changing, according to the state of mind of whoever is looking at it. A picture lives a life like a living creature, undergoing the changes imposed on us by our life from day to day. This is natural enough, as the picture lives only through the man who is looking at it.*

—PABLO PICASSO

INTRODUCTION

As the globalization of the competitive landscape intensifies, a global strategic outlook will become more important to large-size and midsize companies alike. Conventional wisdom has it that large corporations have a better chance of competing successfully in the global arena. Recent evidence, however, indicates that midsize companies often have a distinct advantage. This advantage is rooted in precisely those characteristics once thought to be detrimental to success: size—smaller can mean nimbler, not less capable; pressure to succeed—for smaller companies international sales are a must, not a luxury; and an entrepreneurial culture that more easily accommodates a global vision and creative implementation.

In this chapter we take a closer look at the opportunities and risks associated with staking out a global competitive position and identify the principal dimensions of a global strategy. To set the stage we first take a look at the driving forces behind the emerging global economy and characterize "globalization" in greater detail as an economic, political, social, and technological phenomenon. Industry globalization is the next topic of discussion. In this section we focus on such questions as: "What is a global industry?" "What are the driving forces behind the globalization of industries?" and "What explains the dominance of particular countries or regions in global industries?" The third major topic of this chapter is global strategic thinking. In this section we identify the principal dimensions of global strategy and introduce a framework for global strategic thinking that links global strategy options to the nature of the global industry environment. A major tenet of this discussion is that global strategy, more than strategy at the corporate or business unit levels, increasingly is played out in two arenas—a market and a nonmarket arena. Market dimensions of global strategic thinking concern questions such as "Which markets should we participate in?"; "Why?"; "In what

---

*From an interview with Christian Zervos published as "Conversation avec Picasso," *Cahiers d' Art* X (Paris, 1935): 173–178, as quoted in Herschell B. Chipp, *Theories of Modern Art: A Source Book by Artists and Critics* (Berkeley, Calif.: University of California Press, 1968), 269.

form?"; "To what extent should we standardize products and services?"; "Where should we locate key value-added activities?"; "Should we have a uniform market positioning worldwide?"; and "How do we coordinate competitive moves across the globe?" Market dimensions of global strategy are aimed at creating value through economic performance in a global context. Nonmarket dimensions of global strategy deal with shaping the global competitive environment.

As many executives will attest, the rules of global competition are critical to performance. Consequently, to enhance their global competitiveness, an increasing number of companies have concluded that they need to participate in the political process of shaping those rules. An integrated global strategy therefore consists of market and nonmarket components that act synergistically to create a sustained competitive advantage on a global scale. The effectiveness of different global postures depends importantly on the structure of the global industry. Accordingly, we evaluate the relative effectiveness of different global strategy options in the context of a number of generic global industry settings. In the last section of this chapter we consider the various strategic risk factors associated with a global posture.

TOWARD A GLOBAL ECONOMY

Globalization as a political, economic, social, and technological force appears unstoppable. While boundaries between countries and regions may be meaningful in political terms, they have all but disappeared on the global competitive map. The ever faster flow of information around the world has made people aware of the tastes, preferences, and lifestyles of citizens in other countries. Through this information flow we are all becoming—at varying speeds and at least in economic terms—global citizens. This "Californiazation of need"—the notion that California lifestyles, consumption and work habits, and culture are a bellwether for what globalization will bring to the rest of the world—is controversial, even offensive, to some who consider globalization a threat to their identity and way of life. It is not surprising therefore that globalization has evoked counterforces aimed at preserving, if not deepening, a sense of local identity.

Globalization — Twice

While globalization has become a much-hyped phenomenon, it is, in fact, not exactly new. In the decades before World War I cross-border flows of capital, goods, and people increased at rates comparable to or even higher than today. Then, as now, the principal drivers were falling trade barriers and technological progress (then in the form of reduced transportation costs through the development of the railroads and shipping). This first experience with globalization ended with the outbreak of World War I. In its aftermath, the adoption of protectionist trade policies and limits on capital movement caused the volume of world trade to fall sharply and halted the globalization of the world economy. Even after World War II, capital controls were maintained for some time as the major economic powers agreed to keep their exchange rates fixed under the Bretton Woods Agreement. Eventually, however, they initiated negotiations to gradually reduce tariffs. This led to an ongoing set of discussions focused on creating a new multilaterally agreed upon set of rules governing market access and world trade under the General Agreement on Tariffs and Trade—the GATT—which, in 1995, culminated in the creation of the World Trade Organization, the WTO, a supranational body that plays a key role today in setting global trade policy and resolving trade disputes.

The global capital market was reborn when the Bretton Woods system of fixed exchange rates collapsed in the early 1970s. Aided by technological breakthroughs in the areas of computing and communication and the liberalization of international trade regimes, capital started to flow again across borders. In the nineties, international currency transactions have increased from less than $200 billion to more than $1.2 trillion a day. And while financial markets are not yet totally integrated across the globe, this is simply a matter of time. As Europe embraces the euro, and the Asian economies become more integrated, a vision of seamless around-the-clock movement of capital around the world is now firmly in sight.

A reversal in the course of events is always possible, of course, but appears less likely this time. For one thing, although in the first epoch of globalization only a relatively few countries participated, today more economies than ever have opened their borders to trade and foreign investment. Technology advances are also difficult to stem. And an explosion in new financial instruments has made it far more difficult to impose effective capital controls. Another reason that globalization may be more durable this time around is that it is anchored in stronger international institutions. Withdrawal from global trade through unilateral action now exposes countries to substantial losses and alienation from important sources of growth.

Global Corporations

When *Forbes* magazine published its first issue in 1917, many of the companies that would become household names in the subsequent 60 years were already well established. U.S. Steel was the biggest industrial company at that time, with assets of more than $2 billion. Also among the largest companies were Standard Oil of New Jersey (now Exxon), International Harvester, DuPont, General Electric, and Ford Motor Company.

Between 1917 and 1977, the list of the world's top 50 corporations remained largely unchanged. Critics such as Harvard Professor John Kenneth Galbraith questioned whether the U.S. economic system was truly competitive or whether big corporations just grew bigger at the expense of others. But as recent history has shown, corporate size is no guarantee for survival. In 1977 there were only a handful of countries including the United States, West Germany, Britain, Japan, and France represented by more than one company in the list of the world's largest corporations. The United States dominated the list with 22 out of 50 entries. By 1997, a mere 20 years later, as measured by revenues, Japan and the United States each had 18. Newcomers to the list included companies from Korea and Italy. Industry composition also changed. While the automotive and oil industries remain at the top, the list shows a surge in the number of computer and electronics firms. Interestingly, in terms of market value, U.S. and European companies continue to dominate (Figures 6-1 and 6-2).

In the years to come, the list is likely to change even more dramatically. Global merger and acquisition (M & A) activity continues to increase as companies around the world combine forces and restructure themselves to become more globally competitive and to capitalize on opportunities in emerging world markets. We have already seen megamergers involving financial services, leisure, food-and-drink, and media companies, and proposals for future combinations in the automobile and telecommunications

Global 500 Rank	Company	Revenues $ millions	Global 500 Rank	Company	Revenues $ millions
1	General Motors Corporation	178,174	26	Mobil Corporation	59,978
			27	United States Postal Service	58,216
2	Ford Motor Company	153,627	28	Allianz AG	56,785
3	Mitsui $ Co., Ltd.	142,688	29	Philip Morris Companies Inc.	56,114
4	Mitsubishi Corporation	128,922	30	Sony Corporation	55,033
5	Royal Dutch/Shell Group	128,142	31	Nissan Motor Co., Ltd.	53,478
6	Itochu Corporation	126,632	32	AT&T Corp.	53,261
7	Exxon Corporation	122,379	33	Fiat S.p.A.	52,569
8	Wal-Mart Stores, Inc.	119,299	34	Honda Motor Co., Ltd.	48,876
9	Marubeni Corporation	111,121	35	Unilever N.V./Unilever PLC	48,761
10	Sumitomo Corporation	102,395	36	Nestlé S.A.	48,254
11	Toyota Motor Corporation	95,137	37	Credit Suissse Group	48,242
12	General Electric Copany	90,840	38	The Dai-ichi Mutual Life Insurance Co.	47,442
13	Nissho Iwai Corporation	81,894			
14	International Business Machines Corporation	78,508	39	The Boeing Company	45,800
			40	Texaco Inc.	45,187
15	Nippon Telegraph & Telephone Corporation	76,984	41	Toshiba Corporation	44,467
			42	State Farm Insurance Companies	43,957
16	AXA	76,874			
17	Daimler-Benz AG	71,561	43	Veba AG	43,881
18	Daewoo Group	71,526	44	Elf Aquitaine	43,575
19	Nippon Life Insurance Company	71,388	45	Tomen Corporation	43,400
			46	The Tokyo Electric Power Co., Inc.	42,997
20	The British Petroleum P.L.C.	71,193			
21	Hitachi, Ltd.	68,567	47	Hewlett-Packard Company	42,895
22	Volkswagen AG	65,328	48	Sumitomo Life Insurance Company	42,279
23	Matsushita Electric Industrial Co., Ltd.	64,281			
			49	E.I. du Pont de Nemours and Company, Inc.	41,304
24	Siemens AG	63,755			
25	Chrysler Corporation	61,147	50	Sears, Roebuck and Co.	41,296

FIGURE 6-1 The 1998 Global Top 50 Corporations (Revenue)

Source: Reprinted by permission of Fortune Magazine.

industries. There are good reasons to believe that the global M&A movement is just in its beginning stages; the economics of globalization point to further consolidation in many industries. In Europe, for example, more deregulation and the European Union's (EU's) move toward a single currency will encourage further M&A activity and corporate restructuring.

Countries

As the pace of globalization picks up, the rich countries are getting richer. More importantly, the poor ones are getting richer faster. According to the International Monetary Fund, world output grew by a little more than 4 percent in 1997. And while the

Rank				Market Value
1996	1997			**Billions of U.S. dollars**
1	1	General Electric	U.S.	271.64
2	5	Microsoft	U.S.	208.98
3	3	Royal Dutch/Shell Group	Neth./Britain	195.68
4	2	Coca-Cola	U.S.	193.53
5	6	Exxon	U.S.	172.50
6	9	Merck	U.S.	139.85
7	22	Pfizer	U.S.	133.03
8	4	Nippon Telegraph & Telephone	Japan	130.91
9	20	Wal-Mart Stores	U.S.	123.47
10	7	Intel	U.S.	121.16
11	11	Novartis	Switzerland	116.12
12	12	Procter & Gamble	U.S.	112.42
13	13	International Business Machines	U.S.	110.79
14	18	Bristol-Myers Squibb	U.S.	106.99
15	14	Roche Holding	Switzerland	98.90
16	26	AT&T	U.S.	98.87
17	19	Glaxo Wellcome	Britain	96.07
18	8	Toyota Motor	Japan	94.34
19	56	Lucent Technologies	U.S.	93.07
20	17	Johnson & Johnson	U.S.	92.87
21	10	Philip Morris	U.S.	90.74
22	32	Berkshire Hathaway	U.S.	87.74
23	24	Dupont	U.S.	87.71
24	33	Unilever	Neth./Britain	86.67
25	23	American International Group	U.S.	86.62
26	21	British Petroleum	Britain	85.28
27	38	Nestle	Switzerland	84.40
28	30	Lloyds Tsb Group	Britain	78.28
29	41	Allianz	Germany	77.41
30	47	Cisco System	U.S.	77.36
31	28	Walt Disney	U.S.	77.21
32	25	Deutsche Telekom	Germany	73.64
33	51	Nationsbank	U.S.	72.65
34	31	Sbc Communications	U.S.	71.49
35	78	Bell Atlantic	U.S.	71.12
36	68	Travelers Group	U.S.	70.44
37	36	Eli Lilly	U.S.	67.97
38	34	Citicorp	U.S.	67.39
39	16	Hsbc Holdings	Britain	67.26
40	45	British Telecommunications	Britain	66.26
41	37	Gillette	U.S.	65.79
42	35	Hewlett-Packard	U.S.	64.31
43	70	Ing Group	Netherlands	64.08
44	46	Bell South	U.S.	63.86
45	39	American Home Products	U.S.	63.42
46	48	Ford Motors	U.S.	62.92
47	43	Fannie Mae	U.S.	61.84
48	72	Schering-Plough	U.S.	61.35
49	29	Mobil	U.S.	60.95
50	42	Smithkline Beecham	Britain	60.89

FIGURE 6-2 The 1998 Global Top 50 Corporations (by Market Value)

Source: Reprinted from www. businessweek.com website of Business Week by special permission, copyright © 1999 by The McGraw-Hill Companies, Inc.

seven largest economies, the G7: Canada, France, Germany, Italy, Japan, the United Kingdom, and the United States did well, China's economy expanded by more than 9 percent. And while nobody predicts a straight path to economic prosperity for the lagging Asian, Central European, and Latin American economies, their growth is widely expected to outpace that of the West in the years to come.

GLOBALIZATION: MORE THAN COKE AND LEVIS EVERYWHERE

Globalization as a Process

When we speak of "globalization" it is important to define terms. Although the phenomenon has been with us for more than a hundred years, for many the term "globalization" only recently gained currency.[1] Professor R. F. M. Lubbers, in a series of special lectures at Harvard, suggested that the notion of globalization as a primary process reshaping the world approximately coincides with the collapse of communism in 1989 because it marked the beginning of *political* globalization.[2] He noted that since 1945, international politics had been conducted in the context of the tripartition of the world—the first or "free" world, the second or communist world, and the third world comprised of the "nonaligned" or developing nations. The disappearance of the second world caused the term "nonaligned" to lose its relevance. A number of Pacific Rim economies took off and "nonaligned" countries could no longer be considered as a homogeneous group. As the tripartition of the world dissolved, many countries opted for democracy and market-driven economies. Trade and cross-country investment increased, industries were deregulated, former state enterprises privatized, and capital flows liberated. Free enterprise was adopted on a worldwide scale, thus setting in motion *economic globalization*. This pattern of economic globalization, in turn, would not have been possible without key advances in technology. Indeed, it is unlikely that without the benefits of *technological globalization,* brought on by the technology revolution that brought us modern communication systems, electronics, Silicon Valley, the microchip, routine space travel, CNN, the Internet, global sourcing, and electronic capital flows, economic and political globalization would have taken off. Thus, the three principal components of the globalization process have merged into a set of mutually reinforcing forces.

Frictions and Countereffects

History rarely moves in a straight line. While the forces of globalization are strong and continue to reshape society, frictions and countereffects have developed. Questions are being raised about the role of global politics in the new economic order. Following World War II, the Western democracies laid the groundwork for a more interdependent world by agreeing to a number of intergovernmental initiatives. The Bretton Woods initiative, the General Agreement on Tariffs and Trade (GATT), and the formation of the Organization for Economic Cooperation and Development (OECD) define the early part of this process. By the end of the Cold War the pace of globalization accelerated and the economies of many developing countries took off. These created frictions in international cooperation, many of which are still with us today. Examples include the teething problems of the relatively new World Trade Organization (WTO), the politics of the North Atlantic Treaty Organization (NATO), and the functioning of the Security Council of the United Nations. These frictions on the way toward a global political concept and a global economic framework are likely to stay with us for some time and will have important implications for how corporations can operate globally.

Globalization has also given rise to *countereffects*. Almost a generation ago, sociologists began to draw our attention to concepts such as the "global village."[3] They noted that as the pace of globalization accelerated, people felt a stronger need for a sense of *identity* and predicted that the increasing pressure exerted by the global flow of information and the worldwide availability of products and services would create cultural conflicts. This explains, for example, the recent surge in interest in religion around the world and why countereffects to globalization are often so strong. A "global culture" does not have a history nor does it have any roots. It also reenforces the view that economic and technological globalization are primarily rational phenomena and inherently somewhat more superficial than their more deeply rooted, culture-based counterforces.

A second countereffect is an increase in *environmental* concerns. The well-known book *The Limits to Growth* by D. Meadows warned that unfettered expansion of economic and technological growth would lead to disaster.[4] It raised our consciousness about issues of growth and spurred technological innovation aimed at solving problems of scarcity and ecology.

Concerns about *social justice and economic participation* are also on the rise. Economists warn about the growing disparity of incomes—in the developed countries as well as the developing nations—as a possible source of future social unrest.[5] Discussions about economic progress are increasingly framed in terms of the benefits accruing to the "haves" and the "have nots"; proposals for social programs talk about the dichotomy between "knowledge workers" and those left behind by the technology revolution; and words such as "equity" and "inclusion" are heard with greater frequency. Yet, at the same time, capitalism is sinking its roots more deeply. More than ever before, corporations see entrepreneurial behavior as the key to their competitiveness. Workers' compensation is increasingly tied to performance and only people with the right qualities, for example those that can keep up with the fast pace of change and technological progress, are valued.

A fourth phenomenon—*regionalism*—is somewhat harder to interpret. Increased regional cooperation can be viewed as a stepping stone on the path toward a truly global order. A more pessimistic assessment interprets the rise in regionalism as a countereffect, a proxy for "real solutions" to the problems and pressures created by the globalization process. According to this view, if global solutions seem intractable or infeasible, regional solutions will be tried. If true, this may increase rather than decrease tensions as "like" countries and societies forge economic and political structures that will be hard to change later.

The Diminished Power of the State

Will globalization diminish the power of countries as natural centers of political power? And what will be the consequences either politically, economically, or socially if nation states become weaker? As global economics and politics become more closely intertwined, and the balance of power between multinational corporations and governments shifts in favor of the corporation, the potential loss of authority on the part of the nation state is an issue that should concern politicians, strategists, and citizens alike.

There is reason to be concerned. The efficacy of governments in providing solutions to the problems presented by the globalization process is diminishing precisely because these problems transcend national boundaries. This comes at a time when for many countries traditional "external threats" have largely disappeared making security—traditionally one of government's most important and visible functions—seem less urgent. And increasingly citizens like to control their destiny at the local level; decentralization and devolution of power rank among the most popular political ideas today.

A substantial loss of authority on the part of the nation state, however, would exact a considerable price. The globalization process itself would slow considerably if the nation state, the traditional guarantor of freedom, pluralism, public access, transparency, and accountability, would lose its ability to forge international agreements. In this scenario, international organizations and agreements themselves would have less clout and a reversal of recent trends toward more open trade and global cooperation becomes a distinct possibility.

It would be premature, however, to conclude that nations no longer matter. Nation states are important not just because of the power of their governments but also because they constitute relatively *well-defined* and homogeneous units for aggregating supply and demand, and therefore are natural targets in crafting strategy. Growth rates, purchasing power, financial mechanisms, and tastes and preferences tend to be more homogeneous within than among nations. Customs (driving on the left or the right), conventions (e.g., accounting practices), and environmental factors (climate) also vary considerably between countries. Another reason why national boundaries are still relevant is that some countries or regions are more important than others from a strategic perspective because they offer larger markets, or have the potential to do so, or because they have a high concentration of suppliers and a network of supporting firms, or because they are hotbeds of innovation.[6] We discuss this issue of the geography of global competition at greater length in the following section.

Three groups of countries are of particular interest to global strategists. The G7 nations—Canada, France, Germany, Italy, Japan, the United Kingdom, and the United States—lead the world in economic activity. The so-called "newly industrialized countries" (NICs)—Hong Kong, Singapore, South Korea, and Taiwan—lead in terms of economic growth. And Brazil, China, India, and Mexico—the Emerging Four—stand out for their potential.

INDUSTRY GLOBALIZATION

Global Industries

Increasingly, executives ask whether their industry is becoming global and if so, what strategies they should consider to take advantage of this trend and stake out a sustainable global competitive advantage. This may be the wrong question, however. Simple characterizations such as "The chocolate industry is global" are not particularly useful. A better question is *how* global an industry is or is likely to become. Virtually all industries are global in some respects. Only a handful of industries can be considered truly global today, however, or are likely to become so in the future. Many more will remain hybrids, that is, global in some respects, local in others. *Industry globalization, therefore, is a matter of degree.* What counts is which elements of an industry are becoming global and how they affect strategic choice. In approaching this issue, we must focus on the drivers of the industry globalization and think about how these elements shape strategic choice.

We should also make a distinction between *industry globalization, global competition,* and the degree to which a *company has globalized* its operations. In traditionally global industries competition is mostly waged on a worldwide basis and the leaders have created global corporate structures. But the fact that an industry is not truly global does not prevent global competition. And a global competitive posture does not necessarily require a global reorganization of every aspect of a company's operations. Economies of scale and scope are among the most important drivers of industry globalization; in global industries the minimum volume required for cost efficiency is simply no longer available in a single country or region. Global competition begins when companies cross-subsidize national market-share battles in pursuit of global brand and distribution positions. A global company structure is characterized by production and distribution systems in key markets around the world that enable cross-subsidization, competitive retaliation on a global basis, and world-scale volume.[7]

So why are some industries more global than others? And why do global industries appear to be concentrated in certain countries or regions? Most would consider the oil, auto, and pharmaceutical industries global industries while consumer banking, many retailing sectors, and real estate are mainly domestic in nature. Others, such as furniture, lie somewhere in the middle. What accounts for the difference? The dominant location of global industries also poses interesting questions. Although the machine tool and semiconductor industries originated in the United States, the Far East has emerged as the dominant player in a number of their segments today. What accounts for this shift? Why is the worldwide chemical industry concentrated in Germany while the United States continues to dominate in software and entertainment? Can we predict that France and Italy will remain the global centers for fashion and design? These issues are important to strategists. They are also relevant as a matter of public policy; as governments attempt to shape effective policies to assist the development and retain the most *attractive* industries and companies, they must anticipate changes in global competition and locational advantage.

Industry Globalization Drivers

Research by George Yip has identified four sets of "industry globalization drivers"—the underlying conditions in each industry that create the potential for that industry to become more global and, as a consequence, for the potential viability of a global approach to strategy (Figure 6-3).[8] *Market* drivers—the degree to which customer needs converge around the world, customers procure on a global basis, worldwide channels of distribution develop, marketing platforms are transferable, and "lead" countries can be identified in which most innovation takes place—define how customer behavior distribution patterns evolve. *Economic* globalization drivers—the opportunity for global scale or scope economics, experience effects, sourcing efficiencies reflecting differentials in costs between countries or regions, and technology advantages—shape the economics of the industry. *Competitive* drivers are defined by the actions of competing firms—the extent to which competitors from different continents enter the fray, globalize their strategies and corporate capabilities, and the degree to which they create interdependence between geographical markets. *Government* drivers include such factors as favorable trade policies, a benign regulatory climate, and common product and technology standards.

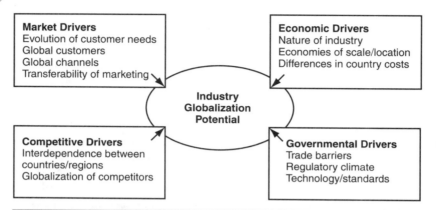

Source: From *Columbia Journal of World Business* Winter 1988, George S. Yip, Pierre M. Loene, and Michael E. Yoshino, "How to Take Your Company to the Global Market," copyright © 1988, pp. 14–26, with permission from Elsevier Science.

Market Drivers   One aspect of globalization is the steady convergence of customer needs. As customers in different parts of the world increasingly demand similar products and services, opportunities for scale arise through the marketing of more or less standardized offerings. How common needs, tastes, and preferences will become varies greatly by product and depends on such factors as the importance of cultural variables, disposable incomes, and the degree of homogeneity in the conditions in which the product is consumed or used. This applies to consumer as well as industrial products and services. Coca-Cola offers similar, but not identical, products around the world. McDonald's, while adapting to local tastes and preferences, has standardized many elements of its operations. Software, oil products, and accounting services increasingly look alike no matter where they may be purchased. The key to exploiting such opportunities for scale is understanding which elements of the product or service can be standardized without sacrificing responsiveness to local preferences and conditions.

Global customers have emerged as needs continue to converge. Large corporations such as Du Pont, I.C.I., or General Motors demand the same level of quality in the products and services they buy no matter where in the world they are procured. In many industries global distribution channels are emerging to satisfy an increasingly global customer base further causing a convergence of needs. Finally, as consumption patterns become more homogeneous, global branding and marketing will become increasingly important to global success.

Economic Drivers   The globalization of customer needs and the opportunities for scale and standardization it brings will fundamentally alter the economics of many industries. Economies of scale and scope, experience effects, and exploiting differences in factor costs for product development, manufacturing, and sourcing in different parts of the world will assume a greater importance as determinants of global strategy. Consequently, a single market will no longer be large enough to support a competitive strategy on a global scale in many industries.

Global scale and scope economics already are having far-reaching effects. On the one hand, the more the new economies of scale and scope shape the strategies of incumbents in global industries, the harder it will be for new entrants to develop an effective competitive threat. Thus, barriers to entry in such industries will get higher. At the same time, the rivalry within such industries is likely to increase reflecting the broadening scope of competition among interdependent national and regional markets, and the fact that true differentiation in such a competitive environment may be harder to achieve.

Competitive Drivers   Industry characteristics such as the degree to which total industry sales are made up by export or import volume, the diversity of competitors in terms of their national origin, and the extent to which major players have globalized their operations and created an interdependence between their competitive strategies in different parts of the world also affect the globalization potential of an industry. High levels of trade, competitive diversity, and interdependence increase the potential for industry globalization. Industry evolution plays a role too. As the underlying characteristics of the industry change, competitors will respond to enhance and preserve their competitive advantage. Sometimes, this causes industry globalization to accelerate. At other times, as in the case of the worldwide major appliance industry, the globalization process may be reversed.

Government Drivers   Government globalization drivers such as the presence or absence of favorable trade policies, technical standards, policies and regulations, and government operated or subsidized competitors or customers affect all the other elements of a global strategy and therefore are important in shaping the global competitive environment in an industry. In the past, multinationals almost exclusively relied on governments to negotiate the rules of global competition. Today, however, this is changing. As the politics and economics of global competition become more closely intertwined, multinational companies are beginning to pay greater attention to the so-called non-market dimensions of their global strategies aimed at shaping the global competitive environment to their advantage (see the following section). This broadening of the scope of global strategy reflects a subtle but real change in the balance of power between national governments and multinational corporations and is likely to have important consequences for how differences in policies and regulations affecting global competitiveness will be settled in the years to come.

As noted earlier, only a few industries such as oil or aircraft are truly global today, that is, their global nature is confirmed by most if not all of these factors. Many industries have the potential of becoming global in some respects but not others. Furthermore, globalization drivers can work in opposite directions—some pointing to increasing globalization while others signaling a less global competitive environment. This, combined with the fact that the conditions defining an industry's globalization potential change over time, suggests that *companies should be careful about defining their global strategic intent and consider partial or incremental initiatives such as globalizing only those aspects of their strategy that directly benefit from a more global posture.*

Global Industry Location

What accounts for the location of a global industry? The classical answer to this question is found in the theory of comparative economic advantage. It holds that as a result of natural endowments some countries or regions of the world are more efficient than others in producing particular goods. Australia, for example, is naturally suited to the mining industry; the United States, with its vast temperate landmass, has a natural advantage in agriculture; while more wooded parts of the world may have a natural advantage in producing timber-based products. This theory is persuasive for industries such as agriculture, mining, and timber. But what about electronics, entertainment, or fashion design? To explain the clustering of these industries in particular countries or regions, a more comprehensive theory of the geography of competition is needed.

Paul Krugman has noted that in the absence of natural comparative advantages, industrial clustering occurs as a result of a relative advantage that is created by the industry itself.[9] Producers tend to locate manufacturing facilities close to their primary customers. If transportation costs are not too high, and there are strong economies of scale in manufacturing, a large geographic area can be served from this single location. This, in turn, attracts suppliers to the industry. A labor market is likely to develop that begins to act like a magnet for "like" industries requiring similar skills. This co-location of "like" industries can lead to technological interdependencies, which further encourage clustering. Clustering, therefore, is the natural outcome of economic forces. A good example is provided by the semiconductor industry. Together, American and Japanese firms supply the entire world's needs. The industry is capital intensive, research and development costs are high, and the manufacturing process highly complex while transportation costs are minimal. Technology interdependencies encourage co-location with suppliers while cost and learning curve effects point to scale efficiencies. Clustering, therefore, is mutually advantageous.

Only when transportation costs are prohibitive or scale economies difficult to realize, that is, when there are disincentives to clustering, do more decentralized patterns of industry location define the natural order. The appliance industry illustrates this. While companies such as General Electric and Whirlpool have globalized their operations in many respects, the fundamental economics of the industry make clustering unattractive. The production of certain value-added components such as compressors or electronic parts can be concentrated to some extent but the bulky nature of the product and high transportation costs make further concentration economically unattractive. Additionally, advances in flexible manufacturing techniques are reducing the minimum scale needed for efficient production. This allows producers to tailor their product offerings more finely to local tastes and preferences further thwarting the globalization of the industry.

While classical economic theory tells us why clustering occurs, it does not fully explain why *particular* regions attract certain global industries. Porter addressed this issue using a framework he calls a "national diamond" shown in Figure 6-4.[10] According to this model, the answer begins with the degree to which a country or region's endowments match the characteristics and requirements of the industry. Such *factor conditions* include natural (climate, minerals) as well as created (skill levels, capital, infrastructure) endowments. But to the extent that such factors are mobile, or can be imitated by other countries or regions, factor conditions alone do not fully explain regional dominance. In fact, the opposite is true. When a particular industry is highly profitable and barriers to entry are low, the forces of imitation and diffusion cause such an industry to spread across international borders.[11] The Japanese compete in a number of industries that originated in the United States, Korean firms imitate Japanese strategies, and Central European nations are conquering industries that were founded in Western Europe. Industries that depend on such mobile factors as capital are particularly susceptible.

A second factor is *nature and size of the demand in the home country*. Simply, large home markets act as a stimulus for industry development. And when a large home mar-

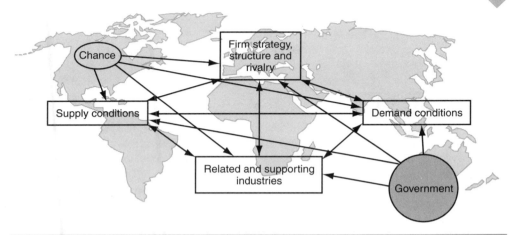

FIGURE 6-4 Porter's Diamond of National Competitive Advantage

Source: Adapted with the permission of The Free Press, a Division of Simon & Schuster, Inc., from *The Competitive Advantage of Nations* by Michael E. Porter. Copyright © 1990 by Michael E. Porter.

ket develops before it takes hold elsewhere in the world, experienced firms have ample incentives to look for business abroad when saturation at home begins to set in. The motorcycle industry in Japan, for example, used its scale advantage to create a global presence following an early start at home.[12] Porter found that it is not just the *location* of early demand but its *composition* that matters. He notes that "a product's fundamental or core design nearly always reflects home market needs."[13] As such, the nature of the home market needs and the sophistication of the home market buyer are important determinants of the potential of the industry to stake out a future global position. It was helpful to the U.S. semiconductor industry, for example, that the government was an early, sophisticated, and relatively cost-insensitive buyer of chips. These conditions encouraged the industry to develop new technologies and provided early opportunities to manufacture on a substantial scale.

The presence of *related and supporting industries* is the third element of Porter's framework. This is similar to our earlier observation about clustering. Hollywood is more than just a cluster of moviemakers. It encompasses a host of suppliers and service providers, and has shaped the labor market in the Los Angeles area.

Firm strategies, the structure and the rivalry in the home industry define the fourth element of the "national diamond" model. In essence, this element summarizes the "five forces" competitive framework described earlier. The more vigorous the level of domestic competition, the more successful firms are likely to be in competing on a global scale. There is plenty of evidence for this assertion. The fierce rivalry that exists among German pharmaceutical companies has made them a formidable force in the global market and the intense battle for domestic market share has strengthened the competitive position of Japanese automobile manufacturers abroad.

Two more elements should be considered: *public policy* and *chance.* There can be no doubt that government policy can—through infrastructure, incentives, subsidies, or temporary protection—nurture global industries. Whether such policies are always effective is less clear. Picking "winners" in the global marketplace has never been the strong suit of governments. The chance element allows for the influence of random events such as where and when fundamental scientific breakthroughs occur, the presence of entrepreneurial initiative, and sheer luck. For example, the early U.S. domination of the photography industry is as much due to the fact that George Eastman (Eastman Kodak) and Edwin Land (Polaroid) were born here as to any other factor.

WHAT IS A GLOBAL STRATEGY?

"Going global" is often described as a more or less gradual process starting with increased exports, followed by a modest international presence, and ultimately evolving into a global posture. This appearance of gradualism, however, is deceptive. It obscures key changes in a company's mission, core competencies, structure, processes, and culture, and thereby the enormous differences between managing international operations, a multinational enterprise, and managing a global corporation. Just as it is difficult to speak of a global industry, the term *global strategy*—while convenient for everyday use—is equally ambiguous. Specific *elements* of a strategy such as market coverage or production can be globalized. Truly global strategies, or strategies that are global in all respects, are relatively rare.

To successfully transform a global vision into reality, a company must carefully define what globalization means for its particular business. As we have seen, this greatly depends on the industry, the product or service, and the extent to which global success requires insider status in different parts of the world. For Coca-Cola, it meant duplicating virtually the entire value creation process in all parts of the world, from product formulation to marketing and delivery, with little local variation. For Intel, it meant attaining technological leadership and preferred component supplier status on a global basis. For a midsize company it may mean setting up a host of small foreign subsidiaries and forging numerous alliances. For still others, it means something entirely different. Thus, while it is tempting to think of global strategy in universal terms, it is important to recognize that globalization is a company- and industry-specific issue. Globalization forces a company to rethink its strategic intent, global architecture, core competencies, and its entire current product and service mix. As many companies have found, the outcome may well call for dramatic changes in the way the company does business—with whom, how, and why.

Market Dimensions of Global Strategy

George Yip identified five "global strategy levers", dimensions that define market-based aspects of a global strategy directed at developing and sustaining a position of global competitive advantage. In essence, these choices determine a strategy's focus on a continuum from a truly global orientation to a more local one.

Market Participation   A key question for many companies is "How many and which countries or regions should we compete in?" Few companies can afford to enter all markets open to them. Even the world's top international companies such as General Electric must exercise strategic discipline in choosing the markets they serve and weigh the relative advantages of a direct or indirect presence in different regions of the world. For midsize companies, the choices are even starker. For them, as for their larger rivals, the key to gaining global competitive advantage lies in creating a worldwide resource network through alliances with suppliers, customers, and yes, competitors. And what is good for one company may have little chance of succeeding in another. Experience suggests that winning strategies are highly selective in terms of market participation; they target realistic market share and profit objectives, and balance "stretch" with current capabilities.

Developing a global presence takes time and money. Ideally, the pace of overseas expansion is dictated by customer demand. It may, however, be necessary to expand ahead of direct opportunity in order to secure a long-term competitive advantage. This can make it difficult to earn a satisfactory return on capital invested. As a result, an increasing number of companies, particularly smaller and midsize corporations, favor global expansion strategies that minimize direct investment. Strategic alliances have made vertical or horizontal integration less important to profitability and shareholder value in many industries. Alliances boost contribution to fixed cost while expanding a company's global reach. At the same time, they can be powerful windows on technology and greatly expand opportunities to create the core competencies needed to effectively compete on a worldwide basis.

Products/Services   Ideally, products and services are tailored to local customer needs. As tastes, preferences, and product regulations become more homogeneous, however, many companies seek opportunities to standardize core products and services. Reducing cost is the primary motivation for product standardization. A second benefit is a greater potential for quality improvement. Yip noted, however, that with a few exceptions the idea of an identical, fully standardized global product is a myth.[14] Product standardization, as many other dimensions of global strategy, should be viewed along a continuum. While substantial benefits can be achieved by standardizing the core product or parts of it, others must be customized. Sony, for example, standardizes substantial portions of its consumer electronics products except for the parts that must meet different national electric standards.

Activity Concentration   To enhance their global competitiveness, many companies are reexamining the extent of their participation in the various steps of the value chain and seeking to reduce costs through initiatives such as eliminating duplicate operations in different parts of the world and outsourcing the production of some components while reducing the number of manufacturing sites for others. There are many factors to consider in selecting the right location for key value-added activities. Factor conditions, the presence of supporting industrial activity, the nature and location of the demand for the product, and industry rivalry all should be considered. In addition, such issues as tax consequences, the ability to repatriate profits, currency and political risk, the ability to manage and coordinate in different locations, and synergies with other elements of the company's overall strategy should be factored in.

Experience has shown that concentrating value-added activities and rationalizing operations on a global scale to focus on core skills and technologies are difficult to implement. They can play havoc with a company's organization chart, create staffing problems, and increase performance risk at a time when the dependence of one unit on others—the company's own or those of its strategic partners—is increased. Many companies, therefore, are adopting a more cautious, incremental approach to this aspect of globalizing their operations. Several pharmaceutical companies, for example, have focused primarily on concentrating only those elements of the value chain that are more easily separated from others, such as R&D. Only a few companies, in global industries such as oil or aircraft manufacturing, have fully globalized all of their value-added activities. This too may change. The issue is one of balancing risks and returns in developing a global posture.

Increased standardization or concentrating value-added components in key locations do not necessarily preclude responsiveness to local demands. The key question is which parts of the value creation process to standardize or concentrate. A major engineering and construction firm, for example, found that parts of its value-creation process—financing large projects among them—could best be handled globally while customer contact-intensive services such as project management and building maintenance were best managed locally. At the same time, the company globalized its entire estimating, project tracking, and programming services by constructing a state-of-the-art global information network with standardized software worldwide.

Market Positioning   As markets become more global, customer tastes and preferences more homogeneous, and global distribution channels more prevalent, companies will increasingly adopt a more global marketing position. As with the other market dimensions of a global strategy, this does not mean they will standardize all elements of the marketing mix or the process by which marketing decisions are made. Rather, it foreshadows a more global, cost-benefit approach to formulating marketing strategy that balances flexibility with uniformity. Companies such as Nestlé, Coca-Cola, Ford, Unilever, IBM, and Disney have all realized that a more global marketing approach can have important benefits. The use of global branding, for example, helps in building brand recognition and enhancing customer preference, and may in fact reduce worldwide marketing costs.

Coordination of Decision Making   Ultimately, the degree to which decision making has been integrated on a global scale defines the extent to which globalization has been implemented successfully. Many companies have found that to be effective on a global scale coordination of activity is as important as control. Concern for global performance based on local success is the guiding principle, not competition for resources on a worldwide basis.

Nonmarket Dimensions of Global Strategy

An essential difference between formulating strategy in a global and a primarily domestic context concerns the relative importance of nonmarket factors in shaping the competitive environment and hence, their potential impact on corporate performance. The global business environment consists of two principal components: a *market* environment—governed by economic forces and private agreements—and a *nonmarket* environment—defined by social, political, and legal arrangements that directly affect the market environment but are primarily determined and intermediated by public institutions. There is a growing body of evidence that nonmarket factors are more important in a global than in a domestic context.[15] This reflects the heterogeneity of the emerging global economy. Different countries have different political, economic, and legal systems. Cultures vary dramatically from country to country, as does the education and skill level of the population. And different countries are at various stages of economic development.[16] These differences have profound implications for the rules that shape global competition and, as a consequence, for global strategy. An effective global strategy addresses both elements. It has market dimensions that seek to create value through economic performance and nonmarket strategy dimensions aimed at unlocking competitive opportunity. The nonmarket environment is often nation or region specific; it is defined by the institutions, culture, and organization of political and economic interests in individual countries or regions. Nonmarket elements therefore tend to be less global or, to be more precise, more multidomestic than the market dimension of a global strategy.

The importance of integrating the market dimensions of a global strategy with nonmarket dimensions is illustrated by the ongoing battle between Kodak and Fujifilm. Frustrated by a lack of open access to the Japanese market, Kodak, in 1995, with the help of the U.S. government, initiated a trade action. It alleged that the Japanese government tolerated anticompetitive practices, which effectively prevented Kodak from competing with Fuji in a substantial portion of the primary distribution system for photographic products in Japan. Such issues of control of opportunity and interests by governments are likely to arise more frequently in the future as industry globalization drivers gain strength. They are important because they have a direct impact on the market-based elements of a global strategy. Fujifilm's quasi monopoly in a major portion of the domestic market has provided it with a "profit sanctuary," which it allegedly used to fund competitive action elsewhere in the world. In the words of Kodak's CEO George Fisher: "While Fuji competes with Kodak on a global basis, it makes virtually all of its profits in Japan, using those proceeds to finance low-price sales outside Japan."[17]

In response, Kodak has embarked upon an integrated global strategy, which takes advantage of possible synergies between its market and nonmarket dimensions. Its objectives are to become more competitive in the Japanese market, to contest its constrained access to the Japanese distribution system, and thereby to weaken Fuji's profit sanctuary. To achieve this, Kodak must exploit both its market and nonmarket opportunities. It must maintain product leadership through continued innovation, leverage, and enhancement of its brand equity, organize itself more effectively in Japan—possibly by seeking additional partnerships—and use all available avenues to gain greater market access.[18] This integrated strategy is depicted in Figure 6-5. It recognizes that the battle for global dominance is not just waged in the competitive arena. It consists of market and nonmarket components, each of which is crucial to the ultimate outcome.

Toward a Global Strategy Framework

Porter's generic strategies for a business unit—low cost, differentiation, and focus—can also be applied in a multinational setting. Low-cost strategies are often followed by competitors based in countries with low factor costs and a large domestic demand. By keeping the value-added process centralized and seeking further economies of scale and scope, they sometimes can translate their domestic low-cost advantage into a worldwide low-cost position. Countries with advanced and specialized factor endowments are natural home bases for companies seeking to follow an international differentiation strategy. Sharp Corporation, for example, has been able to capitalize globally on its lead in liquid crystal displays. Finally, Italy's ceramic tile industry demonstrates the viability of international focus players.

Ghoshal developed a more insightful framework that integrates much of the previous discussion. According to this model, in order to develop a worldwide competitive advantage, a company must achieve three strategic objectives. Through revenue enhancement and cost reduction, it must create *global-scale efficiency* in all of its operations; it must seek *multinational flexibility* in managing diverse country risks and opportunities;

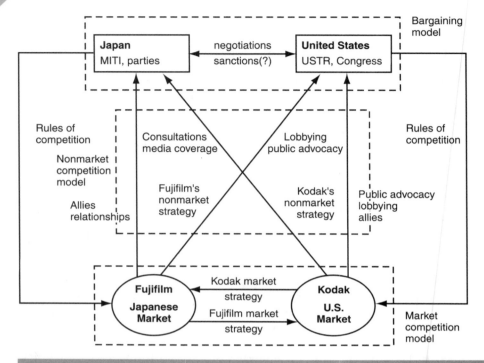

FIGURE 6-5 Kodak's Integrated Strategy

Source: Copyright © 1997, by The Regents of the University of California. Reprinted from the *California Management Review,* vol. 39, no. 2. By permission of The Regents.

and it must retain adaptability to changing competitive conditions through *global learning.* The model identifies three principal approaches or tools by which these objectives can be achieved. A multinational company can *exploit regional differences* through its approach to the market or in its value creation, for example, through sourcing; it can focus on *leveraging synergies and economies of scope* among its diverse worldwide activities; and/or it can build *economies of scale.* The strategic challenge is to exploit these three sources of competitive advantage—regional differences, opportunities for synergy and economies of scope, and scale economies—to optimize global efficiencies, multinational flexibility, and worldwide learning.[19] Figure 6-6 provides examples of factors to consider under each combination of the different goals and means for achieving them.

A related characterization of different approaches to achieving a worldwide competitive advantage distinguishes between *multinational* (or *multidomestic*), *international, transnational,* and *global* strategies.[20] As the name suggests, *a multinational or multidomestic* approach is applicable when customer needs and industry conditions vary considerably from country to country, and a high degree of localization is required. In terms of the previous framework, it focuses heavily on one of the different means—exploiting regional differences—to achieve its strategic objectives. Many of the world's best-known food companies follow this type of strategy to allow them to adapt to differences in local taste preferences and distribution structures. Under a multidomestic

Strategic Objectives	Sources of Competitive Advantage		
	National Differences	*Scale Economies*	*Scope Economies*
Achieving efficiency in current operations	Benefiting from differences in factor costs—wages and cost of capital	Expanding and exploiting potential scale economies in each activity	Sharing of investments and costs across products, markets, and businesses
Managing risks	Managing different kinds of risks arising from market or policy-induced changes in comparative advantages of different countries	Balancing scale with strategic and operational flexibility	Portfolio diversification of risks and creation of options and side-bets
Innovation learning and adaptation	Learning from societal differences in organizational and managerial processes and systems	Benefiting from experience—cost reduction and innovation	Shared learning across organizational components in different products, markets, or businesses

FIGURE 6-6 Global Strategy: An Organizing Framework

Source: S. Ghoshal, "Global Strategy: an Organizing Framework," in *Strategic Management Journal*, Sept/Oct. 1987, vol. 8. Copyright © 1987 John Wiley & Sons Limited. Reproduced with permission.

posture, most strategic and operating decisions are made at the local level, that is, they are decentralized to the business unit in each country.

In industries in which global strategic advantage heavily depends on effectively developing and managing new products and processes in the home market and then sequentially diffusing these innovations to foreign markets through affiliate organizations, an *international* strategic posture is required. The name reflects the importance of managing the international product life cycle through transferring technologies to foreign markets. This strategic posture is common in high-tech industries in which exploiting home country innovations is key to global value creation.

A *global* strategic posture is appropriate when substantial standardization in products and services and in marketing and other aspects of strategy is possible. Coca-Cola is an example. Although there are regional variations in the product and in methods of delivery, a substantial amount of standardization is possible. As a consequence, this approach uses all possible means—exploiting regional differences, synergies and economies of scope, and scale economics—to achieve a worldwide competitive advantage.

A *transnational* strategic posture represents a hybrid and may well be the most challenging to implement. It fits businesses in which parts of the value chain can be standardized but others must be tailored to local demands. Car manufacturing is a good example. While substantial parts of the vehicle production process can be standardized, differences in customer preferences, driving conditions, and related factors mandate a substantial amount of local adaptation. A transnational strategy therefore attempts to achieve global efficiencies while preserving local responsiveness. Implementing such as strategy is difficult because it relies heavily on "flexible coordination" rather than direct control.[21]

GLOBAL STRATEGY AND INDUSTRY STRUCTURE*

We can be more specific about the relative attractiveness of different global strategy options by considering a number of generic global industry settings. As will be readily apparent, the globalization of industries can take different paths depending on, among other factors, the dynamics that shape competition in the industry and the role governments play in stimulating or obstructing the globalization process.[22]

The Importance of Industry Structure — Extended "Strategic" Trade Theory

Strategic trade theory, the successor to the classical theory of trade advanced by Adam Smith and David Ricardo, which explained international trade in terms of absolute and comparative advantage and the more recent theories of trade rooted in the comparative advantage of nations, advanced earlier thinking about the determinants of international trade by directly confronting two issues the classical theories had trouble explaining: the presence of market imperfections and intervention by governments.[23] It recognizes that international trade and investment can occur in the presence of such "imperfections" as an oligopolistic market structure, barriers to entry, economics of scale and scope, and experience curve effects. Additionally, the theory demonstrates that the presence of such imperfections sometimes justifies government intervention. These two fundamental departures from earlier thinking make the theory "strategic"; it allows that some industries can generate substantial profits for a nation and may have "spillover" effects for other parts of the economy, and that trade patterns are not always the result of unencumbered free trade.

The new model integrates the major premises of strategic trade theory with observations about the strategies followed by and the internal workings of multinational corporations. This is important because most economic theory portrays multinationals as simple rational organizations with a single production location that seek to optimize profits. In reality, today's global giants have multiple production, R&D, sales and marketing centers, serve the world's markets from several locations, and are far too complex to be characterized in terms of a simple, profit-maximizing production function.

Five Propositions

This extended framework explains international trade and investment in terms of the interplay of five sets of factors: *country advantages, global industry structure, organizational and strategic attributes of multinational firms in the industry, government policies, and corporate inertia.* Specifically, David Yoffie offers the following five propositions:[24]

1. *When industries are relatively fragmented and competitive, national environments (factors of production, domestic market and domestic demand, and so forth) will largely shape the international advantage of domestically headquartered firms and the patterns of trade.* A correlate to this proposition is that *in emerging industries, country advantages also play a dominant role in determining global competitive advantage.* In other words, in fragmented industries rela-

---

*This section is largely based on David B. Yoffie *Beyond Free Trade: Firms, Governments, and Global Competition,* Boston: Harvard Business School Press, 1993.

tive cost is a key determinant of global success, and because countries differ in terms of their factor costs; as long as entry barriers remain low, production will gravitate to the lowest cost, highest efficiency manufacturing location. Another way of saying this is that *the presence of multinational firms, by itself, should not influence the pattern of international trade in globally competitive, fragmented industries: other things being equal, country factors determine the location of production and the direction of exports.* Oligopolistic global industry structures define a very different strategic context, as the next proposition illustrates.

2. *If an industry becomes globally concentrated with high barriers to entry, location, activity concentration, export and other strategic decisions by multinational companies are determined to a greater extent by the nature of the global oligopolistic rivalry.* Thus, while in concentrated industries country characteristics remain important, the dynamics of the global, oligopolistic competitive climate become the principal drivers of global strategy. This is intuitive. In global oligopolies, more so than in fragmented market structures, the success of one firm is directly affected by that of a few, immediate competitors. Entry into the industry is often restricted in some way by factors such as economies of scale or scope, high levels of capital investment, or by restrictions imposed by governments. Furthermore, in many global oligopolies, participating firms earn above-average returns, which may make the difference in cost between producing locally and exporting a less critical determinant of strategy. Opportunities to cross-subsidize businesses and geographies further reduce the importance of geography in production or export decisions. As a consequence, the moves and countermoves of direct global competitors heavily influence company strategies. For example, it is quite common for companies to enter some other firm's home market, not just because that market is likely to generate additional profits but mainly to weaken its global competitive position. This line of reasoning directly leads to a third proposition, which relates organizational and strategic attributes of global competitors to global strategic choice.

3. *In global oligopolies, specific firm characteristics—the structure of ownership, strategies employed, and organizational factors, to name a few—directly affect strategic posture, the pattern of trade and sometimes, the competitiveness of nations.* In global oligopolies with a relatively small number of competitors, issues such as *who* owns the resources necessary for creating value and *who* sets the global priorities take on a greater strategic significance. Executives from different cultures approach strategy differently; state-owned enterprises are often more motivated by public policy considerations, employment, and other nonprofit concerns. These differences can have a direct impact on the relative attractiveness of global strategy options. The influence of governments in global markets is captured further in the fourth proposition.

4. *Extensive government intervention in global oligopolistic industries can alter the relative balance between firms of different countries; even in fragmented industries it can alter the direction of trade and affect major corporate trade decisions.* The degree and influence of government intervention varies from industry to industry. Whereas in fragmented industries the influence of governments is naturally somewhat limited by market conditions, government intervention can have a pronounced influence in industries with significant economies of

scale effects or other market imperfections. For example, governments can protect "infant" industries with such characteristics. While a case can be made for the temporary protection of strategically important industries, in reality such protection is rarely temporary. This can create a global strategic environment in which anticipating and capitalizing on the actions of governments become the driving forces of global strategy.

5. *In industries where firms make long-term commitments, corporate adjustments and patterns of trade tend to be "sticky."* This fifth and final proposition addresses the issue of corporate inertia. Although the global competitive climate changes every day, choices made by multinational companies and governments tend to have an enduring impact on the industry environment. This proposition has at least two implications. First, the study of how industries evolve globally, what decisions different competitors made and how they made them, is relevant to understanding what drives strategy in a particular global context. Second, the commitments already made by industry participants and governments may spell opportunity or impose constraints for years to come.

Global Strategy and Industry Structure

The five aforementioned propositions provide two principal dimensions for classifying global industries according to the nature of the global strategic challenge they represent: *the degree of global concentration and the extent to which governments intervene* (Figure 6-7).

As noted, in industries with a relatively low degree of concentration and little government intervention, the classical economic laws of *comparative advantage* are the primary drivers of international competition. Here, factor costs are a primary determinant of global competitiveness. It would seem natural, therefore, to focus on a global strat-

FIGURE 6-7 Global Strategy and Industry Structure

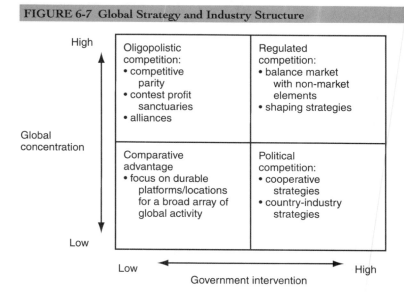

egy aimed at minimizing costs. But this can be extremely difficult in a fast-changing world. Comparative country costs change continuously. As Yoffie notes, in cars, semi-conductors, and computers, among other industries, the comparative (cost) advantage has shifted a number of times since World War II—from the United States to Japan to East Asia to Southeast Asia. Furthermore, there is good reason to believe it will shift again, perhaps to Africa or Latin America. And, with new technological breakthroughs, Western nations may once again become the low-cost production centers. So what should companies do? He argues that while companies should definitely take advantage of opportunities to minimize costs, especially in their initial investments, long-term global strategic choices should emphasize *commitments to countries that are likely to act as the best platforms over time for a broad array of activities.*[25]

In globally concentrated industries in which the role of governments is limited and characterized by *oligopolistic competition,* company strategies are often heavily influenced by the moves and countermoves of direct competitors. Strategies such as making significant investments in competitors' markets regardless of their short- or medium-run profitability, which would not work in highly competitive markets, can only be explained in terms of a strategic posture aimed at maintaining a long-term global competitive balance between the various participants. Caterpillar invested heavily in Japan while Komatsu and European construction equipment manufacturers moved into the United States at a time when such moves offered limited immediate returns. In this kind of competitive environment, the potential for overglobalization—the globalization of different aspects of strategy well in advance of proven benefits—exists as the relatively small number of competitors and high barriers to entry encourage "follow-the-leader" competitive behavior. On the other hand, not responding directly to major competitors can be equally dangerous. Komatsu's challenge to Caterpillar in part was made possible because early on Caterpillar focused its strategy on keeping John Deere, International Harvester, and Dresser Industries at bay rather than on beating Komatsu. This suggests a number of strategic implications. First, *while imitation cannot be the sole basis for developing strategy, in oligopolies it may be necessary at times to match a competitor in order to reduce the risk of competitive disadvantage.* A related implication is *that in global oligopolies companies cannot allow their competitors to have uncontested home markets—profit sanctuaries that can be used to subsidize global competitive moves.* This explains Kodak's extraordinary efforts to pry open the Japanese market; it knows Fuji will be at a considerable advantage if it remains dominant in Japan. Finally, *the use of alliances* can make such global moves more affordable, flexible, and effective. Alliances can be powerful vehicles to rapidly enter new countries, acquire new technologies, or otherwise support a global strategy at a relatively low cost.[26]

Dealing effectively with governments is a prerequisite for global success in oligopolistic industries such as telecommunications where extensive government intervention creates a global competitive climate known as *regulated competition.* Here, nonmarket dimensions of global strategy may well be as important as market dimensions. Political involvement may be necessary to create, preserve, or enhance global competitive advantage because government regulations—whether in infant or established industries—are critical to success. As a consequence, *strategy in global regulated industries should be focused as much on shaping the global competitive environment as on capitalizing on the opportunities it offers.*

Finally, *political competition,* characteristic of fragmented industries with significant government intervention, also calls for a judicious mix of market- and nonmarket-based strategic thinking. In contrast to regulated competition in which government policy has a direct impact on individual companies, however, government intervention in political competition often pits one country or region of the world against another. This *encourages a whole range of cooperative strategies between similarly affected players and strategic action at the country-industry level.*

Before deciding on a particular strategy, it is worth remembering that patterns of competition are not static. Industries evolve continuously, sometimes dramatically. In the eighties and nineties the insurance industry has gradually become less fragmented while copper became significantly less concentrated as barriers to entry came down.[27] Similarly, the focus of government action in different industries can change as national priorities change and the global competitive environment evolves.

ENTRY STRATEGIES

Getting started on the road toward a more global strategic posture poses a set of unique challenges. Should a company first establish an export base or license its products to gain experience in a newly targeted country or region, or does the potential associated with first-mover status justify a bolder move such as entering an alliance, making an acquisition, or even starting a new subsidiary? Many companies move from exporting to licensing to a higher investment strategy, in effect treating these choices as a learning curve. Figure 6-8 depicts these choices. Each has distinct advantages and disadvantages. *Exporting,* while relatively low risk, also entails substantial costs and limited control. Exporters typically have little control over the marketing and distribution of their products, face high transportation charges and possible tariffs, and must pay distributors for a variety of services. Furthermore, exporting does not give a company firsthand experience in staking out a competitive position abroad and makes it difficult to customize products and services to local tastes and preferences. While *licensing* reduces cost and also involves limited risk, it does not mitigate the substantial disadvantages associated with operating from a distance. As a rule, licensing strategies inhibit control and produce only moderate returns. *Strategic alliances and joint ventures,* discussed earlier, have become increasingly popular in recent years. They allow companies to share the risks and resources required to enter international markets. And while returns may also have to be shared, they give a company a degree of flexibility not afforded by going it alone through direct investment. Ultimately, most companies will aim at building their own presence through company-owned facilities in important international markets. *Acquisitions* or *greenfield* start-ups represent this ultimate commitment. Acquisition is faster but starting a new wholly owned subsidiary may be indicated if no suitable acquisition candidates can be found.

As the preceding shows, which mode of entry to choose depends on a host of factors.[28] A learning curve starting with exports often makes sense. Licensing can be a helpful step toward a more substantial local presence. Alliances and joint ventures may allow a company to enter more markets than otherwise would be possible. But to secure a strong local presence, acquisitions or greenfield start-ups may be indicated. In making these decisions, executives should pay particular attention to the degree of risk involved, which is the subject of the next section.

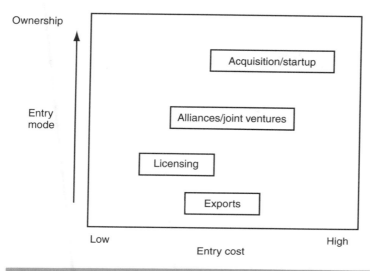

Ownership

Entry
mode

Acquisition/startup

Alliances/joint ventures

Licensing

Exports

Low   High

Entry cost

FIGURE 6-8 International Entry Strategies

GLOBAL STRATEGY AND RISK

Crafting a successful global strategy represents a formidable challenge. As many CEOs have learned, to transform global ambitions into reality strategy and implementation must be considered together. Most globalization strategies represent a significant "stretch" of the company's experience base, resources, and capabilities. New markets may be targeted, often in new—for the company—cultural settings, new technologies sought, or new partnerships initiated. In the process, new and different forms of competition can be anticipated, and it may turn out that the "economics" that got the company to its current position are no longer applicable. Equally important, the management style that proved successful in the past may turn out to be ineffective in a global setting.[29]

Even with the best planning "going global" imposes significant risks. For example, a detailed analysis of global opportunities may lead a company to adopt market share objectives that require earlier or greater commitments to a market than current returns can justify. A more global posture may imply exposure to different cyclical patterns, currency, and political risk. And there are substantial costs associated with coordinating global operations.

Consequently, before deciding to enter a foreign country or continent, companies are well advised to carefully analyze the risks involved. The different risks a company can encounter in the international business environment can be *political, legal, financial/economic,* or of a *sociocultural nature.*

Political risk relates to politically induced actions and policies initiated by a foreign government. Its assessment involves an evaluation of the stability of a country's current government and of its relationships with other countries. High levels of risk affect ownership of physical assets and intellectual property, security of personnel, and, as a consequence, the potential for trouble. Analysts frequently divide political risk into two subcategories: *global* and *country-specific risk.* Global risk affects all of a company's multinational operations whereas country-specific risk relates to investments in a specific foreign country. We can also speak of *macro* and *micro* political risk. Macrorisk is concerned with how foreign investment in general in a particular country is affected. By reviewing the government's past use of *soft* policy instruments, such as blacklisting, indirect control of prices, strikes in particular industries, and so forth, or *hard* policy tools, such as expropriation, confiscation, nationalization, or compulsory local shareholding, a company can be better prepared for potential future government action. At the microlevel, risk analysis is focused on a particular company or group of companies. A weak balance sheet, questionable accounting practices, or a regular breach of contracts should give rise to concerns.

Legal risk concerns risk that multinationals can encounter in the legal arena in a particular country. Legal risk is often closely tied to political country risk. An assessment of legal risk involves an analysis of the foundations of a country's legal system and determining whether the laws are properly enforced. Legal risk analysis therefore involves becoming familiar with a country's enforcement agencies and their scope of operation. As many companies have learned, there are a number of countries that have written laws protecting a multinational's rights but rarely enforce them. Entering such countries can expose a company to a host of risks, including the loss of intellectual property, technology, and trademarks.

Financial/economic risk exposure in a global business environment is analogous to the concept of domestic operating and financial risk. The volatility of a country's macroeconomic performance and the country's ability to meet its financial obligations directly affect performance. A nation's currency competitiveness and fluctuation are important indicators of a country's financial and political stability, and its willingness to embrace changes and innovations. In addition, financial risk assessment should consider such factors as how well the economy is being managed, the level of the country's economic development, working conditions, infrastructure, technological innovation, and the availability of natural/human resources.

Societal/cultural risk deals with the risk associated with operating in a different sociocultural environment. For example, it may be advisable to analyze specific ideologies, the relative importance of ethnic, religious, and nationalistic movements, and the country's ability to cope with changes that will sooner or later be induced by foreign investment. Thus, elements such as the standard of living, patriotism, religious factors, and the presence of charismatic leaders play a significant role in the evaluation of these risks.

SUMMARY

While there are many forces pushing companies to think more globally—meeting foreign competition head-on, better serving an increasingly global customer base, exploiting diverse capabilities and cost advantages, or taking advantage of an easing global regulatory environment—*changing customer expectations* are the primary reason many companies need to strengthen their global posture. Or, as Ohmae puts it: "Today . . . , the pressure for globalization is driven not so much by diversification or competition as by the needs and preferences of customers. Their needs have globalized, and the fixed costs of serving them have soared. That is why we must globalize."[30] Consequently, the real question for many companies is not "whether to globalize" but "to what extent and how."

Although the final chapter of the book on global strategy has not yet been written, a number of lessons have been learned. First, *global strategy is different*. Globalization has produced a competitive environment in which issues of economics and politics are becoming increasingly entangled. As a consequence, strategic thinking forces the consideration of *market* as well as *nonmarket* options. Second, *global strategy is more complex*. This complexity stems from the rapid pace of change and diversity that characterize the global competitive environment. Third, *global competitive strategy is defined by a continuum of action* on a number of key dimensions. How to develop a presence in key regions, segments, and product/service categories, whether or not to standardize core products and services, and how to build and exploit core competencies on a global scale are among the many decisions to be made. Finally, we noted that *global strategies carry significant risk*. Setting realistic market share and profit objectives, and carefully balancing stretch objectives with current capabilities, therefore are equally critical to global success.

Notes

1. As Paul Krugman, noted economist, observes in *Geography and Trade* (Cambridge, Mass.: MIT Press, 1993), the world in the nineteenth century was considerably more international in terms of capital and product flows than today's economy.
2. R. F. M. Lubbers, "Globalization: An Exploration," from lectures given at Harvard University, 1996, available at http://www.globalize.org/review.htm
3. See e.g., McLuhan, M. and B. Powers, *The Global Village: Transformations in World Life and Media in the 21st Century* (New York: Oxford University Press, 1989).
4. D. Meadows, *The Limits to Growth* (New York: Universe Books, 1972).
5. Krugman, *Geography and Trade*.
6. R. Vernon, L. T. Wells Jr., and S. Rangan, *The Manager in the International Economy*, 7th ed. (Upper Saddle River, N.J.: Prentice Hall, 1996), 15.
7. Hamel, G. and C. K. Prahalad, "Do You Really Have A Global Strategy?" *Harvard Business Review* 63 (July–Aug. 1985): 139–148.
8. This section is based on George S. Yip, *Total Global Strategy: Managing for Worldwide Competitive Advantage* (Englewood Cliffs, N.J.: Prentice Hall, 1992), chaps. 1 and 2. As Yip points out, Michael Porter first showed how industry factors affect the potential for global strategy in Michael E. Porter, "Changing Patterns of International Competition," *California Management Review* 28 (winter 1986): 9–40, and in "Competition in Global Industries: A Conceptual Framework," in *Competition in Global Industries*, Michael E. Porter, ed. (Cambridge, Mass.: Harvard Business School Press, 1986). The term "globalization drivers" was first introduced in George S. Yip, Pierre M. Loewe, and Michael Y. Yoshino, "How to Take Your Company to the Global Market," *Columbia Journal of World Business* (winter 1988): 37–48, and in George S. Yip, "Global Strategy … In a World Of Nations?" *Sloan Management Review* (fall 1989): 29–41.
9. Krugman, *Geography and Trade*.
10. Michael Porter, *The Competitive Advantage of Nations* (New York: Free Press, 1990).
11. S. M. Oster, *Modern Competitive Analysis*, 2d ed. (New York: Oxford University Press, 1994).
12. Oster, *Modern Competitive Analysis*, ch. 6.
13. Porter, *The Competitive Advantage*, 87.
14. Yip, *Total Global Strategy*, 85.
15. Baron first introduced the concept of an integrated strategy comprised of market and nonmarket dimensions. For a detailed description of the relationships between strategy, trade policy, and global competition, see David P. Baron, "Integrated Strategy, Trade Policy, and Global Competition," *California Management Review* 39 (winter 1997): 145–169; and David P. Baron, "Integrated Strategy: Market and Non-Market Components," *California Management Review* 37 (winter 1995): 47–65.

16. Charles W. L. Hill, *International Business: Competing in the Global Marketplace,* 2d ed. (Boston, Mass.: Irwin/McGraw-Hill, 1998), 32.

17. *International Trade Reporter,* BNA (June 7, 1995).

18. Baron, *Integrated Strategy,* 145–169.

19. S. Ghoshal, "Global strategy: An organizing framework," *Strategic Management Journal* 8 (Sept.–Oct. 1987): 425–440.

20. C. A. Bartlett and S. Ghoshal, *Transnational Management: Text, Cases, and Readings in Cross-Border Management* (Homewood, Ill.: Irwin, 1992), ch. 1.

21. C. A. Bartlett and S. Ghoshal, *Managing Across Borders: The Transnational Solution* (Boston: Harvard Business School Press, 1989).

22. This section is substantially based on David B. Yoffie (ed.), *Beyond Free Trade: Firms, Governments, and Global Competition* (Boston: Harvard Business School Press, 1993), chaps. 1 and 10. The reader is encouraged to consult this excellent book for further details.

23. For a good summary of how trade theory has evolved, see e.g., Charles W. Hill, *International Business,* chaps. 4 and 5.

24. David B. Yoffie (ed.), *Beyond Free Trade,* 12–18.

25. Ibid., 432.

26. Ibid., 433, 434.

27. Ibid., 21.

28. W. C. Kim and P. Hwang, "Global strategy and multinationals' entry mode choice," *Journal of International Business Studies* 23 (1) (1992): 29–53.

29. For further details on this subject, see e.g., Ellen Goldberg and Dan Haendel, *On Edge: International Banking and Country Risk* (Praeger Publishers, 1987); Ronald L. Sohlberg, *Country Risk Analysis—A Handbook* (Rontledge, Chapman and Hall, 1992); David M. Raddock, *Navigating New Markets Abroad* (Rowman and Littlefeld Publishers, 1993); Erol M. Balkan, *International Banking: Lending and Country Risks,* (Nova Science Publishers, 1995); Ephraim Clark and Bernard Marois, *Managing Risk in International Business* (International Thomson Business Press, 1996); Richard D. Robinson, *Internationalization of Business: An Introduction* (The Dryden Press, 1984).

30. Kenichi Ohmae, "Managing in a Borderless World," *Harvard Business Review* 67 (May–June 1989): 161.

CHAPTER

Strategy and the (R)evolution in Management

The most difficult problem of all is to unite voice and instruments so they blend in the rhythmic motion of a piece and the instruments support and enhance the voice in its emotional expression, for voices and instruments are by their nature opposed to each other . . . .*

—CARL MARIA VON WEBER

INTRODUCTION

Tackling the unprecedented challenges and opportunities the next century will bring will require more than creative strategic thinking. As any executive knows, formulating a good strategy is one thing; successfully implementing a chosen direction is quite another. Effective execution requires imagination, foresight, drive, courage, faith, persistence, and an ability to motivate and inspire others. In the 1980s, chief executives were rewarded for restructuring their corporations, "getting back to the core business," and downsizing in an all-out attempt to restore competitiveness. Rising to the challenges of the next century will make different, even greater demands on top managers; *they will be judged on their ability to shape a global vision and marshal the talent and technologies needed to translate that vision into reality.*

Shaping such a global vision requires a radical shift in mind-set. Competing effectively on a global basis requires adopting a different strategic outlook, paying attention to the needs and concerns of a more diverse set of stakeholders, investing in new skills and technologies, and learning how to operate effectively across organizational and cultural boundaries. Above all, it demands a corporate culture that welcomes rather than fights change. For most companies, this will not be an easy transition to make. "Going global" often represents a significant "stretch" of a company's experience base, resources, and capabilities. New markets may be targeted, often in new (for the company) cultural settings; new technologies sought, or new partnerships initiated. In the process, new and different forms of competition can be anticipated, and it may turn out that the "economics" that got the company to its current position is no longer applicable. Equally important, the management style that proved successful in the past may be less suitable in a global setting. And, as we have seen, even with the best planning "going global" imposes significant risks. A global strategy may require earlier or greater commitments to a market than current returns can justify. A more global posture may imply exposure to different cyclical patterns, currency, and political risk. And there are substantial costs associated with coordinating global operations.

---

*From an article on the metronome markings to Euryanthe, 1824, as quoted in Josiah Fisk (ed.), *Composers on Music: Eight Centuries of Writings* (Boston: Northwestern University Press, 1956), 63.

This chapter briefly looks at two topics that are relevant to both strategy and its implementation. First, we argue that the need for effective *leadership*—at all levels of the organization—has never been greater. Second, we look at how companies are experimenting with new forms of *organization*. This reinvention of the corporation reflects a broader paradigm shift to what management is all about. Getting comfortable with change is not an option any more, it is a requirement for success. After all, no matter how well crafted a strategy is, success begins with implementation. And as many executives have learned, "Successful implementation is secured through commitment, not compliance."

THE INCREASING IMPORTANCE OF LEADERSHIP

The New Mind-Set

While increased competitive intensity has created a *greater need* for leadership at all levels of the organization, the higher pace of change and greater uncertainty in the strategic environment have increased the *difficulty* of providing effective leadership.[1] This explains the extensive reexamination of all aspects of the job of managing in recent years. Just as principles of strategy formulation can become obsolete as the competitive environment changes, so can assumptions about other aspects of management. Executives understand that to prosper in the competitive environment of the twenty-first century keeping up with or adapting to the latest change is not good enough anymore, so they are actively seeking to regain a measure of control over their destiny by making continuous adaptation an organizational core competency itself. The traditional hierarchical "command and control" model of organization may be one of the casualties of this management (r)evolution. A growing number of corporations are experimenting with new network-based forms of organization, which emphasize horizontal communication and coordination over traditional vertical hierarchical decision making. A *Fortune* article describes today's managerial challenge as the ultimate paradox: (1) keep everything running efficiently and profitably, while, at the same time, (2) change everything.[2]

Paradigm Shift

This new focus on reinventing the corporation reflects a major shift in managerial thinking. Instead of thinking about the strategic environment as essentially in equilibrium, subject to occasional shocks and disturbances that strategies must confront, the new paradigm emphasizes constant, often chaotic change. Trying to control things back into some stable equilibrium is all but impossible in this new world; there is no alternative but to get comfortable with continuous change.

The depth of this (r)evolution is illustrated by the new terms—the twenty-first-century organization, the collaborative organization, the empowered organization, and the new-age organization—that have been added to our vocabulary. In the next section we will discuss two other well-known descriptions—a "learning organization" and a "centerless corporation."[3]

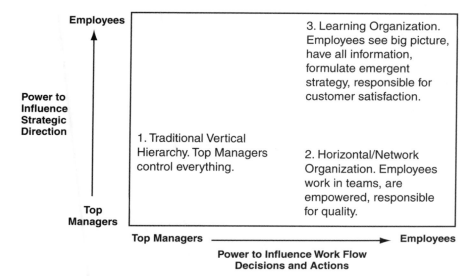

FIGURE 7-1 Toward a Learning Organization

Source: From Richard L. Daft, *Management,* 4th edition. Copyright © 1997 Harcourt Brace, Orlando, FL.

RETHINKING THE ORGANIZATION

Toward a Learning Organization

A *learning organization* is defined as an organization in which everyone—from the lowest ranking employee on the shop floor to the most senior executive—is involved in identifying and solving problems. This enables the organization to continuously experiment and change and improve; thus increasing its capacity to grow, learn, and achieve its purpose.[4] The concept does not imply a specific structure. Rather, it is a vision of and an attitude about what an organization can become. It is the envisioned outcome of an organization's evolution from a traditional hierarchical model in which strategy formulation and implementation are centrally controlled by top management to a more horizontal or network model characterized by teamwork, and from an empowered workforce to a learning organization in which strategy emerges from the coordinated activities of employee teams (Figure 7-1).

A true learning organization as previously defined is probably a Utopian vision. It assumes everyone in the organization has access to a virtually unlimited amount of information, is able to take a strategic perspective about his or her area of work, and that such perspectives harmoniously fit together into an overall emergent strategy for the organization. This is unlikely. Ultimately, someone will have to make the key decisions and "hierarchy" will therefore remain an element of organization. Nevertheless, the principles on which the concept of a learning organization is based are worth thinking about. Senge's original vision focused on five disciplines managers should concentrate on in building a learning organization: (1) encouraging more *systems thinking*—letting employees know how the company really works and how and where they fit in, (2) fostering a *shared vision*—developing a common purpose and commitment, (3) *challenging existing mental models*—questioning old ways of doing things and encouraging "out-of-the-box" thinking, (4) enhancing *team learning*—emphasizing collective over individual contributions and learning, and (5) motivating employees to improve their *personal mastery* of their jobs.[5] There can be little question that the pursuit of these objectives will help companies adapt more effectively to a changing competitive environment and improve the chances of successfully implementing strategic change.

The Centerless Corporation

Extensive research into the mismatch between the emerging business environment and the classic organizational "command and control" model conducted by consultants Booz·Allen & Hamilton has produced the concept of the "centerless corporation." This model was formulated by Bruce Pasternack and Albert Viscio and is described as follows:

> Imagine a corporation that has a core but not a center. Imagine a corporation that is built around resources (people, knowledge, capabilities) rather than the assets that get lined up on financial balance sheets—one that manages its people with a relationship we call the "new people partnership" rather than downsizing lists and that places great stock in its knowledge department and its chief executive officer. Imagine a corporation that is characterized by the interdependence rather than the independence of its parts. This is the centerless corporation.[6]

Figure 7-2 illustrates this new vision. It depicts two concentric rings; the inner ring houses the *global core, business units, services,* and *governance;* the outer ring represents "a sort of free-flowing glue that contains *people, knowledge,* and *coherence.*"[7] The *global core* is the modern-day equivalent of the old corporate headquarters. As in the traditional model, it consists of the CEO, the senior executive team, and key corporate services but with a few important differences. First, it has only five key missions: (1) pro-

FIGURE 7-2 The Centerless Corporation

Source: Bruce A. Pasternack and Albert J. Viscio, "The Centerless Corporation: A Model for Tomorrow," in *Strategy & Business,* third quarter 1998, issue 12. Copyright © 1998 Booz·Allen and Hamilton, New York, NY. Reprinted by permission.

vide strategic leadership, (2) help distribute and provide access to capabilities, (3) create an appropriate identity, (4) ensure access to low-cost capital, and (5) exert control over the enterprise as a whole. Second, the core is not bound to a single physical location; it is distributed so that the five missions can be carried out where they are needed. Third, its focus is on adding value where the businesses cannot. The new model envisions a different style of managing *business units*; instead of acting as independent units with relatively well-defined boundaries the focus is on interaction and flexibility through permeable boundaries. Key *services*—payroll, accounts payable, benefit administration, and so forth—are shared by all other units of the corporation. And the role of *governance* is expanded from the traditional oversight role of the corporation as a whole by the board of directors to include two new dimensions: the governance of intercorporate entities such as alliances and joint ventures and oversight of intracorporate entities like shared services.

The outer ring of the model defines the three principal axes along which the centerless corporation is built: people, knowledge, and coherence. It reinforces the notion that *people* are a company's most important strategic resource; that *knowledge* has never been as critical to competitiveness as it is today; and that *coherence* between different organizational entities and activities, through communication and systems, is key to successful strategy implementation.

As Pasternack and Viscio readily admit, there probably is no corporation today that functions exactly this way. But elements of the centerless model already exist in many companies. This illustrates the ongoing (r)evolution in strategic and managerial thinking that will shape competitive behavior in the next century.

Notes

1. John P. Kotter, *The Leadership Factor* (New York: Free Press, 1988), 12.
2. John Huey, "Managing in the Midst of Chaos," *Fortune* (April 5, 1993):38–48.
3. Peter Senge popularized the term "learning organization." See e.g., Peter Senge, *The Fifth Discipline: The Art and Practice of Learning Organizations* (New York: Doubleday/Currency, 1990), or Peter Senge, "The Leader's New Work: Building Learning Organizations," *Sloan Management Review* (fall 1990):7–20. The term "centerless corporation" comes from Bruce A. Pasternack and Albert J. Viscio, *The Centerless Corporation: A New Model for Transforming Your Organization for Growth and Prosperity* (New York: Simon & Schuster, 1998). See also Bruce A. Pasternack and Albert J. Viscio, "The Centerless Corporation: A Model for Tomorrow," *Strategy & Business*, no. 12 (1998):10–21.
4. Richard L. Daft, *Management*, 4th ed. (Dryden Press, 1997), 751.
5. Ibid., 750.
6. Bruce A. Pasternack and Albert J. Viscio, "The Centerless Corporation: A Model for Tomorrow," 12.
7. Ibid.

Index